Lecture Notes in Artificial Intelligence   1788

Subseries of Lecture Notes in Computer Science
Edited by J. G. Carbonell and J. Siekmann

Lecture Notes in Computer Science

Edited by G. Goos, J. Hartmanis and J. van Leeuwen

Springer
Berlin
Heidelberg
New York
Barcelona
Hong Kong
London
Milan
Paris
Singapore
Tokyo

Alexandros Moukas   Carles Sierra
Fredrik Ygge (Eds.)

Agent Mediated Electronic Commerce II

Towards Next-Generation Agent-Based
Electronic Commerce Systems

Springer

Series Editors

Jaime G. Carbonell,Carnegie Mellon University, Pittsburgh, PA, USA
Jörg Siekmann, University of Saarland, Saarbrücken, Germany

Volume Editors

Alexandros Moukas
MIT Media Laboratory and Frictionless Commerce Inc.
20 Ames Street
Cambridge, MA 02142, USA
E-mail: moux@media.mit.edu

Carles Sierra
IIIA-Institut d'Investigació en Intel.ligencia
CSIC-Spanish Scientific Research Council
Campus UAB
08193 Bellaterra, Catalonia Spain
E-mail: sierra@iiia.csic.es

Fredrik Ygge
EnerSearch AB and Uppsala University
Chalmers Science Park
412 88 Gothenburg, Sweden
E-mail: ygge@enersearch.se

Cataloging-in-Publication Data applied for

Die Deutsche Bibliothek - CIP-Einheitsaufnahme

Agent mediated electronic commerce / Alexandros Moukas ... (ed.). -
Berlin ; Heidelberg ; New York ; Barcelona ; Hong Kong ; London ;
Milan ; Paris ; Singapore ; Tokyo : Springer
2. Towards next generation agent based electronic commerce
systems. - 2000
  (Lecture notes in computer science ; 1788 : Lecture notes in
  artificial intelligence)
  ISBN 3-540-67773-9
CR Subject Classification (1998): I.2.11, K.4.4, C.2, H.3.4-5, H.4.3, H.5.3, I.2, J.1,
K.5

ISBN 3-540-67773-9 Springer-Verlag Berlin Heidelberg New York

Springer-Verlag Berlin Heidelberg New York
a member of BertelsmannSpringer Science+Business Media GmbH
© Springer-Verlag Berlin Heidelberg 2000
Printed in Germany

Typesetting: Camera-ready by author, data conversion by Christian Grosche, Hamburg
Printed on acid-free paper   SPIN 10720026   06/3142   5 4 3 2 1 0

Preface

The Internet is spawning many new markets and electronic commerce is changing many market conventions. Not only are old commercial practices being adapted to the new conditions of immediacy brought forth by the global networks, but new products and services, as well as new practices, are beginning to appear. There is already ample evidence that agent-based technologies will be crucial for these developments. However many theoretical, technological, sociological, and legal aspects will need to be addressed before such opportunities become a significant reality.

In addition to streamlining traditional transactions, agents enable new types of transactions. For example, the elusive one-to-one marketing becomes more of a reality when consumer agents capture and share (or sell) consumer demographics. Prices and other transaction dimensions need no longer to be fixed; selling agents can dynamically tailor merchant offerings to each consumer. Economies of scale become feasible in new markets when agents negotiate on special arbitration contracts. Dynamic business relationships will give rise to more competitively agile organizations. It is these new opportunities combined with substantial reduction in transaction costs that will revolutionize electronic commerce.

The first generation of agent-mediated electronic commerce systems are already creating new markets and beginning to reduce search and transaction costs in a variety of business practices. However, we still have a long way to go before software agents transform how businesses conduct business. This change will occur as technology matures to better manage ambiguous content, personalized preferences, complex goals, changing environments, and disconnected parties, but more importantly, as standards are adopted to succinctly and universally define goods and services, consumer and merchant profiles, value added services, secure payment mechanisms, inter-business electronic forms, etc.

During this next generation of agent-mediated electronic commerce systems, agents will streamline business-to-business transactions, reducing transaction costs at every stage of the supply chain. At some critical threshold, new types of transactions will emerge in the form of dynamic relationships among previously unknown parties. Agents will strategically form and reform coalitions to bid on contracts and leverage economies of scale - in essence, creating dynamic business partnerships that exist only as long as necessary. It is in this third generation of agent-mediated electronic commerce where virtual and non-virtual companies will be at their most agile and marketplaces will approach perfect efficiency. This book sets the scene for the assessment of the challenges that agent-based electronic commerce faces as well as the opportunities it creates. By focusing on agent mediated interactions we brought together specialists from different disciplines who are contributing theoretical, methodological, and application perspectives in the narrowly focused topic that nevertheless involves wide ranging concerns such as: agent architectures, institutionalization, economic-theoretic, modeling, legal frameworks, and policy guidelines.

The workshop on whose proceedings this book is based was held during the Sixteenth International Joint Conference on Artificial Intelligence in Stockholm, Sweden in July 1999. The six papers that were presented during the workshop were augmented with six additional manuscripts that were invited to contribute to this book in order to provide a more complete picture of the practical, theoretical, institutional, and legal issues of agents in electronic commerce.

The papers covered a wide range of topics: Greenwald and Kephart's *Shopbots and Pricebots* contribution focuses on agents that collect information about pricing and specifications information for products and services on the Web. The authors include findings on the tradeoffs between profitability and computational complexity of the pricebots algorithms. Dellarocas and Klein's paper on *Civil Agent Societies* introduces a framework and the infrastructure support tools that can assist in the design of open marketplaces that will provide quality of service guarantees to their members. Conan et al. in *Privacy Protection and Internet Agents* discuss privacy issues in a variety of agent mediation scenarios in electronic commerce, from agents that represent the users, to agents that represent the sellers, to agents that are acting as third party middlemen. Ygge presents an overview in his paper *Energy Resellers - An Endangered Species?* describing important issues related to implementing electronic power trade. An overview paper called *Modeling Supply Chain Formation in Multi-agent Systems* describing the importance of supply chain formation and its most major promises and difficulties is authored by Walsh and Wellman. Yoon et al. in their *Jangter: A Novel Agent-Based Electronic Marketplace* paper discuss the design and implementation of a marketplace that provides brokering, negotiation, and reputation capabilities, while addressing ontological and computational complexity issues. Collins et al. introduce a bid evaluation framework that supports the assessment of multiple criteria in a multi-agent automated contracted environment. Boutilier et al. in *Resource Allocation Using Sequential Auctions* discuss a model for agent bidding in a resource allocation environment where the agents are coming up with policies that govern their bidding behavior. Dailianas et al. in *Profit-Driven Matching in E-Marketplaces: Trading Composable Commodities* provide insight in highly computationally efficient matching heuristics in a marketplace for soft composable commodities (bandwidth products.) In *Two-Sided Learning in an Economy for Information Bundles*, Kephart, Das, and MacKie-Mason investigate the price dynamics in an information bundling economy with learning producers and consumers. Parkes' paper *Optimal Auction Design for Agents with Hard Valuation Problems* describes the interplay between the complexity of the agents' valuation problems and the outcome of specific auctions; the interesting issue of making the right agents deliberate at the right time is carefully examined. Finally, Esteva's and Padget's contribution *Auctions without Auctioneers: Distributed Auction Protocols* analyze the concept of "interagent", and use p-calculus to specify the protocols of first-price, second-price English and Dutch auctions.

In addition to the papers presented at the workshop and included above, a set of additional events occurred: A demonstration of the *Diplomat* system and a report from a strongly related workshop at AAAI, was given by Grosof. Furthermore, a very stimulating competition proposal called *A Trading Agent Competition for the Research Community* by Wellman and Wurman presented a trading competition. The competition will take place as a workshop at ICMAS 2000, and researchers in the field were encouraged to design their agents for the competition. More information about the competition can be otained from Michael P. Wellman, University of Michigan (wellman@umich.edu) or by visiting: http://tac.eecs.umich.edu.

Finally, two panels, one on practical issues and one on theoretical issues were also held at the workshop. The panels were indeed lively and interesting, reflecting many of the challenges facing the researchers in the field. Some of the practical issues are legal, security aspects, integrity aspects, as well as issues related to what auctions to use in what situations etc. In the theory session, one issue that was discussed was related to the agent-mediated electronic commerce as a field of study. Some argued that there are no original theoretic contributions in this field - they belong to economics, game theory, or other fields, whereas others insisted that there are new issues in the interplay between computation/communication and economics which belong to this field.

We would like to thank all the members of the program committee and the reviewers of submitted papers for their guidance and their valuable suggestions to authors and organizers. Finally, we would like to mention the encouragement and support we received from the IJCAI-99 conference organizers and staff, and from Alfred Hofmann of Springer-Verlag for the publication of this volume.

March 2000   Alexandros Moukas, Carles Sierra, Fredrik Ygge

Organization

The workshop was organized in conjunction with the Sixteenth International Joint Conference on Artificial Intelligence (IJCAI-99) held in Stockholm, Sweden. Alexandros Moukas (MIT Media Laboratory / Frictionless Commerce Incorporated, USA), Carles Sierra (IIIA-Institut d'Investigació en Intelligència Artificial, Spain) and Fredrik Ygge (EnerSearch AB, and Uppsala University, Sweden) co-chaired the event.

Program Committee

Ken Binmore	University College London, UK
Frank Dignum	U. Eindhoven, The Netherlands
Fausto Giunchiglia	IRST, Italy
Robert Guttman	Frictionless Commerce Inc., USA
Sverker Janson	Swedish Institute of Computer Science
Nick R. Jennings	Queen Mary and Westfield College, UK
Sarit Kraus	Bar-Ilan U., Israel
Yannis Labrou	UMBC, USA
Jack Lang	ESI, UK
Pattie Maes	MIT Media Lab, USA
Joerg Muller	Siemens, UK
Pablo Noriega	LANIA, Mexico
Julian Padget	University of Bath, UK
Jeff Rosenschein	Hebrew University, Israel
Tuomas Sandholm	Washington University, USA
Katia Sycara	Carnegie Mellon University, USA
Aphrodite Tsalgatidou	University of Athens, Greece
Hans Voss	GMD, Germany
Mike Wooldridge	Queen Mary and Westfield College, UK

Acknowledgements

We would like to thank the travel support given to Carles Sierra by the European Network of Excellence, AgentLink.

Table of Contents

Shopbots and Pricebots..1
Amy R. Greenwald and Jeffrey O. Kephart (IBM T.J. Watson Research Center, USA)

Civil Agent Societies: Tools for Inventing Open Agent-Mediated Electronic
Marketplaces...24
Chrysanthos Dellarocas and Mark Klein (Massachusetts Institute of Technology, USA)

Legal Issues for Personalised Advertising on Internet: The AIMedia Case Study............40
Vania Conan, Marten Foss, Peter Lenda, Sophie Louveaux, and Anne Salaun
(AIM Media Project, Spain, and ECLIPSE Project, Germany)

Energy Resellers - An Endangered Species? 68
Fredrik Ygge (EnerSearch, AB, Sweden)

Modeling Supply Chain Formation in Multiagent Systems. 94
William E. Walsh and Michael P. Wellman (University of Michigan, USA)

Jangter: A Novel Agent-Based Electronic Marketplace...................................102
Shim Yoon, Ju Young Yun, SooWoong Kim, and Juneha Kim (Samsung Ltd, Korea)

Bid Selection Strategies for Multi-agent Contracting in the Presence of
Scheduling Constraints. 113
John Collins, Rashmi Sundareswara, Maria Gini, and Bamshad Mobasher
(University of Minessota, USA and DePaul University, USA)

Resource Allocation Using Sequential Auctions. 131
Craig Boutilier, Moisés Goldszmidt, Claire Monteleoni, and Bikash Sabata
(University of Toronto, Canada, and Stanford University, USA)

Profit-Driven Matching in E-Marketplaces: Trading Composable Commodities. 153
Apostolos Dailianas, Jakka Sairamesh, Vibby Gottemukkala, and Anant Jhingran
(IBM T.J. Watson, USA)

Two-Sided Learning in an Agent Economy for Information Bundles............................180
Jeffrey O. Kephart, Rajarshi Das, and Jeffrey K. MacKie-Mason
(IBM T.J. Watson Center, USA, and University of Michigan, USA)

Optimal Auction Design for Agents with Hard Valuation Problems. 206
David C. Parkes (University of Pennsylvania, USA)

Auctions without Auctioneers: Distributed Auction Protocols. 220
Marc Esteva and Julian Padget (IIIA, Spain and University of Bath, UK)

Author Index....239

Shopbots and Pricebots

Amy R. Greenwald and Jeffrey O. Kephart

IBM Institute for Advanced Commerce
IBM Thomas J. Watson Research Center
Yorktown Heights, NY 10598
amygreen@cs.nyu.edu, kephart@watson.ibm.com

Abstract. *Shopbots* are software agents that automatically gather and collate information from multiple on-line vendors about the price and quality of consumer goods and services. Rapidly increasing in number and sophistication, shopbots are helping more and more buyers minimize expenditure and maximize satisfaction. In response to this trend, it is anticipated that sellers will come to rely on *pricebots*, automated agents that employ price-setting algorithms in an attempt to maximize profits. In this paper, a simple economic model is proposed and analyzed, which is intended to characterize some of the likely impacts of a proliferation of shopbots and pricebots.

In addition to describing theoretical investigations, this paper also aims toward a practical understanding of the tradeoffs between profitability and computational and informational complexity of pricebot algorithms. A comparative study of a series of price-setting strategies is presented, including: game-theoretic (GT), myoptimal (MY), derivative following (DF), and no regret learning (NR). The dynamic behavior that arises among collections of pricebots and shopbot-assisted buyers is simulated, and it is found that game-theoretic equilibria can dynamically arise in our model of shopbots and pricebots.

1   Introduction

Shopbots — automated Web agents that query multiple on-line vendors to gather information about prices and other attributes of consumer goods and services — herald a future in which automated agents are an essential component of electronic commerce [6, 10, 24, 31]. Shopbots outperform and out-inform humans, providing extensive product coverage in a few seconds, far more than a patient and determined human shopper could ever achieve, even after hours of manual search. Rapidly increasing in number and sophistication, shopbots are helping more and more buyers to minimize expenditure and maximize satisfaction.

Since the launch of BargainFinder [26] — a CD shopbot — on June 30, 1995, the range of products represented by shopbots has expanded dramatically. A shopbot available at shopper.com claims to compare 1,000,000 prices on 100,000 computer-oriented products. DealPilot.com (formerly acses.com) is a shopbot that gathers, collates and sorts prices and expected delivery times of books, CDs, and movies offered for sale on-line. One of the most popular shopbots, mysimon.com, compares office supplies, groceries, toys, apparel, and consumer

A. Moukas, C. Sierra, and F. Ygge (Eds.): AMEC'99, LNAI 1788, pp. 1–23, 2000.

electronics, just to name a few of the items on its product line. As the range of products covered by shopbots expands to include more complex products such as consumer electronics, the level of shopbot sophistication is rising accordingly. On August 16th, 1999, mysimon.com incorporated technology that, for products with multiple features such as digital cameras, uses a series of questions to elicit multi-attribute utilities from buyers, and then sorts products according to the buyer's specified utility. Also on that day, lycos.com licensed similar technology from frictionless.com.

Shopbots are undoubtedly a boon to buyers who use them. Moreover, when shopbots become adopted by a sufficient portion of the buyer population, it seems likely that sellers will be compelled to decrease prices and improve quality, benefiting even those buyers who do not shop with bots. How the widespread utilization of shopbots might affect sellers, on the other hand, is not quite so apparent. Less established sellers may welcome shopbots as an opportunity to attract buyers who might not otherwise have access to information about them, but more established sellers may feel threatened. Some larger players have even been known to deliberately block automated agents from their web sites [8]. This practice seems to be waning, however; today, sellers like Amazon.com and BarnesandNoble.com tolerate queries from agents such as DealPilot.com on the grounds that buyers take brand name and image as well as price into account.

As more and more buyers rely on shopbots to supplement their awareness about products and prices, it is becoming advantageous for sellers to increase flexibility in their pricing strategies, perhaps via *pricebots* — software agents that utilize automatic price-setting algorithms in an attempt to maximize profits. Indeed, an early pricebot is already available at books.com, an on-line bookseller. When a prospective buyer expresses interest in a book at books.com, a pricebot automatically queries Amazon.com, Borders.com, and BarnesandNoble.com to determine the price that is being offered at those sites. books.com then slightly undercuts the lowest of the three quoted prices, typically by 1% of the retail price. Real-time dynamic pricing on millions of titles is impossible to achieve manually, yet can easily be implemented with a modest amount of programming.

As more and more sellers automate their price-setting, pricebots are destined to interact with one another, yielding unexpected price and profit dynamics. This paper reaches toward an understanding of pricebot dynamics via analysis and simulation of a series of candidate price-setting strategies, which differ in their informational and computational demands: game-theoretic pricing (GT), myoptimal pricing (MY), derivative following (DF), and no regret learning (NR). Previously, we studied the dynamics that ensue when shopbot-assisted buyers interact with pricebots utilizing only a subset of these strategies [19, 25, 29]. In this work, we simulate additional, more sophisticated, pricebot strategies, and find that the game-theoretic equilibrium can arise dynamically as the outcome of adaptive learning in our model of shopbots and pricebots.

This paper is organized as follows. The next section presents our model of an economy that consists of shopbots and pricebots. This model is analyzed from a game-theoretic point of view in Sec. 3. In Sec. 4, we discuss the price-setting strategies of interest: game-theoretic, myoptimal pricing, derivative following, and no regret learning. Sec. 5 describes simulations of pricebots that implement these strategies, while Sec. 6 discusses one possible evolution of shopbots and pricebots, and Sec. 7 presents our conclusions.

2 Model

We consider an economy in which there is a single homogeneous good that is offered for sale by S sellers and of interest to B buyers, with $B \gg S$. Each buyer b generates purchase orders at random times, with rate ρ_b, while each seller s reconsiders (and potentially resets) its price p_s at random times, with rate ρ_s. The value of the good to buyer b is v_b; the cost of production for seller s is c_s.

A buyer b's utility for the good is a function of price:

$$u_b(p) = \begin{cases} v_b - p & \text{if } p \le v_b \\ 0 & \text{otherwise} \end{cases} \tag{1}$$

which states that a buyer obtains positive utility if and only if the seller's price is less than the buyer's valuation of the good; otherwise, the buyer's utility is zero. We do not assume that buyers are utility maximizers; instead we assume that they consider the prices offered by sellers using one of the following strategies:[1]

1. *Any Seller:* Buyer selects seller at random, and purchases the good if the price charged by that seller is less than the buyer's valuation.

2. *Bargain Hunter:* Buyer checks the offer price of all sellers, determines the seller with the lowest price, and purchases the good if that lowest price is less than the buyer's valuation. (This type of buyer corresponds to those who take advantage of shopbots.)

The buyer population consists of a mixture of buyers employing one of these strategies, with a fraction w_A using the *Any Seller* strategy and a fraction w_B using the *Bargain Hunter* strategy, where $w_A + w_B = 1$. Buyers employing these respective strategies are referred to as type A and type B buyers.

A seller s's expected profit per unit time π_s is a function of the price vector $\boldsymbol{p}$, as follows: $\pi_s(\boldsymbol{p}) = (p_s - c_s)D_s(\boldsymbol{p})$, where $D_s(\boldsymbol{p})$ is the rate of demand for the good produced by seller s. This rate of demand is determined by the overall buyer rate of demand, the likelihood of the buyers selecting seller s as their potential seller, and the likelihood that seller s's price p_s does not exceed the buyer's valuation v_b.[2] If $\rho = \sum_b \rho_b$, and if $h_s(\boldsymbol{p})$ denotes the probability that

---

[1] In this framework, it is also possible to consider all buyers as utility maximizers, with the additional cost of searching for the lowest price made explicit in the buyer utility functions. In doing so, the search cost for bargain hunters is taken to be zero, while for those buyers that use the any seller strategy, its value is greater than v_b. The relationship between models of exogenously determined buyer behavior and the endogenous approach which incorporates the cost of information acquisition and explicitly allows for buyer decision-making is further explored in computational settings in Kephart and Greenwald [25]; in the economics literature, see, for example, Burdett and Judd [5] and Wilde and Schwartz [33].

[2] We assume that buyers' valuations are uncorrelated with their buying strategies.

seller s is selected, while $g(p_s)$ denotes the fraction of buyers whose valuations satisfy $v_b \geq p_s$, then $D_s(\boldsymbol{p}) = \rho B h_s(\boldsymbol{p})g(p_s)$. Without loss of generality, define the time scale $s.t.$ $\rho B = 1$. Now $\pi_s(\boldsymbol{p})$ is interpreted as the expected profit for seller s per unit sold systemwide. Moreover, seller s's profit is such that $\pi_s(\boldsymbol{p}) = (p_s - c_s)h_s(\boldsymbol{p})g(p_s)$. We discuss the functions $h_s(\boldsymbol{p})$ and $g(\boldsymbol{p})$ presently.

The probability $h_s(\boldsymbol{p})$ that buyers select seller s as their potential seller depends on the buyer distribution (w_A, w_B) as follows:

$$h_s(\boldsymbol{p}) = w_A f_{s,A}(\boldsymbol{p}) + w_B f_{s,B}(\boldsymbol{p}) \tag{2}$$

where $f_{s,A}(\boldsymbol{p})$ and $f_{s,B}(\boldsymbol{p})$ are the probabilities that seller s is selected by buyers of type A and B, respectively. The probability that a buyer of type A selects a seller s is independent of the ordering of sellers' prices: $f_{s,A}(\boldsymbol{p}) = 1/S$. Buyers of type B, however, select a seller s if and only if s is one of the lowest price sellers. Given that the buyers' strategies depend on the relative ordering of the sellers' prices, it is convenient to define the following functions:

- $\lambda_s(\boldsymbol{p})$ is the number of sellers charging a lower price than s,
- $\tau_s(\boldsymbol{p})$ is the number of sellers charging the same price as s, excluding s itself, and
- $\mu_s(\boldsymbol{p})$ is the number of sellers charging a higher price than s.

Now a buyer of type b selects a seller s iff s is $s.t.$ $\lambda_s(\boldsymbol{p}) = 0$, in which case a buyer selects a particular such seller s with probability $1/(\tau_s(\boldsymbol{p}) + 1)$. Therefore,

$$f_{s,B}(\boldsymbol{p}) = \frac{1}{\tau_s(\boldsymbol{p}) + 1} \delta_{\lambda_s(\boldsymbol{p}),0} \tag{3}$$

where $\delta_{i,j}$ is the Kronecker delta function, equal to 1 whenever $i = j$, and 0 otherwise.

The function $g(p)$ can be expressed as $g(p) = \int_p^\infty \gamma(x)dx$, where $\gamma(x)$ is the probability density function describing the likelihood that a given buyer has valuation x. For example, suppose that the buyers' valuations are uniformly distributed between 0 and v, with $v > 0$; then the integral yields $g(p) = 1 - p/v$. This case was studied in Greenwald, et al. [20]. In this paper, we assume $v_b = v$ for all buyers b, in which case $\gamma(x)$ is the Dirac delta function $\delta(v - x)$, and the integral yields a step function $g(p) = \Theta(v - p)$ as follows:

$$\Theta(v - p) = \begin{cases} 1 & \text{if } p \leq v \\ 0 & \text{otherwise} \end{cases} \tag{4}$$

The preceding results can be assembled to express the profit function π_s for seller s in terms of the distribution of strategies and valuations within the buyer population. Recalling that $v_b = v$ for all buyers b, and assuming $c_s = c$ for all sellers s, yields the following:

$$\pi_s(\boldsymbol{p}) = \begin{cases} (p_s - c)h_s(\boldsymbol{p}) & \text{if } p_s \leq v \\ 0 & \text{otherwise} \end{cases} \tag{5}$$

where

$$h_s(\boldsymbol{p}) = w_A \frac{1}{S} + w_B \frac{1}{\tau_s(\boldsymbol{p}) + 1} \delta_{\lambda_s(\boldsymbol{p}),0} \qquad (6)$$

3   Analysis

In this section, we present a game-theoretic analysis of the prescribed model viewed as a one-shot game.[3] Assuming sellers are profit maximizers, we first show that there is no pure strategy Nash equilibrium, and we then compute the symmetric mixed strategy Nash equilibrium. A Nash equilibrium is a vector of prices $\boldsymbol{p}^* \in \mathbf{R}^S$ at which sellers maximize their individual profits and from which they have no incentive to deviate [28]. Recall that $B \gg S$; in particular, the number of buyers is assumed to be very large, while the number of sellers is a good deal smaller. In accordance with this assumption, it is reasonable to study the strategic decision-making of the sellers alone, since their relatively small number suggests that the behavior of individual sellers indeed influences market dynamics, while the large number of buyers renders the effects of individual buyers' actions negligible.

Traditional economic models consider the case in which all buyers are bargain hunters: *i.e.*, $w_B = 1$. In this case, prices are driven down to marginal cost; in particular, $p_s^* = c$, for all sellers s (see, for example, Tirole [30]). In contrast, consider the case in which all buyers are of type A, meaning that they randomly select a potential seller: *i.e.*, $w_A = 1$. In this situation, tacit collusion arises, in which all sellers charge the monopolistic price, in the absence of explicit coordination; in particular, $p_s^* = v$, for all sellers s. Of particular interest in this study, however, is the dynamics of interaction among buyers of various types: *i.e.*, $0 < w_A, w_B < 1$. Knowing that buyers of type A alone results in all sellers charging the valuation price v, we investigate the impact of buyers of type B, or shopbots, on the marketplace.

Throughout this exposition, we adopt the standard notation $\boldsymbol{p} = (p_s, p_{-s})$, which distinguishes the price offered by seller s from the prices offered by the other sellers. Our analysis begins with the following observation: *at equilibrium, at most one seller s charges $p_s^* < v$.* Suppose that two distinct sellers $s' \neq s$ set their equilibrium prices to be $p_{s'}^* = p_s^* < v$, while all other sellers set their equilibrium prices at the buyers' valuation v. In this case, $\pi_s(p_s^* - \epsilon, p_{-s}^*) = [(1/S)w_A + w_B](p_s^* - \epsilon - c) > [(1/S)w_A + (1/2)w_B](p_s^* - c) = \pi_s(p_s^*, p_{-s}^*)$, for small, positive values of ϵ,[4] which implies that p_s^* is not an equilibrium price for

---

[3] The analysis presented in this section applies to the one-shot version of our model, although the simulation results reported in Sec. 5 focus on repeated settings. We consider the Nash equilibrium of the one-shot game, rather than its iterated counterpart, for at least two reasons, including (i) the Nash equilibrium of the stage game played repeatedly is in fact a Nash equilibrium of the repeated game, and (ii) the Folk Theorem of repeated game theory (see, for example, Fudenberg and Tirole [15]) states that virtually all payoffs in a repeated game correspond to a Nash equilibrium, for sufficiently large values of the discount parameter. Thus, we isolate the stage game Nash equilibrium as an equilibrium of particular interest.

[4] Precisely, $0 < 2\epsilon < \frac{w_B S}{w_A + w_B S}(p_s^* - c)$.

seller s. Now suppose that two distinct sellers $s' \neq s$ set their equilibrium prices to be $p^*_{s'} < p^*_s < v$, while all other sellers set their equilibrium prices at v. In this case, seller s prefers price v to p^*_s, since $\pi_s(v, p^*_{-s}) = [(1/S)w_A](v - c) > [(1/S)w_A](p^*_s - c) = \pi_s(p^*_s, p^*_{-s})$, which again implies that p^*_s is not an equilibrium price for seller s. In sum, no 2 (or more) sellers charge equal equilibrium prices strictly below v, and no 2 (or more) sellers charge unequal equilibrium prices strictly below v. Therefore, at most one seller charges $p^*_s < v$.

On the other hand, *at equilibrium, at least one seller s charges $p^*_s < v$*. Given that all sellers other than s set their equilibrium prices at v, seller s maximizes its profits by charging $v - \epsilon$, since $\pi_s(v - \epsilon, p^*_{-s}) = [(1/S)w_A + w_B](v - \epsilon - c) > [(1/S)(w_A + w_B)](v - c) = \pi_s(v, p^*_{-s})$, for small, positive values of ϵ.[5] Thus, v is not an equilibrium price for seller s. It follows from these two observations that at equilibrium, exactly one seller s sets its price below the buyers' valuation v, while all other sellers $s' \neq s$ set their equilibrium prices $p^*_{s'} \geq v$. Note that $\pi_{s'}(v, p^*_{-s'}) = [(1/S)w_A](v - c) > 0 = \pi_{s'}(v', p^*_{-s'})$, for all $v' > v$, since $w_A > 0$, implying that all other sellers s' maximize their profits by charging price v. The unique form of pure strategy equilibrium which arises in this setting thus requires that a single seller s set its price $p^*_s < v$ while all other sellers $s' \neq s$ set their prices $p^*_{s'} = v$. The price vector (p^*_s, p^*_{-s}), with $p^*_{-s} = (v, \ldots, v)$, however, is not a Nash equilibrium. While v is in fact an optimal response to p^*_s, since the profits of seller $s' \neq s$ are maximized at v given that there exists low-priced seller s, p^*_s is not an optimal response to v. On the contrary, $\pi_s(p^*_s, v, \ldots, v) < \pi_s(v - \epsilon, v, \ldots, v)$, whenever $\epsilon < v - p^*_s$. In particular, the low-priced seller s has incentive to deviate. It follows that there is no pure strategy Nash equilibrium in the proposed shopbot model.[6]

There does, however, exist a symmetric mixed strategy Nash equilibrium. Let $f(p)$ denote the probability density function according to which sellers set their equilibrium prices, and let $F(p)$ be the corresponding cumulative distribution function. Following Varian [32], we note that in the range for which it is defined, $F(p)$ has no mass points, since otherwise a seller could decrease its price by an arbitrarily small amount and experience a discontinuous increase in profits. Moreover, there are no gaps in the said distribution, since otherwise prices would not be optimal — a seller charging a price at the low end of the gap could increase its price to fill the gap while retaining its market share, thereby increasing its profits. In this probabilistic setting, the event that seller s is the low-priced seller occurs with probability $[1 - F(p)]^{S-1}$. Rewriting Eq. 2, we obtain the demand expected by seller s:[7]

$$h_s(p) = w_A \frac{1}{S} + w_B[1 - F(p)]^{S-1} \tag{7}$$

---

[5] Precisely, $0 < \epsilon < \frac{w_B(S-1)}{w_A + w_B S}(v - c)$.

[6] This argument rests on the fact that price selection is made within a continuous strategy space; the existence of pure strategy Nash equilibria as an outcome of price discretization is discussed in Appendix A.

[7] In Eq. 7, $h_s(p)$ is expressed as a function of seller s's scalar price p, given that probability distribution $F(p)$ describes the other sellers' expected prices.

A Nash equilibrium in mixed strategies requires that (i) sellers maximize individual profits, given the other sellers' strategic profiles, so as there is no incentive to deviate, and (ii) all prices assigned positive probability yield equal profits, otherwise it would not be optimal to randomize. Following condition (ii), we define equilibrium profits $\pi \equiv \pi_s(p) = (p - c)h_s(p)$, for all prices p. The precise value of π can be derived by considering the maximum price that sellers are willing to charge, say p_m. At this boundary, $F(p_m) = 1$, which by Eq. 7 implies that $h_s(p_m) = (1/S)w_A$. Moreover, the function $\pi_s(p)$ attains its maximal value at price $p_m = v$, yielding equilibrium profits $\pi = (1/S)w_A(v - c)$. Now, by setting $(p - c)h_s(p)$ equal to this value and solving for $F(p)$, we obtain:

$$F(p) = 1 - \left[\left(\frac{w_A}{w_B S} \right) \left(\frac{v - p}{p - c} \right) \right]^{\frac{1}{S-1}} \tag{8}$$

which implicitly defines p and $F(p)$ in terms of one another. Since $F(p)$ is a cumulative probability distribution, it is only valid in the domain for which its valuation is between 0 and 1. As noted previously, the upper boundary is $p = v$; the lower boundary is computed by setting $F(p) = 0$ in Eq. 8, which yields:

$$p^* \equiv p = c + \frac{w_A(v - c)}{w_A + w_B S} \tag{9}$$

Thus, Eq. 8 is valid in the range $p^* \leq p \leq v$. A similar derivation of this mixed strategy equilibrium appears in Varian [32]. Greenwald, et al. [20] presents various generalizations of this model.

Figs 1 (a) and (b), respectively, exhibit plots of the functions $F(p)$ and $f(p)$ under varying distributions of buyer strategies — in particular, the fraction of shopbot users $w_B \in \{.1, .25, .5, .75, .9\}$ — with $S = 5$, $v = 1$, and $c = 0.5$. When w_B exceeds a critical threshold $w_B^{\text{crit}} = \frac{S-2}{S^2+S-2}$ (equal to 0.1071 for $S = 5$), $f(p)$ is bimodal. In this regime, as either w_B or S increases, the probability density concentrates either just below v, where sellers expect high margins but low volume, or just above p^*, where they expect low margins but high volume, with the latter solution becoming increasingly probable. Since p^* itself decreases under these conditions (see Eq. 9), it follows that both the average price paid by buyers and the average profit earned by sellers decrease. These relationships have a simple interpretation: buyers' use of shopbots catalyzes competition among sellers, and moreover, small fractions of shopbot users induce competition among large numbers of sellers.

Recall that the profit earned by each seller is $(1/S)w_A$, which is strictly positive so long as $w_A > 0$. It is as though only buyers of type A are contributing to sellers' profits, although the actual distribution of contributions from buyers of type A vs. buyers of type B is not as one-sided as it appears. In reality, buyers of type A are charged less than v on average, and buyers of type B are charged more than c on average, although total profits are equivalent to what they would be if the sellers practiced perfect price discrimination. Buyers of type A exert negative externalities on buyers of type B, by creating surplus profits for sellers.

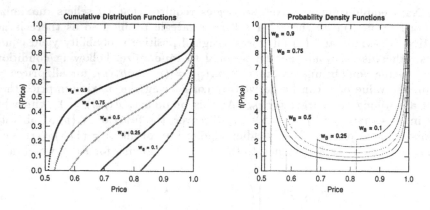

Fig. 1. Nash Equilibria for $S = 5, v = 1, c = .5$, and $w_B \in \{.1, .25, .5, .75, .9\}$

4   Strategies

When sufficiently widespread adoption of shopbots by buyers forces sellers to become more competitive, it is likely that sellers will respond with the creation of *pricebots* that automatically set prices in attempt to maximize profitability. It seems unrealistic, however, to expect that pricebots will simply compute a Nash equilibrium and fix prices accordingly. The real business world is fraught with uncertainties, undermining the validity of traditional game-theoretic analyses: sellers lack perfect knowledge of buyer demands, and they have an incomplete understanding of their competitors' strategies. In order to be deemed profitable, pricebots will need to learn from and adapt to changing market conditions.

In this section, we introduce a series of pricebot strategies, and which we later simulate in order to compare the resulting price and profit dynamics with the game-theoretic equilibrium. In 1838, Cournot showed that the outcome of learning via a simple best-reply dynamic is a pure strategy Nash equilibrium in a quantity-setting model of duopoly [7]. Recently, empirical studies of more sophisticated learning algorithms have revealed that learning tends to converge to pure strategy Nash equilibria in games for which such equilibria exist [17]. As there does not exist a pure strategy Nash equilibrium in the shopbot model, it is of particular interest to study the outcome of adaptive pricing schemes.

We consider several pricing strategies, each of which makes different demands on the required level of informational and computational power of agents:

GT The *game-theoretic* strategy is designed to reproduce the mixed strategy Nash equilibrium. It therefore generates a price chosen at random according to the probability density function derived in the previous section, assuming its competitors utilize game-theoretic pricing as well, and making full use of information about the buyer population. GT is a constant function that ignores historical observations.

MY The myopically optimal, or *myoptimal*, [8] pricing strategy (see, for example, [24]) uses information about all the buyer characteristics that factor into the buyer demand function, as well as competitors' prices, but makes no attempt to account for competitors' pricing strategies. Instead, it is based on the assumption of static expectations: even if one seller is contemplating a price change under myoptimal pricing, this seller does not consider that this will elicit a response from its competitors.

The myoptimal seller s uses all available information and the assumption of static expectations to perform an exhaustive search for the price p_s^* that maximizes its expected profit π_s. The computational demands of MY can be reduced greatly if the price quantum ϵ — the smallest amount by which one seller may undercut another — is sufficiently small (see Appendix A). Under such circumstances, the optimal price p_s^* is guaranteed to be either the monopolistic price p_m or ϵ below some competitor's price, limiting the search for p_s^* to S possible values. In our simulations, we choose $\epsilon = 0.002$.

DF The *derivative-following* strategy is less informationally intensive than either the myoptimal or the game-theoretic pricing strategies. In particular, this strategy can be used in the absence of any knowledge or assumptions about one's competitors or the buyer demand function. A derivative follower simply experiments with incremental increases (or decreases) in price, continuing to move its price in the same direction until the observed profitability level falls, at which point the direction of movement is reversed. The price increment δ is chosen randomly from a specified probability distribution; in the simulations described here the distribution was uniform between 0.01 and 0.02.

NR The *no regret* pricing strategies are probabilistic learning algorithms which specify that players *explore* the space of actions by playing all actions with some non-zero probability, and *exploit* successful actions by increasing the probability of employing those actions that generate high profits. In this study, we confine our attention to the no external regret algorithm due to Freund and Schapire [14] and the no internal regret algorithm of Foster and Vohra [12].[9] As the no regret algorithms are inherently non-deterministic, they are candidates for learning mixed strategy equilibria.

5   Simulations

We simulated an economy with 1000 buyers and (unless otherwise specified) 5 pricebots. employing the aforementioned pricing strategies. In the simulations depicted below, each buyer's valuation of the good $v = 1$, and each seller's production cost $c = 0.5$. The mixture of buyer types is set at $w_B = 0.75, i.e.,$ 75% are bargain hunters, or shopbot users. The simulations were asynchronous:

---

[8] In the game-theoretic literature, this strategy is often referred to as Cournot best-reply dynamics [7]; however, price is being set, rather than quantity.

[9] For completeness, the details of these algorithms are presented in App. B.

at each time step, a buyer or seller was randomly selected to carry out an action (e.g., buying an item or resetting a price). The chance that a given agent was selected for action was determined by its rate; the rate ρ_b at which a given buyer b attempts to purchase the good was set to 0.001, while the rate ρ_s at which a given seller reconsiders its price was 0.00002 (except where otherwise specified). Each simulation was iterated for 100 million time steps.

5.1   GT Pricebots

Simulations verify that, if agents are GT strategists, the cumulative distribution of prices closely resembles the derived $F(p)$ (to within statistical error), and moreover, the time-averaged profit for each seller is $\bar{\pi} = 0.0255 \pm 0.0003$, which is nearly the theoretical value of 0.0250. (Not shown.)

5.2   MY Pricebots

Fig. 2(a) illustrates cyclical price wars that typically occur when 5 pricebots use the myoptimal pricing strategy. Regardless of the initial value of the price vector, a pattern quickly emerges in which prices are positioned near the monopolistic price $v = 1$, followed by a long episode during which pricebots successively undercut one another by ϵ. During this latter phase, no two prices differ by more than $(S - 1)\epsilon$, and the prices fall linearly with time. Eventually, when the lowest-priced seller is within ϵ above the value $p^* = 0.53125$, the next seller finds it unprofitable to undercut, and instead resets its price to $v = 1$. The other pricebots follow suit, until all but the lowest-priced seller are charging $v = 1$. At this point, the lowest-priced seller finds that it can maintain its market share but increase its profit dramatically — from $p^* - .5 = 0.03125$ to $0.5 - \epsilon$ — by raising its price to $1 - \epsilon$. No sooner than the lowest-priced seller raises its price does the next seller to reset its price undercut, thereby igniting the next cycle of the price war.

Fig. 2(b) shows the sellers' profits averaged during the intervals between successive resetting of prices. The upper curve represents a linear decrease in the average profit attained by the lowest-priced seller as price decreases, whichever seller that happens to be. The lower curve represents the average profit attained by sellers that are not currently the lowest-priced; near the end of the cycle they suffer from both low market share and low margin. The expected average profit can be computed by averaging the profit given by Eqs. 5 and 6 over one price-war cycle:

$$\pi_s^{MY} = \frac{1}{S}\left[\frac{1}{2}(v + p^*) - c\right] \tag{10}$$

which yields $\pi_s^{MY} = 0.053125$ in this instance. The simulation results match this closely: the average profit per time step is 0.0515, which is just over twice the average profit obtained via the game-theoretic pricing strategy.

Since prices fluctuate over time, it is of interest to compute the probability distribution of prices. Fig. 2(a) depicts the cumulative distribution function for myoptimal pricing. This measured cumulative density function has exactly the same endpoints $p^* = 0.53125$ and $v = 1$ as those of the theoretical mixed strategy equilibrium, but the linear shape between those endpoints (which reflects the linear price war) is quite different from what is displayed in Fig. 1(a).

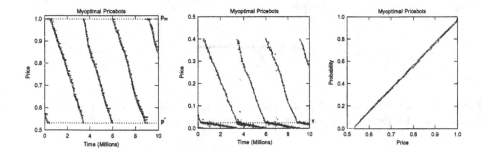

Fig. 2. (a) and (b) Price and profit dynamics, respectively, for 5 MY pricebots. (c) Cumulative distribution of prices observed between times 10 and 100 million.

5.3   DF Pricebots

Fig. 3(a) shows the price dynamics that result when 5 derivative followers are pitted against one another. Recall that derivative following pricebots do not base their pricing decisions on any information that pertains to other agents in the system — neither pricebots' price-setting tendencies nor buyers' preferences. Nonetheless, their behavior tends towards what is in effect a collusive state in which *all* pricebots charge nearly the monopolistic price.[10] This is tacit collusion as defined, for example, in Tirole [30], and so-called because the agents do not communicate at all so there is consequently nothing illegal about their collusive behavior. By exhibiting such behavior, derivative followers accumulate greater wealth than myoptimal or game-theoretic pricebots. According to Fig. 3(b), pricebots that are currently lowest-priced can expect an average profit of 0.30 to 0.35, while the others can expect roughly the game-theoretic profit of 0.025. Averaging over the last 90 million time steps (to eliminate transient effects), we find that the average profit per seller is 0.0841. This value is not far off from the absolute collusive limit of $(1/S)(v - c) = 0.10$.

How do derivative followers manage to collude? Like myoptimal pricebots, DFs are capable of engaging in price wars; such dynamics are visible in Fig. 3(a). These price wars, however, are easily quelled, making upward trends more likely than downward trends. Suppose X and Y are the two lowest-priced pricebots engaged in a mini-price war. Assume X's price is initially above Y's, but that X soon undercuts Y. This yields profits for seller X obtained from the entire population of type B buyers while it is lower-priced, and from its share of type A buyers all throughout. Now suppose Y undercuts X, but soon after X again

---

[10] It has similarly been observed by Huck, *et al.* [23] that derivative followers tend towards collusive behavior in models of Cournot duopoly.

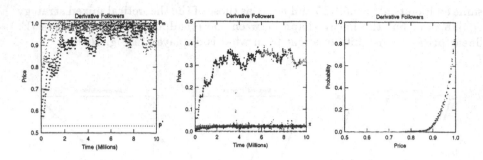

Fig. 3. (a) and (b) Price and profit dynamics, respectively, for 5 DF pricebots. (c) Cumulative distribution of prices observed between times 10 and 100 million.

undercuts Y. This yields profits for seller X once again obtained from the entire population of type B buyers during the period in which it is lower-priced, and from its share of type A buyers all throughout. In other words, given equivalent rates of price adjustment for both pricebots, market share remains fixed during mini-price wars of this kind. Thus, the only variable in computing profits is price, leaving pricebots with the incentive to increases prices more often than not. The tendency of a society of DF pricebots to reach and maintain high prices is reflected in the cumulative distribution function, shown in Fig. 3(c).

5.4   NR Pricebots

Finally, we present simulation results for two no regret pricing strategies, namely no external regret (NER) and no internal regret (NIR). As described in [16], there are a number of learning algorithms that satisfy the no external regret optimality criterion (*e.g.*, Foster and Vohra [11] and Freund and Schapire [14]); similarly, the no internal regret optimality criterion is satisfied by algorithms due to both Foster and Vohra [12] and Hart and Mas-Colell [22]. In this section, we discuss simulations of NER pricebots *á la* Freund and Schapire and NIR pricebots *á la* Foster and Vohra. Rather than consider 5 pricebots as above, we limit our attention to merely 2 NR pricebots, since the dynamics of 2 such pricebots converges more readily than does that of 5. As no regret algorithms are inherently non-deterministic as well as myopic, they are candidates for learning mixed strategy equilibria of stage games.

Although the no external regret algorithm of Freund and Schapire has been observed to converge to Nash equilibrium in games of 2 actions (*e.g.*, the Santa Fe bar problem, see Greenwald, *et al.* [18]), NER pricebots cycle exponentially from price p_m to price p^* in the prescribed model, which entertains $n > 2$ possible actions[11] (see Fig. 4(a)). In fact, the outcome of play of NER pricebots in the shopbot game is reminiscent of the outcome of both NER learning and

---

[11]   Technically, there is a continuum of prices in our model. For the purpose of simulating no regret learning, this continuum was discretized into 100 equally sized intervals.

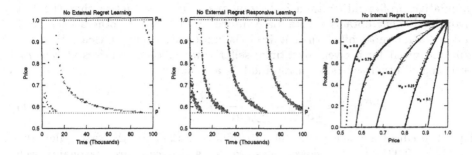

Fig. 4. (a) and (b) Price dynamics for 2 NER pricebots with learning rate $\beta = 0.1$, and $\gamma = 0$ and $\gamma = 0.0001$, respectively. (c) CDFs generated from simulation tape of 2 NIR pricebots with theoretical Nash equilibrium overlayed.

fictitious play in the Shapley game, a game of 3 strategies for which there is no pure strategy Nash equilibrium (see Greenwald, *et al.* [17]). Fig. 4(b) depicts simulations of NER pricebots in which we introduce a responsiveness parameter $0 < \gamma \leq 1$ that exponentially weights the observed history, effectively limiting its length to the finite value $1/\gamma$, thereby allowing NER pricebots to more readily respond to environmental changes. Interestingly, the empirical frequency of play during these finite cycles mimics the symmetric mixed strategy Nash equilibrium of the stage game; this result will be further explored in a future publication.

We now investigate the properties of no internal regret (NIR) learning in our model of shopbots and pricebots. Learning algorithms that satisfy the no internal regret optimality criteria are known to converge to correlated equilibria [2, 12], a superset of the set of Nash equilibria which allows for dependence among players' strategies. Despite several negative theoretical results on the rational learning of Nash equilibria (*e.g.*, Foster and Young [13], Nachbar [27], and Greenwald *et al.* [18]), in practice, no internal regret learning — a form of boundedly rational learning — seems to learn Nash equilibria. In our present simulations we observe convergence to the symmetric mixed strategy Nash equilibrium. Fig. 4(c) depicts the cumulative distribution functions generated from simulation tapes of the no internal regret learning algorithm designed by Foster and Vohra [12]. In these simulations, we consider 2 NIR pricebots, and we let buyer distributions range from $(w_A, w_B) = (0.1, 0.9)$ to $(w_A, w_B) = (0.9, 0.1)$. These plots closely match the theoretical Nash equilibria given 2 sellers, which are overlayed in this figure.

6 Evolution of Shopbots and Pricebots

We now revisit the situation in which all five sellers utilize the myoptimal pricing strategy, but we allow one of the sellers to reset its price five times as quickly as all the others. These price dynamics are illustrated in Fig. 5(a). As in Fig. 2(a), we experience price wars; in this case, however, they are accelerated, which is apparent from the increase in the number of cycles that occur during the simulation run. From the individual profit curves, which in Fig. 5(b) depict cumulative profits rather than instantaneous profits, we notice that the fast myoptimal agent obtains substantially more profit than the others because it undercuts far more often than it itself is undercut. Analysis yields that the expected profit for a given myoptimal seller s who resets its prices at rate ρ_s, assuming all other sellers are myoptimal, is as follows:

$$\pi_s^{my}(p_s) = \left[\frac{1}{S}w_A + \frac{\rho_s}{\sum_{s'}\rho_{s'}}w_B\right]\left[\frac{1}{2}(v + p^*) - c\right] \tag{11}$$

Eq. 11 predicts average profits of $119/960 = 0.1240$ for the fast seller and $34/960 = 0.0354$ for the slower ones, values which compare reasonably well with those obtained by averaging over the last 10 complete cycles of the price war, namely 0.1111 and 0.0351, respectively.

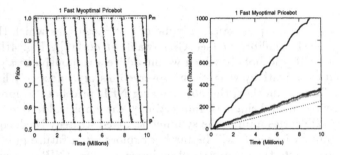

Fig. 5. (a) and (b) Price and profit dynamics, respectively, with 1 Fast MY pricebot.

Evidently, myoptimal pricebots stand to gain by resetting their prices at faster, rather than slower, rates, particularly when a large proportion of the buyer population is shopbot-assisted (see Eq. 11). If MY pricebots were to reprice their goods with ever-increasing frequency, a sort of arms race would develop, leading to arbitrarily fast price-war cycles. This observation is not specific to myoptimal agents. In additional simulations, we have observed sufficiently fast DF pricebots who obtain the upper hand over slower derivative following and myoptimal agents. In the absence of any throttling mechanism, it is advantageous for pricebots to re-price their goods as quickly as possible.

Let us carry the arms race scenario a bit further. In a world in which sellers are inclined to reset prices at ever-increasing rates, human price setters would undoubtedly be too inefficient. Sellers, therefore, would necessarily come to rely on pricebots, perhaps sophisticated variants of one of the strategies proposed in Sec. 4. Quite possibly, pricebot strategies would utilize information about the buyer population, which could be purchased from other agents. Even more likely, pricebot strategies would require knowledge of their competitors' prices. How would up-to-date information be obtained? From shopbots, of course!

With each seller seeking to re-price its products faster than its competitors, shopbots would quickly become overloaded with requests. Imagine a scenario in which a large player like amazon.com were to use the following simple price-setting strategy: every 10 minutes, submit 2 million or so queries to one or more shopbots (one for each title carried by Amazon.com), then charge 1 cent less than the minimum price returned on each title! Since the job of shopbots is to query individual sellers for prices, it would in turn pass this load back to Amazon.com's competitors. The rate of pricing requests made by sellers could easily dwarf the rate at which similar requests would be made by human buyers, thereby eliminating the potential of shopbots to ameliorate market frictions.

A typical solution to an excess demand for shopbot services would be for shopbots to charge pricebots for price information. Today, shopbots tend to make a living by selling advertising space on their Web pages. This appears to be an adequate business model so long as requests are made by humans. Agents, however, are unwelcome customers because they are are not influenced by advertisements; as a result, agents are either barely tolerated or excluded intentionally. By charging for the information services they provide, shopbots would be economically-motivated agents, creating the proper incentives to deter excess demand, and welcoming business from other agents.

Once shopbots begin to charge for pricing information, it would seem natural for sellers — the actual owners of the desired information — to themselves charge shopbots for price information. In fact, sellers could use another form of pricebot to dynamically price this information. This scenario illustrates how the need for agents to dynamically price their services could quickly percolate through an entire economy of software agents. The alternative is "meltdown" due to overload which could occur as agents become more prevalent on the Internet. Rules of etiquette followed voluntarily today by web crawlers and related programs [9] could be trampled in the rush for competitive advantage.

7   Conclusion

Game-theoretic analysis of a model of a simple commodity market established a quantitative relationship between the degree of shopbot usage among buyers and the degree of price competition among sellers. This motivated a comparative study of various *pricebot* algorithms that sellers might employ in an effort to gain an edge in a market in which the presence of shopbots has increased the degree of competition.

MY pricebots were shown to be capable of inducing price wars, yet even so they earn profits that are well above those of GT strategists. DF pricebots were observed to exhibit tacit collusion, leading to cartel-level profits. Finally, game-theoretic equilibria arose dynamically as the outcome of repeated play among certain NR pricebots. In related work (see [20]), we explore the dynamics of prices and profits among pricebots that use non-myopic learning algorithms, such as Q-learning, and we directly compare the profitability of various pricing strategies by simulating heterogeneous collections of pricebots. In future work, we intend to study the dynamics of markets in which more sophisticated shopbots base their search on product attributes as well as price, and in which pricebot strategies are extended accordingly.

Acknowledgments

The authors are grateful to Fredrik Ygge for his careful reading of an earlier version of this paper, in which he isolated some serious flaws in the original analysis. Any remaining errors are surely the fault of the authors. In addition, the authors thank Adam Kalai for discovering certain pure strategy Nash equilibria in the discretized model, which inspired the analysis presented in Appendix A.

References

1. P. Auer, N. Cesa-Bianchi, Y. Freund, and R. Schapire. Gambling in a rigged casino: The adversarial multi-armed bandit problem. In *Proceedings of the 36th Annual Symposium on Foundations of Computer Science*, pages 322–331. ACM Press, November 1995.
2. R. Aumann. Subjectivity and correlation in randomized strategies. *Journal of Mathematical Economics*, 1:67–96, 1974.
3. A. Banos. On pseudo games. *The Annals of Mathematical Statistics*, 39:1932–1945, 1968.
4. D. Blackwell. An analog of the minimax theorem for vector payoffs. *Pacific Journal of Mathematics*, 6:1–8, 1956.
5. K. Burdett and K. L. Judd. Equilibrium price dispersion. *Econometrica*, 51(4):955–969, July 1983.
6. Anthony Chavez and Pattie Maes. Kasbah: an agent marketplace for buying and selling goods. In *Proceedings of the First International Conference on the Practical Application of Intelligent Agents and Multi-Agent Technology*, London, U.K., April 1996.
7. A. Cournot. *Recherches sur les Principes Mathematics de la Theorie de la Richesse*. Hachette, 1838.
8. J. Bradford DeLong and A. Michael Froomkin. The next economy? In Deborah Hurley, Brian Kahin, and Hal Varian, editors, *Internet Publishing and Beyond: The Economics of Digital Information and Intellecutal Property*. MIT Press, Cambridge, Massachusetts, 1998.
9. David Eichmann. Ethical web agents. In *Proceedings of the Second World Wide Web Conference '94: Mosaic and the Web*, 1994.
10. Joakim Eriksson, Niclas Finne, and Sverker Janson. Information and interaction in MarketSpace — towards an open agent-based market infrastructure. In *Proceedings of the Second USENIX Workshop on Electronic Commerce*, November 1996.
11. D. Foster and R. Vohra. A randomization rule for selecting forecasts. *Operations Research*, 41(4):704–709, 1993.
12. D. Foster and R. Vohra. Regret in the on-line decision problem. *Games and Economic Behavior*, 21:40–55, 1997.
13. D. Foster and P. Young. When rational learning fails. Mimeo, 1998.
14. Y. Freund and R. Schapire. Game theory, on-line prediction, and boosting. In *Proceedings of the 9th Annual Conference on Computational Learning Theory*, pages 325–332. ACM Press, May 1996.
15. D. Fudenberg and J. Tirole. *Game Theory*. MIT Press, Cambridge, 1991.
16. A. Greenwald. *Learning to Play Network Games*. PhD thesis, Courant Institute of Mathematical Sciences, New York University, New York, May 1999.
17. A. Greenwald, E. Friedman, and S. Shenker. Learning in network contexts: Results from experimental simulations. *Games and Economic Behavior: Special Issue on Economics and Artificial Intelligence*, Forthcoming 1999.

18. A. Greenwald, B. Mishra, and R. Parikh. The Santa Fe bar problem revisited: Theoretical and practical implications. Presented at *Stonybrook Festival on Game Theory: Interactive Dynamics and Learning*, July 1998.

19. A.R. Greenwald and J.O. Kephart. Shopbots and pricebots. In *Proceedings of Sixteenth International Joint Conference on Artificial Intelligence*, volume 1, pages 506–511, August 1999.

20. A.R. Greenwald, J.O. Kephart, and G.J. Tesauro. Strategic pricebot dynamics. In *Proceedings of First ACM Conference on Electronic Commerce*, To Appear, November 1999.

21. J. Hannan. Approximation to Bayes risk in repeated plays. In M. Dresher, A.W. Tucker, and P. Wolfe, editors, *Contributions to the Theory of Games*, volume 3, pages 97–139. Princeton University Press, 1957.

22. S. Hart and A. Mas Colell. A simple adaptive procedure leading to correlated equilibrium. Technical report, Center for Rationality and Interactive Decision Theory, 1997.

23. S. Huck, H-T. Normann, and Jörg Oechssler. Learning in a cournot duopoly – an experiment. Unpublished Manuscript, July 1997.

24. J. O. Kephart, J. E. Hanson, D. W. Levine, B. N. Grosof, J. Sairamesh, R. B. Segal, and S. R. White. Dynamics of an information filtering economy. In *Proceedings of the Second International Workshop on Cooperative Information Agents*, 1998.

25. J.O. Kephart and A.R. Greenwald. Shopbot economics. In *Proceedings of Fifth European Conference on Symbolic and Quantitative Approaches to Reasoning with Uncertainty*, pages 208–220, July 1999.

26. B. Krulwich. The BargainFinder agent: Comparison price shopping on the Internet. In J. Williams, editor, *Agents, Bots and Other Internet Beasties*, pages 257–263. SAMS.NET publishing (MacMillan), 1996. URLs: http://bf.cstar.ac.com/bf, http://www.geocities.com/ResearchTriangle/9430.

27. J. Nachbar. Prediction, optimization, and learning in repeated games. *Econometrica*, 65:275–309, 1997.

28. J. Nash. Non-cooperative games. *Annals of Mathematics*, 54:286–295, 1951.

29. G.J. Tesauro and J.O. Kephart. Pricing in agent economies using multi-agent q-learning. In *Proceedings of Fifth European Conference on Symbolic and Quantitative Approaches to Reasoning with Uncertainty*, pages 71–86, July 1999.

30. Jean Tirole. *The Theory of Industrial Organization*. The MIT Press, Cambridge, MA, 1988.

31. M. Tsvetovatyy, M. Gini, B. Mobasher, and Z. Wieckowski. MAGMA: an agent-based virtual market for electronic commerce. *Applied Artificial Intelligence*, 1997.

32. H. Varian. A model of sales. *American Economic Review, Papers and Proceedings*, 70(4):651–659, September 1980.

33. L. L. Wilde and A. Schwartz. Comparison shopping as a simultaneous move game. *Economic Journal*, 102:562–569, 1992.

A   Pure Strategy Nash Equilibria

This appendix revisits the existence of pure strategy Nash equilibria (PNE) in the prescribed model of shopbots and pricebots whenever $0 < w_A, w_B < 1$. It has previously been established (see Sec. 3) that no PNE exist when prices are selected from a continuous strategy space. Here, we assume that prices are chosen from a strategy space that is discrete rather than continuous, and we derive the set of pure strategy Nash equilibria. This set is symmetric in the case of 2 sellers, but is often asymmetric in the case of $S > 2$ sellers.

Recall from Sec. 2 that the profits for seller s are determined as follows, assuming $v_b = v$ for all buyers b, and $c_s = c$ for all sellers s:

$$\pi_s(\boldsymbol{p}) = \begin{cases} (p_s - c)h_s(\boldsymbol{p}) & \text{if } p_s \leq v \\ 0 & \text{otherwise} \end{cases} \qquad (12)$$

where

$$h_s(\boldsymbol{p}) = w_A \frac{1}{S} + w_B \frac{1}{\tau_s(\boldsymbol{p}) + 1} \delta_{\lambda_s(\boldsymbol{p}),0} \qquad (13)$$

- δ is the Kronecker δ function,
- $\lambda_s(\boldsymbol{p})$ is the number of sellers charging a lower price than s, and
- $\tau_s(\boldsymbol{p})$ is the number of sellers charging the same price as s, excluding s itself.

The equilibrium derivation that follows concerns the case of discrete strategy spaces, characterized by some parameter $\epsilon > 0$, which dictates the sellers' space of strategies as follows: $|P| = \{0, \epsilon, 2\epsilon, \ldots\}$. If we assume $c \bmod \epsilon = 0$, then this strategy space contains prices of the form $p_i = c \pm i\epsilon$, where $i \in \{x \in \mathbf{Z} | x \geq c/\epsilon\}$. For convenience, we further assume $v \bmod \epsilon = 0$.[12]

The derivation of the set of pure strategy Nash equilibria is based on the following observations, which dictate the structure of its elements: at equilibrium,

1. No seller charges price $p_i > v$.
2. No seller charges price $p_i \leq c$.
3. At least two sellers charge prices $c < p_i < v$.
4. Those sellers who charge prices $c < p_i < v$ charge equal prices.

The first two observations follow from the fact that the profits obtained by charging the monopoly price v are strictly positive, whereas the profits obtained by charging either $p_i > v$ or $p_i \leq c$ are zero. At least two sellers charge $c < p_i < v$ since (i) if all sellers were to charge v, seller s would stand to gain by instead charging $v - \epsilon$ (assuming $\epsilon < v - c$) and (ii) if only one seller were to charge $c < p_i < v$, then p_i must equal $v - \epsilon$, in which case the other sellers would stand to gain by charging $v - 2\epsilon$ (assuming $2\epsilon < v - c$). Finally, if seller s' were to charge $c < p'_i < v$, while seller s were charging $c < p_i < p'_i < v$, then seller s' would prefer price v to price p'_i, implying that p'_i is not an equilibrium price. Therefore, PNE are structured such that $n \geq 2$ sellers charge p_i for $0 < i < (v - c)/\epsilon$, while

---

[12] Otherwise, v is everywhere replaced by $v' = c + \epsilon \lfloor \frac{v-c}{\epsilon} \rfloor$ in the discussion that follows.

the remaining $S - n$ sellers charge the monopoly price v (unless $\epsilon \geq v - c$, in which case PNE exist of the form (v, v), or $\epsilon \geq (v - c)/2$, in which case PNE exist of the form $(v - \epsilon, v - \epsilon)$).

Given the prescribed structure, the existence of pure strategy Nash equilibria is ensured whenever the following conditions are satisfied: for all sellers s,

1. No low-priced seller charging $c < p_i < v$ prefers the monopoly price v: i.e., $\pi_s(p_i) \geq \pi_s(v)$, where $\pi_s(p_i)$ is computed assuming p_i is charged by n low-priced sellers. Expanding this condition leads to the following:

$$i\epsilon \geq \frac{w_A(v - c)}{w_A + \frac{1}{n}w_B S} \qquad (14)$$

This condition implies that $p_i = c + i\epsilon > p^*$, since $n \geq 2$.[13]

2. No seller charging v prefers to undercut the low-priced sellers charging p_i and charge p_{i-1}: i.e., $\pi_s(v) \geq \pi_s(p_{i-1})$, where $\pi_s(p_{i-1})$ are the profits obtained if seller s is the unique, lowest-priced seller. Expanding this condition yields:

$$\frac{w_A(v - c)}{w_A + w_B S} \geq (i - 1)\epsilon \qquad (15)$$

For $i = 1$ this condition reduces to $\pi_s(v) \geq \pi_s(c) = 0$, which is tautological; hence this constraint is only of interest when $i > 1$.

3. No low-priced seller charging p_i prefers to undercut its cohorts by charging p_{i-1}: i.e., $\pi_s(p_i) \geq \pi_s(p_{i-1})$, which incidentally is implied by Conds. 14 and 15, so long as some seller charges v. This yields a constraint on the value of i (or stated otherwise, n) for which PNE exist, namely:

$$\frac{i}{i - 1} \geq \frac{w_A + w_B S}{w_A + \frac{1}{n}w_B S} \qquad (16)$$

Like the previous condition, this constraint is only applicable when $i > 1$.

Together Conds. 14, 15, and 16 are mathematical statements of the conditions for the existence of pure strategy Nash equilibria of the prescribed structure.

We now construct a series of examples, assuming production cost is $c = 0.5$, buyers have constant valuations $v = 1$, and $w_A = 0.25$ and $w_B = 0.75$. Initially, we consider only 2 sellers. By the prescribed structure of PNE, both sellers charge equal prices $c < p_i < v$, for some $0 < i < (v-c)/\epsilon$, assuming $\epsilon < (v-c)/2 = 0.25$. Since no seller charges v, Cond. 15 is not a relevant constraint. Cond. 16 requires that $\frac{i}{i-1} \geq w_A + 2w_B = 1.75$, which is impossible for integer values of $i > 2$. Thus, our interest is confined to values of $i \leq 2$ and $\epsilon < 0.25$ satisfying Cond. 14. In particular, if $i = 1$, then PNE exist whenever $0.25 > \epsilon \geq w_A(v - c) = 0.125$;

---

[13] The value of p^* derived in Eq. 9 for the continuous case is applicable in the discrete case, unless $v \bmod \epsilon \neq 0$, in which case v is replaced by v' in Eq. 9 (see Foot. 12).

if $i = 2$, then PNE exist whenever $0.25 > \epsilon \geq w_A(v - c) = 0.0625$. The complete set of PNE for $S = 2$ is listed in Table A. Notice that PNE cease to exist when $|P| > 9$; for $S = 3$, PNE cease to exist when $|P| > 12$; in general, PNE cease to exist whenever $|P| > \lfloor 1 + i^*[1 + (w_B/w_A)(S/n)] \rfloor$ where i^* is the maximum integer value i satisfying Cond. 16, which can be rearranged to give an upper bound on i.

$|P|$	$\epsilon = \frac{v-c}{|P|-1}$	i	PNE
1	∞	0	(1.0, 1.0)
2	0.5	1	(1.0, 1.0)
3	0.25	1	(0.75, 0.75)
4	$0.1\overline{6}$	1,2	$(0.\overline{6}, 0.\overline{6})$, $(0.8\overline{3}, 0.8\overline{3})$
5	0.125	1,2	(0.625, 0.625), (0.75, 0.75)
6	0.1	2	(0.7, 0.7)
7	$0.08\overline{3}$	2	$(0.\overline{6}, 0.\overline{6})$
8	0.0714	2	(0.643, 0.643)
9	0.0625	2	(0.625, 0.625)
10	$0.0\overline{5}$	-	DNE

Table 1. The set of PNE for $S = 2$. DNE stands for does not exist, implying the non-existence of pure strategy Nash equilibria, although the existence of mixed strategy equilibria is established in Nash [28].

Now consider a larger number of sellers; for concreteness, say $S = 100$. We first let $i = 1$, which limits our concern to Cond. 14. It follows from this condition that when the number of sellers is large, PNE exist even for small values of ϵ so long as n is also small. In particular, if $n = 2$ then PNE exist for $\epsilon \geq 0.003311$; specifically, if $\epsilon = 0.00\overline{3}$, then an asymmetric solution arises in which sellers who charge price p_1 earn profits of roughly 0.00126, while sellers who charge price v earn 0.00125. At the other extreme, if $n = 100$, then symmetric PNE exist iff $\epsilon \geq 0.125$. A full range of asymmetric PNE exist when $i = 1$ for the values of ϵ specified by Cond. 14 that arise for values of n ranging from 2 to 100.

Still assuming a large number of sellers, let $i > 1$. Restating Cond. 16 as a bound on n and taking the limit as $S \to \infty$, we find that $n \leq i/(i-1) \leq 2$. But since $n \geq 2$ at equilibrium, it follows that at any PNE exactly 2 sellers charge price p_i. Again rewriting Cond. 16, this time as a bound on i and then taking the limit as $S \to \infty$, we also find it necessary that $i \leq n/(n-1) \leq 2$. Thus, for sufficiently large numbers of sellers, PNE exist in which exactly 2 low-priced sellers charge price p_2, but no PNE exist in which any sellers charge p_i for $i > 2$.

It is nonetheless possible for equilibria to arise in which $i > 2$, however not for the assignments of w_A and w_B assumed throughout our examples. Consider instead $w_A = 0.75$ and $w_B = 0.25$. Now for $S = 2$, an equilibrium arises in which $n = 2$, $i = 5$, and $\epsilon = 0.08\overline{3}$, namely $(0.91\overline{6}, 0.91\overline{6})$. Using Cond. 16, we note that as $w_A \to 1$, i is bounded above only by $(v-c)/\epsilon$; in other words, high equilibrium prices prevail. On the other hand, as $w_B \to 1$, n is bounded above only by S, implying that more and more sellers prefer to charge low prices. Finally, through simulations we have observed pure strategy Nash equilibria to be the outcome of myoptimal pricing and no internal regret learning in the discretized model of shopbots and pricebots.

B   No Regret Learning

This appendix describes the no regret learning algorithms which are simulated in Sec. 5.4. There are two no regret criteria of interest, namely no external regret and no internal regret. Computational learning theorists consider the difference between the expected payoffs that are achieved by the strategies prescribed by a given algorithm, as compared to the payoffs that could be achieved by any other fixed sequence of decisions, in the worst-case. If the difference between these two sums is negligible, then the algorithm exhibits *no external regret*. Early no external regret algorithms appeared in Blackwell [4], Hannan [21], and Banos [3]. Game theorists Foster and Vohra [12] study an alternative measure of worst-case performance. If the difference between the cumulative payoffs that are achieved by a sequence of strategies generated by a given algorithm in comparison with the cumulative payoffs that could be achieved by a remapped sequence of strategies is insignificant, then the algorithm is said to exhibit *no internal regret*.[14] No internal regret implies no external regret.

   The no regret algorithms are presented from the point of view of an individual player, as if that player were playing a game against nature, where nature is taken to be a conglomeration of all its opponents. From this perspective, let r_i^t denote the payoffs obtained by the player of interest at time t via strategy i. Mixed strategy weights at time t are given by the probability vector (w_i^t), for $1 \leq i \leq S$, where S is the number of strategies.

B.1   No External Regret Learning

Freund and Schapire [14] derive an algorithm that achieves no external regret via multiplicative updating. Their algorithm is dependent on the cumulative payoffs achieved by all strategies, including the surmised payoffs of strategies which are not played. In particular, let ρ_i^t denote the cumulative payoffs obtained through time t via strategy i, which is computed as follows: $\rho_i^t = \sum_{x=0}^t r_i^x$. Now the weight assigned to strategy i at time $t+1$, for $\beta > 0$, is given by:

$$w_i^{t+1} = \frac{(1+\beta)^{\rho_i^t}}{\sum_{j=1}^S (1+\beta)^{\rho_j^t}} \tag{17}$$

The multiplicative updating rule given in Equation 17 can be modified to become applicable in naive settings, where complete payoff information is not available, but rather the only payoff information known at time t is that which pertains

---

[14] A sequence is remapped if there is a mapping f of the strategy space into itself s.t. for each occurrence of strategy s_i in the original sequence, the mapped strategy $f(s_i)$ appears in the remapped sequence.

to the strategy which was in fact employed at time t. Such a variant of this multiplicative updating algorithm appears in Auer, Cesa-Bianchi, Freund, and Schapire [1]. It remains to perform simulations of this naive algorithm in our model of shopbots and pricebots.

B.2   No Internal Regret Learning

We now describe an algorithm due to Foster and Vohra [12] which achieves no internal regret, and a simple implementation due to Hart and Mas-Colell [22]. Learning via the following no internal regret algorithms converges to correlated equilibrium [2, 12].

The regret felt by a player at time t is formulated as the difference between the payoffs obtained by utilizing strategy the player's strategy of choice, say i, and the payoffs that could have been achieved had strategy $j \neq i$ been played instead:

$$\mathrm{R}^t_{i \to j} = \mathbf{1}^t_i(r^t_j - r^t_i) \tag{18}$$

where $\mathbf{1}^t_i$ is the indicator function, which has value 1 if strategy i is employed at time t, and has value 0 otherwise. Now the cumulative regret $\mathrm{R}^T_{i \to j}$ is the summation of regrets from i to j through time T:

$$\mathrm{R}^T_{i \to j} = \sum_{t=0}^{T} \mathrm{R}^t_{i \to j} \tag{19}$$

Internal regret is defined as follows:

$$\mathrm{IR}^T_{i \to j} = (\mathrm{R}^T_{i \to j})^+ \tag{20}$$

where $X^+ = max\{X, 0\}$. Finally, the cumulative internal regret felt for playing all other strategies but for not having played strategy j throughout the course of a game is given by:

$$\mathrm{IR}^T_{S \to j} = \sum_{i=1}^{S} \mathrm{IR}^T_{i \to j} \tag{21}$$

Given the above definitions, consider the case of a 2-strategy informed game, with strategies X and Y. The no internal regret learning algorithm updates the components of the weight vector, namely w^{t+1}_X and w^{t+1}_Y, according to the following formulae, which reflect cumulative feelings of regret:

$$w^{t+1}_X = \frac{\mathrm{IR}^t_{Y \to X}}{\mathrm{IR}^t_{X \to Y} + \mathrm{IR}^t_{Y \to X}} \quad \text{and} \quad w^{t+1}_Y = \frac{\mathrm{IR}^t_{X \to Y}}{\mathrm{IR}^t_{X \to Y} + \mathrm{IR}^t_{Y \to X}} \tag{22}$$

If the regret for having played strategy j rather than strategy i is significant, then the algorithm updates weights such that the probability of playing strategy i is increased. In general, if strategy i is played at time t,

$$w^{t+1}_j = \frac{1}{\mu} \mathrm{IR}^t_{i \to j} \quad \text{and} \quad w^{t+1}_i = 1 - \sum_{j \neq i} w^{t+1}_j \tag{23}$$

where μ is a normalizing term that is chosen *s.t.*:

$$\mu > (|S| - 1) \max_{j \in S} \mathrm{IR}^t_{i \to j} \tag{24}$$

This generalized algorithm is due to Hart and Mas-Colell [22].

Like the no external regret algorithm of Freund and Schapire [14], the above no internal regret algorithm depends on complete payoff information at all times t, including information that pertains to strategies that were not employed at time t. The no internal regret learning algorithm has also been studied in naive settings, where complete payoff information is not available (see Foster and Vohra [11] and Greenwald [16]). It remains to simulate the naive variant of the no internal regret learning algorithm in our model of shopbots and pricebots.

Civil Agent Societies: Tools for Inventing Open Agent-Mediated Electronic Marketplaces

Chrysanthos Dellarocas and Mark Klein

Sloan School of Management
Massachusetts Institute of Technology
Room E53-315, Cambridge, MA 02139
{dell,m_klein}@mit.edu

Abstract. In the emerging model of 21st century electronic commerce, a variety of open agent marketplaces will be competing with one another for participants. The most successful marketplaces will be those that provide the best "quality of service" guarantees (in terms of security, fairness, efficiency, etc.), while meeting such challenges as agent heterogeneity, limited trust, and potential for systemic dysfunctions. Civil human societies provide a useful model for designing the infrastructure needed to achieve these guarantees. Successful civil human societies build on well-designed "social contracts", i.e. agreed-upon constraints on agent behavior made in exchange for quality of service assurances backed up by social institutions. Civil Agent Societies can be defined in an analogous way. The objective of our work is to provide tools that help developers systematically explore the space of possible Civil Agent Societies, helping them invent the electronic marketplaces that work best for their intended purposes. We present a framework that captures the fundamental elements and processes of Civil Agent Societies and a methodology for designing, prototyping and evaluating a wide range of "civil" open marketplaces. We also discuss how these ideas are currently being applied to the design of open marketplaces of contract net agents, a useful abstraction of agent-mediated business-to-business e-commerce.

1 Introduction

Software agent technologies promise substantial increases in productivity by automating several of the most time-consuming stages of electronic commerce processes. Agents are software systems, which are capable of interacting with other agents in a flexible and autonomous way, in order to meet the design objectives of their creators [9]. In the context of electronic commerce, we can already point to several examples of agents used to compare information about products, buy products, sell products, etc. [15].

Electronic agent marketplaces are formed by collections of software agents, which interact with one another in order to automatically trade products and services through the Internet. For example, one vision for the future of business-to-business electronic commerce consists of electronic marketplaces, where sets of contractor and

A. Moukas, C. Sierra, and F. Ygge (Eds.): AMEC'99, LNAI 1788, pp. 24–39, 2000.
© Springer-Verlag Berlin Heidelberg 2000

subcontractor agents connect with one another and form virtual supply chains for providing goods and services [7].

In the emerging model of 21st century electronic commerce, a variety of open electronic marketplaces will be competing with one another for participants. Independently developed agents will be entering and leaving marketplaces at will, in pretty much the same way that human investors enter and leave different financial markets today. The stakeholders of electronic marketplaces will, therefore, have an interest in making them as attractive to prospective "customers" as possible. One expects that the most successful marketplaces will be the ones that have the lowest barriers to entry (in terms of required agent sophistication) and provide the best "quality of service" guarantees (in terms of security, fairness, efficiency, etc.). The proper design of open electronic marketplaces thus emerges as an important research and practical question.

A lot of the early work on the design of agent marketplaces focused on agent *mechanism design*, that is, on the design of "optimal" rules of behavior to be followed by individual agents [23]. The underlying assumption behind this line of work is that if all agents follow the "right" mechanism, the emerging society will exhibit stable and efficient behavior.

Such research typically assumes that agents will be homogeneous and rational, that their infrastructure will be reliable, and therefore that their relatively simple and "optimistic" rules of behavior will be "intelligent" enough to avoid or cope with whatever deviant behavior or systemic dysfunctions they encounter. The contract net protocol, for example, one of the best-known mechanisms for structuring contractor and subcontractor marketplaces [21] owes its simplicity to many assumptions about agent behavior, some of which are listed in Figure 1. Although such assumptions are possible to guarantee in closed environments, where all agents are developed by the same team, they are becoming less realistic in the open world of the Internet.

Designing efficient and robust open electronic marketplaces, whose participants will be independently developed software agents, each attempting to satisfy the goals of its creator is a difficult problem. Some of the most important challenges include:

- *Heterogeneity.* Open marketplaces cannot expect that all of their members will have an equal level of sophistication. For example, in a contract net marketplace, some subcontractor agents may be able to respond to cancellation of their task by their contractor, while other agents may lack this capability. If they hope to attract a wide enough membership, open marketplaces should be able to provide a certain level of support, even to less sophisticated agents.
- *Limited trust.* Independently developed agents can not always be trusted to follow the rules properly due to bugs, bounded rationality, malice and so on. For example, subcontractor agents may crash or fail to deliver a promised service on time, contractor agents may refuse to pay, etc. Open marketplaces should be prepared to deal with potential fraud or other deviant behavior.
- *Possibility of systemic failures.* Almost any set of social rules of behavior, especially those simple enough to be reasonable for implementation and efficient in execution in a large set of agents, will have "holes" in terms of the potential for unintended emergent dysfunctional behaviors. This is especially true since agent societies operate in a realm where relative coordination, communication and

computational costs and capabilities can be radically different from those in human society, leading to behaviors with which we have little previous experience. It has been argued, for example, that 1987's stock crash was due in part to the action of computer-based "program traders" that were able to execute trade decisions at a speed and volume that was unprecedented in human experience and thus led to unprecedented stock market volatility [22].

- *Need for rapid adaptation.* Just as their "real world" counterparts, open agent marketplaces should be viewed as dynamic, adaptable systems, sensitive and responsive to demands of their members or to other important changes of the competitive landscape.

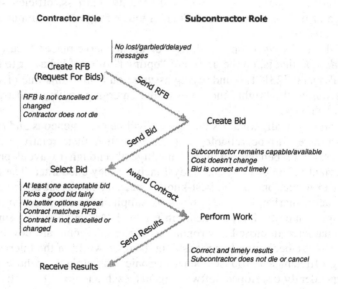

Fig. 1. Simplified description of the contract net protocol. Some of the protocol assumptions are listed in italics.

The typical response of multi-agent system researchers to the previous challenges has been to require all agents of a society to implement more complex, mutually compatible, versions of a mechanism, with hard-coded support for dealing with some of the above issues (see [4, 18, 19] for examples).

Agent societies that emerge in this way are similar to "survivalist societies" of early human history because their members are expected to completely fend for themselves. There is no control or safety net in case things go wrong. There is also no room for agents, which are less capable, or simply slightly "different". This increases the barriers for participation in these societies. Often, these complex mechanisms impose a significant performance penalty and, in any case, they cover only a subset of the possible exception types. In fact, researchers have proven that for some classes of interaction (e.g. voting) there can be no mechanism, which completely avoids all possible systemic dysfunctions [1]. Finally, by "hard-coding" interaction mechanisms entirely within individual agents, such societies are not particularly easy to adapt.

Civil human societies have successfully coped with similar challenges by developing social institutions that set and enforce laws (e.g. courts, police), monitor for and respond to emergencies (e.g. ambulance system), prevent and recover from disasters (e.g. coast guard, firefighters), etc. In that way, civil societies allow citizens to utilize relatively simple, optimistic and efficient rules of behavior, offloading the prevention and recovery of many problem types to social institutions that can handle them efficiently and effectively by virtue of their economies of scale and widely-accepted legitimacy. Successful civil societies have thus achieved a division of labor between individuals and institutions that decreases the "barriers to survival" for each citizen, while helping increase the welfare of the society as a whole. In an analogous manner, we believe that the design of the right electronic social institutions will be a crucial success factor in the new universe of open electronic marketplaces.

Isolated examples of useful "electronic social institutions" have been proposed and analyzed by software agent researchers (for example, social monitors in [10]; reputation mechanisms in [24]). However, up to this date, there has been no methodology or framework for systematically deciding what social institutions are needed in a given context and providing guidance on how to design, evaluate and adapt them.

Our work aims to fill this gap. The long-term goal of our research is to use the civil society metaphor in order to develop methodologies and tools for systematically designing open electronic marketplaces. Our work complements a lot of the current research in designing agent-mediated electronic marketplaces by focusing on the design of appropriate *social* (infrastructure) mechanisms that complement the mechanisms of (possibly independently developed) *individual* agents in order to improve the flexibility, robustness and efficiency of the resulting systems. Although this paper focuses on the design of open electronic marketplaces, we would like to emphasize that the results of our work can be applied to the design of any open multi-agent society.

The rest of the paper is organized as follows: Section 2 gives an overview of the Civil Agent Society architectural framework, which allows the rapid prototyping of a wide range of open agent marketplaces. Section 3 presents our methodology for constructing Civil Agent Societies and describes how it has been applied to develop an open marketplace of contract net agents. Section 4 discusses related work. Finally, Section 5 summarizes our conclusions and presents directions for future research.

2   A Civil Agent Society Framework for Constructing Open Agent Marketplaces

Sociologists have observed that, despite their diversity, human societies can be described through a relatively small set of core elements and processes [13, 16]. These elements and processes thus form a design space that can be used to define a wide range of different societies (Figure 2). Our goal is to define an equivalent design space for software agent societies, supported by a methodology and architectural framework for designing, implementing and experimenting with societies in that space. It is our hope that these tools will enable our research community to better explore the space of possible agent marketplaces and, eventually, to develop guidelines for the design of "good" marketplaces within that space.

Elements	Comprehensive or Master Processes
1. Beliefs (knowledge)	1. Communication
2. Sentiments	2. Boundary maintenance
3. Goals or objectives	3. Systemic linkage
4. Norms	4. Institutionalization
5. Status-roles (positions)	5. Socialization
6. Rank	6. Social control
7. Power	
8. Sanctions	
9. Facilities	

Fig. 2. Elements and master processes of social systems (adapted from [13]).

The following sections present the results of our ongoing work on developing an extensible architectural framework for implementing "civil" open agent marketplaces.

2.1   Core Elements of Civil Agent Societies

Civil societies provide an infrastructure for facilitating the conduct of social interactions. From a design perspective they represent a tradeoff between individual autonomy and social support. Societies constrain the behavior of their citizens by specifying a set of *norms*. Conforming to the norms is the cost that citizens have to pay in order to belong to a civil society. In return, civil societies provide *social institutions* that protect citizens from the actions of other citizens as well as from systemic dysfunctions. In order for citizens to have full access to the protection of the society, they typically need to formalize their interactions through *contracts*.

We can see, therefore, that the three core elements of a civil society are its norms, its institutions and mechanisms for formalizing social interactions as contracts. Below we describe how each of these elements is implemented in the Civil Agent Society framework (Figure 3).

Social Norms

Marketplaces are a relatively simple type of society. Marketplace "citizens" usually interact with one another through short-lived, transactional relationships with a well-specified beginning and end. Furthermore, each marketplace supports a relatively small number of different transaction types. Based on these observations, Civil Agent Societies represent norms using a knowledge base, which enumerates the set of agent roles and the set of role interaction protocols that are permissible within a given marketplace. Agent roles and interaction protocols are organized in a specialization hierarchy. This way, new roles and protocols can be added relatively easily as special cases of existing ones. Figure 4 depicts a subset of the social norms knowledge base for a Civil Society of contract net agents.

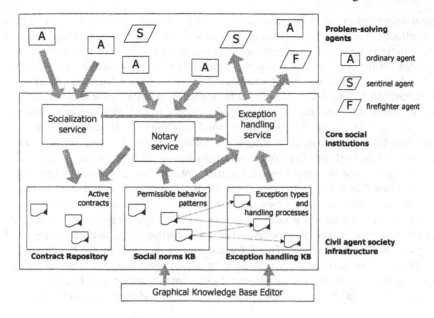

Fig. 3. Architectural overview of the Civil Agent Society framework.

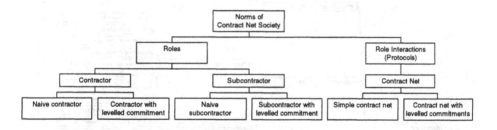

Fig. 4. The social norms knowledge base is organized as a specialization hierarchy of permissible roles and role interaction protocols for a given civil society.

Exception Handling Social Institutions

Given the self-interested and transactional nature of most "social" interactions within a marketplace, an important role of social institutions in marketplaces in that of handling exceptions. The Civil Agent Society framework implements exception handling social institutions as the collection of processes, which anticipate, avoid, detect and resolve all known exception types of all interaction protocols contained in the social norms knowledge base of a civil society.

We define exceptions as any deviation from an ideal sequence of agent behavior, which may jeopardize the achievement of some individual or social goals [6, 11]. We further distinguish exceptions into local and systemic. *Local exceptions* are violations of normal agent behavior in the context of a single multi-agent interaction (e.g. a single contract). Local exceptions may be caused by programming bugs, system crashes, malicious behavior or incompatible protocols among heterogeneous agents. In the context of the contract net protocol, an example of a local exception would be a situation where a contractor agent crashes after it has awarded a contract to a subcontractor, but before it has paid the subcontractor. Another example would be a situation in which the subcontractor delivers the contracted service late and with low quality. *Systemic exceptions* describe unintended emergent dysfunctional behaviors. Resource poaching [4], a situation where all subcontractors are tied up with low-priority tasks while high-priority contractors remain unsatisfied, is an example of a systemic exception that has been observed in the context of contract net marketplaces.

The exception handling knowledge base of the framework (Figure 3) contains representations of all exception types that are associated with at least one protocol stored in the social norms knowledge base. For each exception type, the knowledge base stores representations of processes for anticipating, avoiding, detecting and resolving exceptions of that type. This information is generated during the exception analysis phase of our methodology (see Section 3.2). Figure 5 shows a partial list of the exception type taxonomy for a civil society of contract net agents. Finally, Figure 6 shows how the social norms and exception handling knowledge bases relate to each other.

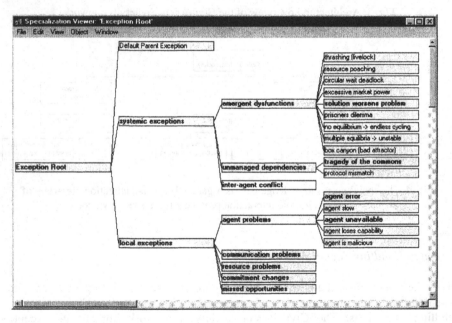

Fig. 5. A subset of the exception types taxonomy for a civil society of contract net agents.

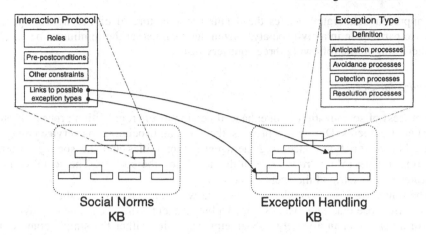

Fig. 6. Overview of the social norms and exception handling knowledge bases.

Contracts

Agents join societies in order to interact with other agents. Contracts make such interactions "visible" to the social institutions. A contract defines a joint commitment of a number of citizens to engage in a "legally acceptable" social interaction in order to achieve a mutually desirable outcome. A social interaction is "legally acceptable" if it conforms to the norms of the given society. The value of contracts in civil societies is that their existence implies the commitment of the society to enforce them, i.e. mobilize its institutions in order to protect the parties involved from contract breaches and other exceptions.

The Civil Agent Society framework supports two classes of contracts:

- *Private contracts*, that is, commitments of two or more society members to engage in a "legal" transaction. The society then commits to protect the agents from local exceptions for the duration of the contract.
- *Social contracts*, that is, commitments of an agent to participate in a society and obey its norms. In return, the society commits to enforce the agent's private contracts and to protect the agent from systemic exceptions for the duration of the agent's membership in the society.

2.2   Core Services of Civil Agent Societies

During run-time, the Civil Agent Society framework relies on a small set of core services to provide the benefits of a civil society to all "citizen" agents. Core services are responsible for generating new social contracts (i.e. admitting new agents to the society), generating new private contracts and mobilizing the exception handling institutions in order to protect citizens from local and systemic exceptions. Although our approach deliberately leaves the detailed architecture of citizen agents open, in order to participate in a civil society, citizen agents must, at the minimum, be capable of interfacing to the following three core services:

Socialization Service

The process of socialization is an enhanced version of the registration process of other agent environments. During this process, the agent and socialization service engage in an explicit negotiation concerning the agent's capabilities and the society's norms, resulting in a *social contract* between the agent and the society. The social contract indicates membership of the agent in the society.

The following is an example scenario of how agents interact with the socialization service. Suppose that we have developed a buyer agent, who is capable of playing the role of a contractor in a variety of marketplaces, using either the simple contract net protocol described in [21] or the leveled commitment contract net protocol described in [20]. The agent wishes to become a citizen of civil marketplace XYZ and trade with other subcontractors who are citizens of the same marketplace. It contacts the socialization service of marketplace XYZ and declares itself a contractor agent who is capable of interacting through either of the above two variants of the contract net protocol. The socialization agent responds that in marketplace XYZ, only the leveled commitment contract net protocol is acceptable. In addition, the agent needs to pay a membership fee of $5. Our agent pays the fee and commits to only use the allowed protocol. The marketplace then creates a social contract, which identifies the agent as a member. It also mobilizes the exception handling mechanism of the society in order to "protect" the agent from local or systemic exceptions.

Notary Service

Once admitted into a civil society, "citizen" agents are free to contact one another and engage in informal "friendly" interactions. The society does not get involved in those interactions. However, whenever a set of agents intends to engage in a transaction, which requires the protection of the society, they contact the notary service. The notary service verifies that the intended interaction is legal (by comparing it against the set of legal interactions enumerated in the social norms knowledge base), verifies that all agents jointly commit to that interaction and its outcome and generates an appropriate private contract structure. A *private contract*[1] is a data structure, which specifies:

1. A pointer to a legal pattern of interaction, which must be an instance of one of the protocols contained in the social norms knowledge base

---

[1] Private (agent-to-agent) contracts are distinguished from social (agent-to-society) contracts. Social contracts are created by the socialization service and indicate membership of an agent to a society.

2. A set of attributes that define the specifics of this particular instance of the interaction (for example, in the case of a contract, the promised delivery date, payment amount, cancellation penalties, etc.)
3. A set of agents who commit to play the roles defined in (1) in order to meet the outcomes specified in (2)

Exception Handling Service

The exception handling service is triggered whenever new contracts are created, or change status (e.g. become canceled, discharged, released, etc.). Such contracts include both the 'agent to agent' private contracts recorded by the notary service, as well as the 'agent to society' social contracts created by the socialization service. In the latter case, the exception handling service initiates the mechanisms, which look for symptoms of potential systemic dysfunctions.

Upon contract creation, the exception handling service first anticipates all exception types that are associated with the type of interaction defined in the contract. This is achieved by locating the corresponding interaction protocol template in the social norms knowledge base and following the links between that protocol template and its characteristic exception types (Figure 6). Based on the information contained in the exception handling knowledge base, the exception handling service starts a number of "sentinel" agents, whose role is either to try to avoid a given type of exception, or to detect some of its symptoms.

Sentinels work by monitoring some of the communication between agents or by pro-actively querying agents about their status. In addition, citizen agents may explicitly call the exception handling service, for example, when they believe that a contract they have signed has been breached. Whenever an exception symptom has been detected, the diagnostic component of the exception handling service is triggered. After the exception cause has been determined, the resolution component selects one of the resolution strategies present in the knowledge base and starts "firefighter" agents in order to enact it and bring the society back to an acceptable state. The exception handling service is described in more detail in [12].

3   A Methodology for Developing Civil Agent Societies

The framework presented in the previous section is meant to be the basis for a systematic, exploratory methodology for designing open marketplaces. This section describes our ongoing experience with using the framework in order to construct and evaluate "civil society" versions of contract net marketplaces.

3.1   Design Social Norms

The first step of our methodology defines the norms of the target electronic marketplace. As explained in Section 2.1, this involves an enumeration of all roles and interaction protocol variants that are permissible in an open version of the marketplace. Each role and interaction protocol is subsequently modeled as a finite automaton and added to the social norms knowledge base.

In the case of a contract net marketplace, there are two basic roles (contractor, subcontractor) and one basic protocol (contract net). To accommodate "diversity", variations of the basic roles and protocols can be easily added as specializations of the basic ones (Figure 4).

3.2   Design Exception Handling Social Institutions

For each protocol variant identified in the previous step, a systematic identification of possible exceptions that may arise in an open environment is performed. In our previous work we have developed methodologies and tools that can be used to facilitate the systematic discovery of exception types [6, 11]. We have applied these methodologies in the context of the contract net protocol family and developed a list of possible exceptions, some of which are listed in Figure 5.

For each such identified exception type, a set of processes for avoiding, detecting, diagnosing and resolving it is designed. This collection of processes is added to the exception handling knowledge base of the framework. Finally, links are established between the protocols stored in the social norms knowledge base and their characteristic exception types, as shown in Figure 6.

Figure 7 presents a partial summary of the exception handling analysis performed for two sample exception types. A comprehensive description of our analysis appears in [2].

3.3   Prototype and Evaluate

The final step in our methodology consists of developing prototype implementations of the citizen agents (i.e. the contractor and subcontractor agents in the case of contract net) and performing deductive or simulation-based analysis of our prototype agent society. The purpose of the analysis is to evaluate the effectiveness of the norms and institutions designed during the previous steps. Effectiveness is usually measured against our basic design objectives of open societies, such as the ability to cope with heterogeneity, limited trust, unreliable infrastructure and systemic dysfunctions. However, different societies may have different design objectives.

As a first test of our approach, we have implemented a prototype version of a "civil" marketplace of contract net agents and are in the process of evaluating how its various "institutions" affect the efficiency and robustness of the overall system. Figure 8 summarizes a typical simulation experiment. The goal of this experiment is to measure the usefulness of a "social monitor" institution in a failure-prone contract net agent environment. This institution is designed to alleviate the negative performance effects caused by subcontractor agents that may crash unexpectedly after they have been awarded a task but before they have completed the work. It works by periodically monitoring the "health" of subcontractors and assisting in the immediate reassignment of tasks performed by failed subcontractors. In essence, this institution implements the processes labeled **Detection-Process-2** and **Resolution-Process-2** in the analysis of exception type "Delay from Subcontractor Death" (see Figure 7).

Type	Delay from Subcontractor Death
For Protocol	Contract Net
Class	Local
Definition	A subcontractor dies after it has been awarded a contract but before it has completed its task
Criticality	This exception can have a potentially high performance impact when subtasks take a long time.
Anticipation Processes	**Anticipation-Process-1** (Maintain a "reliability history" which tracks past crashes of all subcontractors; raise a flag if subcontractor has been unreliable in the past)
Detection Processes	**Detection-Process-1** (Contractor times out if results are not received on schedule) **Detection-Process-2** (Sentinel periodically polls subcontractor)
Avoidance Processes	**Avoidance-Process-1** (Advise contractors to choose different subcontractor or to frequently poll unreliable subcontractor)
Resolution Processes	**Resolution-Process-1** (Locate substitute subcontractor; reassign task; update contract) **Resolution-Process-2** (Notify contractor when subcontractor dies)

Type	Resource poaching
For Protocol	Contract Net
Class	Systemic
Definition	One or more high-priority tasks are unable to access needed subcontractors because they already have been 'grabbed' by lower priority tasks
Criticality	This exception can have a high fairness impact when there is a significant variation in task priority and the available subcontractors population can be oversubscribed.
Anticipation Processes	**Anticipation-Process-1** (The potential subcontractor population is currently busy with low priority tasks, and a set of high-priority tasks is expected)
Detection Processes	**Detection-Process-1** (The priority of the tasks that have the resources they need is less than the priority of those that do not) **Detection-Process-2** (A high-priority contractor does not get any bids for an offered task within time-out period)
Avoidance Processes	**Avoidance-Process-1** (Require that subcontractors collect several request-for-bids before bidding, and respond preferentially to higher-priority bids)
Resolution Processes	**Resolution-Process-1** (Allow subcontractors to suspend lower-priority tasks and bid on later higher-priority tasks)

Fig. 7. Results of exception handling analysis for two sample exception types.

In the absence of "social monitoring", the particular variant of the contract net protocol used in this experiment only checks for subcontractor death after a task result fails to arrive by the specified deadline. Figure 8 shows how the existence of such a "social monitor" significantly reduces the completion delay of supply chains where at least one of the subcontractors unexpectedly fails.

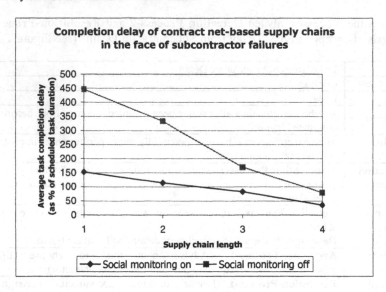

Fig. 8. Effect of a "social monitoring" institution on the completion delay of supply chains where at least one subcontractor agent unexpectedly fails.

4   Related Work

By focusing on the integrative goals of developing architectures and methodologies for building multi-agent marketplaces, our work relates to several aspects of multi-agent system research. Due to space limitations this section is, by necessity, partial and discusses only the most important relationships.

4.1   Computational Market Mechanisms

A significant amount of recent work has focused on the analysis and development of computational market mechanisms. This work has typically made use of normative theories, such as game theory and general equilibrium theory, in order to design a variety of useful mechanisms for areas such as auctions [14], contracting [20, 21], negotiation [17] and task allocation [23]. Mechanisms have typically been analyzed for Pareto efficiency, stability and computational or communication efficiency.

The results of the above work can be considered as the starting point of our approach. Our work complements the above mechanisms with a social infrastructure that aims to improve their performance and robustness in the face of heterogeneity, limited trust, unreliable computation environment and systemic failures. Our contribution in this area is that we are providing a methodology and implementation framework that helps *society* developers (as opposed to *agent* developers) systematically consider the issues that arise when a particular class of mechanisms are used in an open environment, as well as experiment with various design tradeoffs between individual autonomy and social support, in order to build practical, efficient and robust open systems.

4.2   Social Concepts in Multi-agent Systems

Several researchers have studied the concepts of norms, commitments and social relations in the context of multi-agent systems (see [5] for a representative collection of papers). Such work has typically produced ontologies for describing these concepts, as well as their various states and operations. Furthermore, a number of researchers have proposed architectures for developing agents with social awareness. Jennings and Campos [8] propose the concept of socially responsible agents, which retain their local autonomy but draw from, and provide resources to the larger community. Castelfranchi, et. al. [3] discuss normative agents, that is, agents capable of recognizing, adopting and following norms.

We believe, again, that our work is complementary to these efforts. Instead of proposing a specific architecture for building citizen agents, we take the perspective of the society designer. Our work focuses on how norms and contracts can be represented and used by the society infrastructure in order to build stable, robust systems in the face of heterogeneous agents whose internal architecture may not be reliably known.

5   Conclusions and Future Research

In the emerging model of 21st century electronic commerce, a variety of open agent marketplaces will be competing with one another for participants. The most successful marketplaces will, in all likelihood, be those that provide the best "quality of service" guarantees (in terms of security, fairness, efficiency, etc.), while meeting such challenges as agent heterogeneity, limited trust, and potential for systemic dysfunctions.

We believe that civil human societies provide a useful model for designing the infrastructure needed to achieve these guarantees. Civil societies have successfully dealt with many of the issues that confront open electronic marketplaces. Through the development of a set of core social elements and processes (Figure 2), successful civil societies have managed to leverage the capabilities of their members, reducing the "barriers to survival" while increasing the total social welfare.

We presented a framework that captures some of the fundamental elements and processes of Civil Agent Societies and helps agent marketplace developers design, prototype and evaluate "civil society" versions of open agent marketplaces. Our aim is to help marketplace developers systematically consider the issues that arise when a particular class of market mechanisms are used in an open environment, as well as experiment with various design tradeoffs between individual autonomy and social support, in order to build practical, efficient and robust open systems.

This is a long-term, ambitious project. The results presented in this paper describe only our first phase of exploration. The following paragraphs describe some of the directions of our ongoing work:

- *Extend the Civil Agent Society framework.* Compared to the elements and processes of human social systems listed in Figure 2 the framework described in Section 2 currently only supports a subset of the elements (roles, norms, sanctions) and processes (socialization, social control). We are working to capture the remaining core elements of civil agent societies as design dimensions that can be easily prototyped and varied within the framework. For example, we are interested in exploring the meaning of *power* in an agent society, including the various alternative ways that power can be exercised and related to the processes of socialization, social control and communication; the *institutionalization* process, that is, the process of dynamically setting and changing the norms and institutions of an agent society; the *systemic linkages* that an agent society should maintain with other agent societies, especially in the context of competing agent marketplaces. Understanding these dimensions can have far-reaching implications, not only for designing agent marketplaces, but also in the more general issues of Internet legislation and governance.

- *Develop guidelines for building "citizen agents".* One of the motivations behind civil agent societies is the need to accommodate independently developed agents with possibly different internal architectures. Nevertheless, all citizens of civil societies should exhibit a minimum set of capabilities, such as the ability to articulate and reason about norms and contracts. We are working towards formalizing these requirements into minimal interfaces and languages that agents should support in order to participate in civil societies.

- *Develop a "design handbook" for open electronic marketplaces.* The ultimate goal of constructing frameworks is increased understanding and guidelines for action. As we are refining our methodology and framework, we are applying them in order to construct "civil society" versions of the best-known electronic market mechanisms. Our ultimate goal is to organize our findings in a "handbook" for designing open electronic marketplaces.

References

1. Arrow, K. J. "Social Choice and Individual Values", 2nd ed., Yale University Press, New Haven, CT, 1963.
2. Aryananda, L."An Exception Handling Service for the Contract Net Protocol Family", Master's thesis, MIT Department of Electrical Engineering and Computer Science, May 1999.
3. Castelfranchi, C., Dignum, F., Jonker, C.M. and Treur, J. "Deliberate Normative Agents: Principles and Architecture", Proceedings of The Sixth International Workshop on Agent Theories, Architectures, and Languages (ATAL-99), Orlando, FL, July 1999.
4. Chia, M.H., Neiman, D.E., and Lesser, V.R. "Poaching and distraction in asynchronous agent activities", in Proceedings of the Third International Conference on Multi-Agent Systems, Paris, France, July 1998, pp.88-95.

5. Conte R., Falcone R. and Sartor G. editors, "Special Issue on Agents and Norms", Artificial Intelligence and Law, 7 (1), March 1999.
6. Dellarocas, C. and Klein, M. "A Knowledge-Based Approach for Handling Exceptions in Business Processes", Information Technology and Management, forthcoming.
7. Jennings, N.R., Faratin, P., Johnson, M.J., Norman, T.J., O'Brien, P. and Wiegand, M.E. "Agent-based business process management", International Journal of Cooperative Information Systems, 5 (2&3), 1996, 105-130.
8. Jennings, N.R. and Campos, J.R. "Towards a Social Level Characterisation of Socially Responsible Agents", IEE Proceedings on Software Engineering, 144 (1), pp. 11-25.
9. Jennings N.R., Sycara K. and Wooldridge M. "A Roadmap of Agent Research and Development", Autonomous Agents and Multi-Agent Systems 1 (1), 1998, pp. 7-38.
10. Kaminka, G and Tambe, M. "I'm OK, You're OK, We're OK: Experiments in Distributed and Centralized Socially Attentive Monitoring", Proceedings of the Third International Conference on Autonomous Agents, Seattle, Washington, May 1999, pp. 213-20.
11. Klein, M. and Dellarocas, C. "A Knowledge-Based Approach to Handling Exceptions in Workflow Systems", Computer Supported Cooperative Work (CSCW), forthcoming.
12. Klein, M., and Dellarocas, C. "Exception Handling in Agent Systems" in Proceedings of the Third International Conference on Autonomous Agents, Seattle, Washington, May 1999, pp. 62-68.
13. Loomis, C.P. "Social Systems: Essays on their Persistence and Change", D. Van Nostrand Company, Inc., 1960.
14. McAfee, R.P. and McMillan, J. "Auctions and Bidding", Journal of Economic Literature 25, 1987, pp. 699-738.
15. Maes, P., Guttman, R.H. and Moukas A. "Agents that Buy and Sell", Communications of the ACM 42 (3), March 1999, pp. 81-91.
16. Parsons, T. "The Social System", The Free Press, 1964.
17. Rosenschein, J.S. and Zlotkin, G. "Rules of Encounter: Designing Conventions for Automated Negotiation Among Computers", MIT Press, Cambridge, MA, 1994.
18. Saad, A., Kawamura, K., Biswas, G., Johnson, M.E. and Salama, A. "Evaluating a contract net-based hierarchical scheduling approach for flexible manufacturing", Proceedings of the IEEE International Symposium on Assembly and Task Planning, Pittsburgh, PA, August 1995, pp.147-152.
19. Sandholm, T.W. and Lesser, V.R. "Issues in automated negotiation and electronic commerce: Extending the contract net framework", Proceedings of the First International Conference on Multi-Agent Systems, San Francisco, California, June 1995, pp. 328-35.
20. Sandholm, T.W. and Lesser, V.R. "Advantages of a leveled commitment contracting protocol", Proceedings of the National Conference on Artificial Intelligence (AAAI), Portland, OR, August 1996, pp. 126-133.
21. Smith, R.G. "The contract net protocol: high level communication and control in a distributed problem solver", IEEE Transactions on Computers 29 (12), December 1980, pp.1104-1113.
22. Waldrop, M. "Computers amplify Black Monday", Science (238), Oct. 30 1987, pp. 602-604.
23. Wellman, M.P. and Wurman P.R. "Market-Aware Agents for a Multiagent World", Robotics and Autonomous Systems (24), 1998, pp. 115-125.
24. Zacharia, G., Moukas, A. and Maes, P. "Collaborative Reputation Mechanisms in Online Marketplaces", Proceedings of 32th Hawaii International Conference on System Sciences (HICSS-32), Maui, Hawaii, January 1999.

Legal Issues for Personalised Advertising on Internet: The AIMedia Case Study

Vania Conan[1], Marten Foss[2], Peter Lenda[2], Sophie Louveaux[2], and Anne Salaün[2]

[1] AIMedia Project - Personalised Advertising on Interactive Media
http://www.aimedia.org
[2] ECLIP Project - Electronic Commerce Legal Issue Platform
http://www.jura.uni-muenster.de/eclip

Abstract. In this paper we present a study of the legal issues raised by Agent Mediated Electronic Commerce. We propose to explore the problems associated with personalised communication over the Internet, using a home shopping agent scenario as our case study. This work is the result of the collaboration between Esprit projects ECLIP and AIMedia. AIMedia investigates agent technology for personalised advertising over the Internet for retail applications. ECLIP provides legal assistance and expertise. We first present the AIMedia project, its goal and agent approach to personalised communication on the Internet. We then review existing European directives and their national applications, which deal with the relevant legal issues. This entails advertising, personal data protection, and private international law. We conclude with requirements drawn from this study, which we believe to be of general relevance.

1 Introduction

Agent technologies are an active field of research for Internet applications and e-commerce development. Agents are seen, among other things, as a means to personalise each customer's shopping experience. Personalisation is based on the use of 'user profiles', where every person may conceal personal data and express their preferences. Furthermore, agents can also be delegated tasks, and act as the user's representative, making orders, taking part in auctions or negotiations, and eventually purchasing of the behalf of users.

In AMEC, new market models and complex architectures are envisaged. Agent based market places will interconnect large numbers of consumers and product or service providers in a flexible way [1]. Models of consumer's needs, wishes and preferences will form the basis of personalised answers provided by agents [2]. Based on such personal profiles, the web stores are being customised and adapt to each customer [3].

Agent applications when applied to e-commerce therefore raise numerous legal issues. In this paper we do not provide a general presentation of this problem, but we concentrate on a case study, and present a thorough analysis of the legal issues raised

A. Moukas, C. Sierra, and F. Ygge (Eds.): AMEC'99, LNAI 1788, pp. 40–67, 2000.

by agent frameworks for *personalised communication* over the Internet, using home shopping agent scenarios as our case study.

This work is the result of the collaboration between Esprit projects ECLIP and AIMedia. AIMedia investigates agent technology for personalised advertising over the Internet for retail applications. ECLIP provides legal assistance to other projects where this expertise is missing.

The legal analysis contained in this document is a product of the ECLIP Consortium, it represents the Consortium's opinion and is his sole responsibility. It does not bind the European Commission and does not preclude the final conclusions and recommendations the ECLIP project will eventually reach.

We first present the AIMedia project, its goal and agent approach to personalised communication on the Internet (Section 2). We then review existing European directives and their national applications, which deal with the relevant legal issues. This entails advertising (Section 3), personal data protection (Section 4), and private international law (Section 5). We conclude with requirements drawn from this study, which we believe to be of general relevance.

2   The AIMedia Project

In this section, we present the AIMedia Esprit project, *Personalised Advertising over Interactive Media*. The objective is to provide home shoppers with a more interactive agent based shopping experience which either re-creates or exceeds the experience that they currently enjoy by visiting the shop or using a catalogue.

In a first on-line scenario the customer connects to the commercial site, with a definite purpose in mind (e.g. a shopping list). The shopping assistant is the retailer's representative and works at the level of the purchase decision, by pushing products. In a more evolved scenario, the purchase behaviour is mediated by an agent. When an agent is programmed for a certain task, such as finding some products, the problem is specified, the agent is looking for information. The advertising mechanism adds promotions and offers to the answer to the query. The same range of mechanisms is used and the customer is also being proposed personalised offers.

These new approaches to personalisation and advertising raise legal issues, which need to be implemented in a security framework in order to build trust and confidence in e-commerce.

2.1   Agent Architecture

The agent framework involves the user's web client, one agent representing the user, and one representing the retailer (see Figure 1):

- *User Web client.* This is the web browser that each customer is using to connect to the retailer's web site.
- *Personal Agent.* The personal agent manages the user's profile and preferences. Each customer can access their personal profile or preferences through a web interface. They are thus given higher control over their personal data. The Personal Agent can be hosted on the customer's PC or on a trusted third party. From their, the customer may also launch off-line brokering agents which carry out searches based on their preferences.

• *Shopping Assistant.* The retailer's agent representative explores the metaphor of the 'knowledgeable shopping assistant'. This intelligent agent learns about the customer, based on present and past visit as well as on attitudinal or life style information. This agent then accompanies the shopper through their visit, suggesting alternatives and additions to the shopper as they progress through their visit.

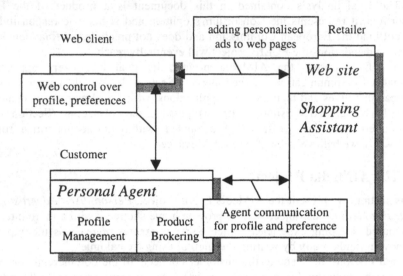

Figure 1. AIMedia Agent Architecture

2.2   Business Scenarios

Let's now turn to two business scenarios, which exemplify well what personalised communication can be used for in home shopping retail applications. These scenarios serve as a basis for AIMedia functional requirements.

2.2.1   Scenario 1: An Enhanced Shopping Site

An initial scenario is suggested as follows :

A customer visits the retailer's home shopping site. The customer enters their reward number, identifying himself or herself to the system. A number of products on offer are selected based on user profile data derived from past shopping trips, reward card data, and any other data available. These products are displayed in different ways that forms part of the project experimentation. If the customer selects a promoted product, it is added to their shopping list. As the shopper chooses products, based on their profile and the items selected so far, they are made customised offers. The selection or non-selection of these promotions is recorded. The customer is offered additional items, services, recipes, or wine offers based on their selection. The customer is asked questions based on their profile and product selection in order to better understand their behaviour / preferences on future visits.

In this scenario there are a number of actions that can be performed by the AIMedia system, for example :

- Offers : An alternative product to one which the customer usually buys because it is on promotion; an existing linked promotion, e.g. a multi-buy deal where buying more quantity gives a discount; a complementary product based on the customer's shopping list, or their selections so far, e.g. offer Parmesan cheese to someone who has bought pasta and a pasta sauce; a discount on types of product that they are not buying, e.g. discounted bread if they are not using the bakery.

- Additional information: e.g. A recipe which fits with some of the items on the list, or looks as if it appeals to the tastes of the customer; prompt the user with a reminder of something that they might have forgotten;

- Special individual rewards: If he or she is a highly valued customer, some sort of treat or special reward might be offered, perhaps linked to answering some questions;

- Experiment with ways of presenting this information, different visualisations etc., to see how the customer responds;

- In each case, if customers do not respond to offers we need to both record this and, as we develop the approach, understand or ask them why, and if they wish to be offered this in future.

2.2.2   Scenario 2: Personal Shoppers

A more radical vision is broadly outlined below. We suggest this as the longer-term goal of the project.

The customer is offered a " shopping agent " who they can brief and ask to shop at Sainsbury's, OTTO and other retailers. (The commercial reality here might be that those retailers form a consortium of non-competing companies.) The shopping agent acts on the customer's behalf to do their shopping for groceries, clothes, and any other products or services offered by the retailers. The agent can operate off-line, without the customer's direction, finding products, offers and information which awaits them next time they use the agent. The customer can control how much information about themselves they wish to share with the retailers' agents. Information from any of the shopping activities may be shared on a common profiling basis between the retailers with the customer's consent. This information is available on request by the customer.

This scenario would still offer the type of marketing opportunities as in scenario one, but would work generically across different types of retailer, with the agent acting as the interface to the offers.

2.2.3   Evaluation

Two prototype applications will be built from the AIMedia framework, one for Otto-Versand, and the other for J. Sainsbury's. These applications will be tested in the beginning of year 2000, and will be evaluated by the two retailers.

2.3 Customer Trust

The success of personalised communication is based on the assumption that the customer are ready to make personal information available to retailers. This requires a trust relationship between the customer and the retailers.

Legislation on advertising and privacy protection provide a basis for building this trust relationship.

Consumers are getting more worried with privacy issues. Many electronic commerce retailers see the increasing awareness of privacy issues by consumers as a "problem". Retailers who wish to gain a competitive advantage should therefore promote privacy issues by introducing safeguards in the form of enhanced security for consumer profiles. AIMedia proposes to address these issues and provide the security features necessary to gain consumer confidence.

The next sections discuss the legal and regulatory constraints.

Two aspects are dealt with : general advertising issues and personal data protection. Each section will outline the legal requirements that partners of the AIMedia project will have to comply with when providing some targeted advertising based on personal user profiles.

We conclude with design constraints the project must integrate as part of the customised secure advertising framework.

3 Advertising

The aim of the project is to develop a personalised and tailored-made advertising in order to promote purchases. According to the project, advertising should be considered as "helpful, exciting and enriching for the customer", but one should keep in mind that advertising can be seen as intrusive.

As the targeted advertising the partners are developing represents a quite large number of communications, mainly individualised on the basis of the consumer's behaviour and purchases' habits, it is important that the consumer receives enough information enabling him to understand the meaning of the advertising and its consequences. Furthermore, it seems obvious that the consumer should be able to refuse such communications through an opposition mean: as this targeted advertising can be interpreted by the consumer as being intrusive, useless and annoying, the advertiser – namely the partners of the project – should prevent the consumer from leaving the site and never come back by offering him the possibility to refuse such advertising.

This section will first concentrate on providing general comments on advertising, i.e. to what extend the advertiser is bound by the content of the advertising, how an advertising can be differentiated from an offer, what consequences the type of medium used has on the advertiser.

Then the rights implied for consumers from this kind advertising will be described, namely any relevant information enabling the consumer to make up his mind on whether he can benefit from the advertising and decide either to accept it or refuse it – on the basis of an opposition right granted by the advertiser - if he believes that the advertising is useless and intrusive.

3.1   Advertising: A Brief Outline

According to Directive 84/450/EC concerning misleading advertising [4], advertising is seen as "the making of a representation in any form in connection with a trade, business, craft or profession in order to promote the supply of goods or services, including immovable property, rights and obligations" (article 2.1).

The obligations and duties described below fall on the advertiser, namely the person responsible for the advertising addressed to the consumer, and its content. In the project the advertiser should be heard as the partners themselves, namely Otto and Sainsbury.

3.1.1   Liability of the Advertiser

As regard the information contained in the advertising, the question raises as to know whether the advertiser is bound for the content of the advertising. This issue is of importance as it has the consequence that the advertiser would not be able to modify the terms described in the advertising when the consumer agrees with this content and decides to conclude the contract.

It can be considered, following what seems to be a dominating opinion in the doctrine [5], that the facts contained in the advertising bound the advertiser who cannot thus modify the content. Otto Versand and Sainsbury's shall therefore be aware of the fact that any information contained in their advertising is bounding: the terms and conditions cannot be modified once the consumer decides to conclude the contract.

3.1.2   Advertising vs. Offer

Another important issue is related to the difference between advertising and offer: under what conditions an advertising can be considered as an offer? What consequences does the qualification of an advertising in offer has on the advertiser?

Legal effects of an advertising depend on its content: either the advertising identifies the essential parts of the contract, i.e. the object of the contract (product or service) and its price, or it does not clearly identify these essential parts.

If any offer to sell a product or supply a service is deemed as an advertising, any advertising is not deemed as an offer. To be considered as an offer, an advertising should clearly identify the object of the contract and the price[1]. In the first case above-described, the advertising should be considered as constituting an offer insofar as both the object and the price are mentioned. The legal consequence of this qualification is that the advertiser has to comply with the information contained in the advertising and to execute the contract according to the terms of the advertising.

Conversely, any advertising where both above-mentioned elements are not identified i.e. where the object of the contract is identified but not the price, would not be considered as an offer, enabling the advertiser to modify slightly the conditions.

---

[1] See Cass. 9 mai 1980, *Pas.* I p. 1127 ; R.C.J.B. 1971 pp. 228-229.

3.1.3   Presentation of the Advert

1. – On-screen messages.

The presentation of the communication chosen by the partners of the AIMedia project is mainly the inclusion of a personalised message directly on the screen, while the consumer is visiting the site. Indeed, partners of the project envisage to target existing consumers, meaning that "it is not until consumers have actually made the decision to visit the site that they will be exposed to the communications".

In this hypothesis, no legal constraints in term of consumer consent are foreseen, as the consumer has taken, at his own initiative, the necessary steps to visit the site.

2. – Individual communications: e-mail messages.

Another hypothesis would be to carry on contacts with the consumer through his e-mail address, as the consumer might, at a particular step of a transaction, introduce personal data including his e-mail address. The advertiser might be attracted to use this address for further individual communications.

Such personalised communications fall under the scope of two European Directives: firstly the distance contracts Directive [6] , secondly the Directive on the protection of individuals with regard to the processing of personal data and the free movement of such data [7]: those two texts provide for a similar principle of *opt-out* in the frame of commercial communications. According to article 14 (b) of the privacy Directive, the data subject shall be provided with the right to "object, on request and free of charge, to the processing of personal data relating to him which the controller anticipates being processed for the purposes of direct marketing (…)". Article 10 § 2 of the distance contracts Directive lays down the opt-out principle: "means of distance communication which allow individual communications may be used only where there is no clear objection from the consumer".

Unlike the opt-in technique, the advertiser has no need to require the prior consent of the consumer to receive the advertising, but he should be aware of the possible objection to receive individual communications.

Consequently, the advertiser shall take the necessary arrangements to be informed of a possible opposition of the consumer to receive such individual communications. The privacy Directive goes further by stating that the data subject (in this case the consumer) shall be "informed before personal data are disclosed for the first time to third parties or used on their behalf for the purposes of direct marketing, and to be expressly offered the right to object free of charge to such disclosures or uses". The Directive imposes upon the Member States the obligation to take the necessary measures to ensure that data subjects are aware of the existence of this right but it does not mention on who this obligation should be imposed.

3.2   Information of the Consumer

When broadcasting their advertisements, Otto Versand and Sainsbury have a double duty of information: they shall first inform their consumers about the advertising itself: what is the aim? What consequences does it have for them? etc. Then, they shall offer them the possibility to object to this kind of advertising with, here again, an information on the consequences of the objection.

Such obligations of information are not stated in any text at the European level, but it does correspond to concrete expectations of consumers: if the screen is overwhelmed by commercial communications, consumers might feel frustrated if no prior explanations has been forwarded to them about those communications, the risk being that they decide to stop the connection with the site. A similar explanation applies to the possibility to object: consumers feel better understood if they are given a rational choice to make, up to their own wills and expectations.

3.2.1   Time and Content of the Information

1. – When does the consumer shall be informed?

Targeted consumers are, according to the statements of the project, existing consumers, meaning consumers having already entered the site and who know already the site. It is without doubt that these consumers will see a major change on the site, as such targeted advertising did not exist at the time of their previous visits. Therefore, as soon as the consumer enters the site and is "in the shop", he shall receive information about the targeted advertising.

2. – How the consumer shall be informed?

Concretely, the site should mention on its first page the existence of the targeted advertising and should incite consumers to call for further information. An icon could be appropriate but should be made attractive enough in order to incite consumers to click on it. However, a minimum information should, at least, be placed on the screen. A difficulty might appear if the consumer does not go for information: unless the site blocks further access if the information has not been consulted - which is rather uncertain - it cannot oblige the consultation. The site should thus leaves the possibility to come back to the information later during the visit and at any time of the visit.

3. – What information shall the consumer receive?

Comprehensive information shall be forwarded to the consumer. It is crucial that he understands the goal of the advertising and how he can benefit from it.

Having these points in mind, it is considered that the following information should be granted to the consumer (the list is indicative and may be subject to changes): what is the aim of the advertising (i.e. it should be stated clearly that the aim is to increase purchases, not only to inform consumer on other products), how the advertising is made personal, how the advertising is presented, what practical consequences does it have as far as the connection is concerned: does it increase the length of connection, does it imply additional costs charged to the consumer, etc. how frequent advertising appears on the screen, how the consumer can take advantage of the advertising, etc.

Actually, the information forwarded to the consumer shall make him able to decide whether he agrees to receive it or not: any relevant information to help him make up his mind should be granted. Finally, the consumer should receive the information about the possibility to object to this kind of advertising.

3.2.2   Right to Object

The possibility to refuse receiving targeted advertising should be given to the consumer without giving any reason and without charges.

1. – Form of the objection.

The objection could be materialised in a form to fill or a icon to click on. However, it is recommended not to limit the opposition to a simple click, in order to avoid any misuse and involuntary objections.

Whether the choice is made between a form to fill, an icon to click or any other possibility, it would be relevant to impose a confirmation of the choice.

2. – Time of objection.

Like the information on the advertising, it is necessary that the consumer be offered the possibility to object at different time of the visit. The objection could be given: at the time the information on the advertising is given, or later during the visit, or at the occasion of a next visit.

The site could also envisage the possibility for the consumer to come back on the objection and to decide to agree on receiving targeted advertising.

3. – Consequences of the objection.

In the "objection form" or in the "objection icon", information should be given on the consequences the objection means for the consumer, especially if Otto Versand and Sainsbury foresee a different treatment between consumers agreeing on receiving the advertising and others.

Likewise, if a possibility to come back on the objection during a next visit is foreseen, consumers should be informed of such possibility and how to manage it.

3.3   Legal and Extra-Legal Rules

3.3.1   The Misleading and Comparative Advertising Directive

An advertising Directive was first adopted in 1984 concerning exclusively misleading advertising [4]. This Directive had to be implemented by the Member States by 1 October 1986 at the latest. Then the European Commission expressed the wish to go further in the protection of consumers in the field of comparative advertising, by allowing it under strict conditions. This new Directive adopted on 16 October 1997, is intended to amend Directive 84/450 [8]. This Directive has to be implemented by Member States at the latest 30 months after its publication in the Official Journal of the European Communities, so by the 23 April 2000.

Misleading Advertising.

Misleading advertising is defined as "any advertising which in any way, including its presentation, deceives or is likely to deceive the persons to whom it is addressed or whom it reaches and which, by reason of its deceptive nature, is likely to affect their economic behaviour or which, for those reasons, injures or is likely to injure a competitor" (article 2(2) in [4]).

In the frame of an administrative or judicial control of those provisions, the Directive mentions that the advertiser may be requested to provide evidence as to the accuracy of factual claims in advertising if, taking into account the legitimate interests of the advertiser and any other party to the proceedings, such a requirement appears appropriate on the basis of the circumstances of the particular case. If such evidence is not furnished by the advertiser or deemed insufficient by the court of the administrative authority, the factual claims will be considered inaccurate, opening either a cessation procedure or a prohibition of publication (see article 4(2)).

Comparative Advertising.

The purpose of the Directive is "to protect consumers, persons carrying on a trade or business or practising a craft or profession and the interests of the public in general against misleading advertising and the unfair consequences thereof and to lay down the conditions under which comparative advertising is permitted" (article 1(2) in [9]).

Comparative advertising is heard as "any advertising which explicitly or by implication identifies a competitor or goods or services offered by a competitor" (article 1(3)).

The conditions for allowing comparative advertising are rather strict as they are, on the one hand, devoted to grant a better information to consumers, but on the other hand the wish is to avoid any distortion in competition through any detriment to competitors and adverse effect on consumers' choice.

3.3.2 2. – Green Paper on Commercial Communications

The advent of the Information Society led the European Commission to formulate four general remarks as far as the commercial communications are concerned [9]:

- Digital communication infrastructures offer a new medium of communication for commercial messages; a large growth of marketing activities on the network is expected;

- Broadcasting speed will ease cross-border commercial communications;

- Distance sales will speed up due to the interactive possibilities of the network;

- Network operators will offer new communication services at lower prices.

4 Privacy Issues

4.1 Introduction

The European Union directive on the protection of individuals with regard to the processing of personal data should be transposed into the legislation of the Member States by October the 24th 1998, and has now become a legally binding instrument [7]. While the directive may require some modifications in the European countries' law, most of these countries already embody the principles of the directive. An overview of the regulatory framework in action in the context of electronic commerce in the United Kingdom and in Germany cannot therefore avoid the analysis of this directive (see section 5, Private International Law).

The aim of this section is to outline the main obligations arising from these legal instruments which must be respected in AIMedia projects such as Otto Versand and Sainsbury.

4.2   Scope and Identification

4.2.1   Personal Data

The directive applies to the processing of personal data wholly or partly by automatic means (see article 3(1)). One of the first questions which arise therefore is to determine whether or not personal data is being processed in the context of the electronic commerce activities developed by Otto Versand or Sainsbury.

The Directive adopts a very broad definition of the term "personal data" so as to include any information relating to an identified or identifiable person ("data subject"). The person may be "directly" identified (by reference to his name, for example) or can be "indirectly" identified by reference to specific characteristics of that person, in particular by reference to an "identification number", or to one or more factors specific to his "physical, psychological, mental, economic, cultural or social identity". It must be underlined that the directive does not therefore apply to data regarding legal persons.

Two types of data can be identified in AIMedia scenarios : Collected data is data collected directly from the data subject either during registration to the service or when filling in a form during the data subject's visit to the site. Extracted data covers data deduced from automatic data mining. For example how can either of the categories of goods purchased, articles ordered, pages visited, catalogue consulted and customer data be correlated to provide additional information than that initially collected from the data subject himself?

4.2.1.1   Collected Data

A distinction must be made here between existing customers entering the site and new prospective customers. In the context of existing customers who enter a customer or card number when entering the website, there is no doubt that personal data about that customer is being processed since this number is linked to identification of the customer (when taking out a card Sainsbury customers are asked to give some basic personal data such as the size of their household, address, age,...). As for new customers they could be asked upon entering into the site to fill in a form requesting personal data. However if no personal data is introduced by the data subject himself will the directive still apply?

To determine whether a person is "identifiable", account should be taken of all the means likely reasonably to be used by the controller, or by any other person, to identify the said person (see §26 of recitals). Indirectly identifiable information is therefore limited to information which can be reasonably linked to an identified person. Does an IP address which reveals the identity of the computer used identify the user behind the computer ? A fixed IP address is more likely to be qualified as personal in the same way as licence plate numbers or telephone numbers have been qualified as personal data by the national data protection authorities. This is even more true in the context of the services offered by Sainsbury and Otto Versand which rely on the identification of the person so as to establish a personalised service.

4.2.1.2   Extracted Data

Extracted data covers any data which is not directly submitted by the data subject himself but is deduced from consumer behaviour for example. To the extent that this information can be linked to an identified or identifiable individual, it must be considered as personal data in the eyes of the directive.

4.2.2   Controller

The directive provides for a number of duties and obligations incumbent on the " controller ". One must therefore determine whether Otto Versand or Sainsbury can be qualified as controllers.

In the processing of data so as to establish personal profiles, a distinction must be made between the simple shopping site service by Otto Versand or Sainsbury and the more complex scenario of a consortium of non competing companies in which personal profiles are established by the sharing of data amongst actors.

In the first scenario Otto Versand and Sainsbury establish their own personal profiles from data collected by the use of their services and by questionnaires filled in by customers visiting their sites. Each company determines the purpose of the service offered and the means by which this service is carried out and must therefore undoubtedly each be qualified as a controller in the terms of the directive. If the retailers share any information amongst themselves so as to establish complete customer profiles, they remain the controllers of the processing and the communication of the data must respect the principles laid down in the directive (see below).

In the context of a consortium of companies, gathering information from the different retailers in a shopping mall so as to establish consumer profiles and dispatching the information to the retailers, the consortium in itself, as a separate legal entity, could be qualified as the controller since it determines the means and purposes of the processing.

4.3   Principles to be Respected

The directive lays down a series of principles which must be respected by the controller. We will examine each one of these principles underlying the main implications for the AIMedia project.

4.3.1   The Purpose Limitation Principle

4.3.1.1   Personal Data Must Be Processed Fairly and Lawfully (Article 6)

"Fair" processing implies a maximum of openness. An individual's personal data cannot be processed for any hidden or occult reasons. Personal data may only be collected in a transparent way (this principle is guaranteed by the right of information, granted to the data subject in articles 10 and 11).

"Lawful" processing implies the respect of the national provisions taken in compliance with Chapter II of the directive.

4.3.1.2   Personal Data Must Be Processed for Specified, Explicit, and Legitimate Purposes

Personal data may only be processed for specified and explicit purposes. This obligation compels the controller to determine at the outcome the exact purpose for which he intends to process personal data. The determination of the purpose by the data controller must be sufficiently precise to enable the data subject to control every use of his personal data. For example, the purpose behind the AIMedia project is not only the sale of goods electronically, but also and more importantly, the processing of personal data so as to establish personal profiles in view of offering a specially customer-tailored range of services, articles and promotions and thus improve seller-consumer-relationships.

The purposes for which personal data are processed must be legitimate and must be determined at the time of collection of the data (article 6.1.b). The very aim of data protection - the respect of the fundamental rights and freedoms of natural persons - implies that the purpose of the processing cannot rightly violate these rights and freedoms without a legitimate cause. The purpose must therefore be necessary in the eyes of a company or of the community in general. One must therefore balance the right of the individual to see his right to privacy preserved with the public or private interest to process the data. The final evaluation of the legitimacy of the purposes depends on the appreciation of the courts or of specialised data protection authorities.

4.3.2   Grounds for Processing of Personal Data

Article 7 of the Directive lays down the grounds justifying the processing of personal data. These grounds correspond to the circumstances considered by the European Community as allowing the processing of personal data. In order to be lawful, the processing of data must rely on one of these grounds, in addition to the fact that it must respect the obligations deriving from the legitimate purpose principle.

In the context of electronic commerce transactions, three justifications laid down in article 7 can more precisely be retained :

i) "The data subject has unambiguously given his consent" (article 7.a) :

Express written consent is not required. Any customer introducing his own personal data in order to purchase a good, could be considered as consenting to the processing of his personal data for this specified purpose. The introduction of further data in order to obtain a personalised service could also be equated to the data subject giving his consent.

The data subject's consent must in any event be freely given: there should be no pressure on the individual to obtain this consent. Free consent also implies that when a user is presented with a screen demanding personal data for further access, the fact that he refuses to go further should not be recorded or held against him.

The interactivity characterising networks offers a special interest as regards the consent. Instead of a consent given once and for all at the start of a series of operations, interactivity enables you to modulate your consent. A message can appear on the screen at different times announcing "if you want to go further, you must consent to give such or such information". You can accept part of the operations but refuse to give more data at a certain point of the processing, or for a certain part of the service offered. Moreover, you can accept certain reuses announced but not all : you can tick off the cases corresponding to the accepted or refused uses of your personal data. Opting-in or -out methods acquire an immediate and effective dimension through interactivity.

ii) "Processing is necessary for the performance of a contract to which the data subject is party or in order to take steps at the request of the data subject prior to entering into a contract" (article 7.b).

A user may be requested to introduce certain personal data in order to obtain certain goods (his name and address so that the goods can be forwarded to him, his credit card number so that the goods can be billed,...). Only the data "necessary" for the performance of the contract may be processed. Therefore when one can do without personal data for the performance of a contract, one should not require it.

iii) "Processing is necessary for the purposes of the legitimate interests pursued by the controller or by the third party or parties to whom the data are disclosed, except where such interests are overridden by the interests or fundamental rights and freedoms of the data subject..." (article 7.f).

This provision justifies the processing of personal data where it is in the legitimate interest of a natural or legal person, provided that the interests of the data subject are not overriding. This means that if the interest of a person in receiving personal data prevails over the data subject's interest not having his data communicated, data may be transferred. This is also true even when the data subject's interest in retaining his data is equivalent to the third party interest. It is only when the data subject's interest prevails, that the data relating to him may not be processed or communicated.

4.3.3   The Prohibition of Processing Sensitive Data (Article 8)

Subject to a number of exceptions set out in article 8.2, the processing of certain categories of data is prohibited according to article 8.1 of the Directive. This prohibition covers any data revealing racial or ethnic origin, political opinions, religious or philosophical beliefs, trade-union membership, and the processing of data concerning health or sex life. Any messages or data bases containing such data, will therefore need to find grounds within article 8.2. in order to be processed.

To the extent that profile information reveals an individual's morals as illustrated by an individual's consumer habits, such profiling comes within the ban of article 8.1. Similarly the electronic commerce activities linked to goods that reveal sensitive information fall within the scope of article.

The data subject's explicit and informed consent is probably the safest course to follow when one decides to process sensitive data relating to an individual (article 8.2.a). The other most obviously eligible ground to process sensitive data is when such data have been manifestly made public by the data subject (article 8(2)) (in answering a questionnaire he has marked his preference for gay activities, or his religion, for example).

4.3.4   Data Quality

The directive requires a level of quality for the personal data that is being processed. The controller must ensure the respect of these principles.

1) Personal data must be adequate, relevant and not excessive in relation to the purposes for which they were collected and/or further processed.

The criteria of data adequacy are designed solely to ensure a necessary and sufficient link between the information and the purpose of the processing. For each finality, one must question whether or not there is a sufficient connection between the purpose and the data collected. Any irrelevant data must be discarded.

In the context of AIMedia, the data collected must therefore always ensure a sufficient link with the purpose of offering a specially customer-tailored range of products, services and promotions. If the collection and use of data such as the customer's name, address, number of persons in their household, hobbies and preferences can be justified as offering a sufficient link with the service offered, this could not be said of data such as the person's passport number or place of birth.

It must be pointed out that the targeted marketing offered requires more information to be given prior to the offering of the service, than the traditional distance selling of goods. Indeed in order be able to offer the most personalised service possible, the vendor will require a number of data before the goods are actually proposed, so as to offer goods corresponding to the person's needs (age, hobbies, sex, …). The criteria of data adequacy could therefore enable the processing of more data than in a traditional environment.

2) Personal data must be accurate and, where necessary, kept up to date.

An actor processing personal data must ensure that this data is accurate. The danger concerning the establishment of personal profiles based on consumer patterns is that the goods purchased may not necessarily correspond to a person's needs or habits: the purchase of a catholic bible does not mean that one is a catholic, one could be buying for someone else…It is recommended in this respect that the data subject is involved in the prior authorisation of the processing and that he is given the possibility to require that inaccurate data be modified (see below, right of rectification).

The personal data must be kept up to date. This implies that it be reviewed on a regular basis. Every reasonable step must be taken so that incomplete or inexact information be modified.

3) Personal data may only be kept for a certain period.

Personal data may only be kept in a form which permits identification of the data subjects for no longer than is necessary for the purposes for which the data were collected and/or for which they are further processed. The data introduced by the consumer in order to purchase certain goods, may only be kept for the period necessary in order to obtain those goods and may not be stored beyond that period unless the controller has been specifically authorised to do so in the context of the profiling of his clientele.

One can question as to whether the vendor will be able to conserve data regarding individuals who enter the site but do not wish to go further and leave the site without having voluntarily entered personal data and without having purchased any goods.

4.4   Rights of Data Subject

4.4.1   Right to Be Informed

According to article 10 and 11 of the directive, there are two particular occasions when the controller must provide information to the data subject. The first is at the time of collection of personal data.

The data subject must be informed at least of :

a) The identity of the controller (and his representative, if any);

b) The purpose or purposes of the processing for which the data are intended.

Further information must also be provided if "necessary in the specific circumstances to ensure a fair processing in respect of the data subject". Such information includes: the recipients or categories of recipients of the data, whether replies to questions are obligatory or voluntary and the possible consequences of failure to reply, and the existence of the data subject's right of access to and the right to rectify the data concerning him.

If personal data on consumers are collected it must be clear to them who is to use the data and what are the purposes for which the data are to be used or disclosed.

It must be pointed out that the features of a network facilitate the provision of information. In the hypothesis of data collected from the data subject, a message can appear on the screen at the beginning of the operations, providing the users with the mandatory information.

The data subject must be informed of the identity of the recipients or categories of recipients. The "recipient" is defined in article 2.g. of the Directive as any person to whom the data are disclosed whether a processor (person processing data on behalf of the controller), third party (any person other than the data subject, the controller, the processor and persons who under the direct authority of the controller or processor, are authorised to process the data), a person in a third country,.... The controller may be requested to provide information as to the identity of these persons to the data subject if deemed necessary in order to guarantee "fair processing" of the data.

4.4.2   Right of Access

The Directive grants every data subject the right to obtain from the controller, without constraint at reasonable intervals and without excessive delay or expense, confirmation as to whether or not data relating to him are being processed and information at least as to the purposes of the processing, the categories of data concerned and the recipients or categories of recipients to whom the data are disclosed.

The data subject may also obtain communication to him in an intelligible form of the data undergoing processing and any "available" information as to their sources. In the context of open networks or shopping malls as those envisaged by OTTO and Sainsbury, the controller will not always be in a position to provide information as to the sources of the data. He will be dispensed from giving this information if it is not "available".

4.4.3   Right of Rectification

Following on from the right of access, article 12. 2 of the directive provides that the data subject is granted, as appropriate, the right to obtain the rectification, erasure or blocking of data, the processing of which does not comply with the provisions of the Directive, in particular because of the incomplete or inaccurate nature of the data. It is up to the controller to ensure that this right is guaranteed.

The Directive further provides that the controller must notify to the third parties to whom the data have been disclosed of any rectification, erasure or blocking of the data, unless this proves impossible or involves a disproportionate effort. In the context of the sharing of information between the different actors, it is important that the notification of the rectification of the data is sent along to the different detainees of the data so that they may dispose of the most adequate and up dated information.

4.4.4   Right to Object

The data subject is granted the right to object on compelling legitimate grounds relating to his particular situation to the processing of data relating to him, save where otherwise provided for by national legislation. Where there is a justified objection, the processing instigated by the controller may no longer involve these data.

This right to object is granted unconditionally as regards the processing of personal data for marketing purposes. In the context of such projects as those developed by AIMedia, therefore it would appear that this right must be granted.

Furthermore, when personal data are to be disclosed for the first time to third parties or used on their behalf for the purposes of direct marketing, the data subject must be informed of this before the data are disclosed and must be offered the right to object free of charge to such disclosures or uses. The sharing of information between actors so as to establish consumer profiles, thus requires the information of the data subject prior to the disclosure of the information.

Different ways of expressing ones right to opt out could be envisaged: by ticking the appropriate box when filling in a questionnaire collecting personal data; by writing; by e-mail or by telephone.

4.4.5   Automated Individual Decisions

Article 15 states that Member States shall grant the right to every person not to be subject to a decision which produces legal effects concerning him or significantly affects him and which is based solely on automated processing of data intended to evaluate certain aspects relating to him, such as his performance at work, creditworthiness, reliability, conduct,...".

This type of provision prevents decisions such as the creditworthiness of a person to be determined by an automated decision, for example, based on the geographical localisation of the person.

4.5   The Controllers' Obligations and Liabilities

4.5.1.1   Security (Article 17)

According to article 17 of the directive, the controller is required to put into place the measures so as to avoid any accidental or unlawful destruction, loss or alteration, against any unauthorised disclosure or access and against any other forms of unlawful processing. The rationale of this article is that the potential danger to the data subject's right of privacy does not only emanate from the controller, who collects, stores, processes and discloses the data for his own purpose, but is also jeopardised if the data subject's data are misused by third parties who have gained access to it, whether authorised (by a processor under the instructions of the controller, for example) or unauthorised.

The security measures can be organisational (designation of a "security officer", documents handed out to the staff with precise security measures to be respected,...) or technical (computers kept under lock and key or in specially protected areas, introduction of access codes, encryption of certain documents, ...). It is left up to the controller to adopt the necessary measures. The measures are the result of the equation of three variables : the risks of the processing, the nature of the data and the state of the art and cost of implementation of the measures.

The introduction of computers and networks increase the risks, notably the threat of access to the data by unauthorised persons and the unauthorised use of the data by authorised users.

Account must be taken of the nature of the data. Processing of sensitive data (medical data, for example) will imply the requirement of a higher level of protection.

The security measures adopted will also be dependent on the state of the art and the cost of their implementation. This provision implies that the controller is under the positive obligation to keep himself informed of the new security measures available and to ensure that the level of security is adequate vis a vis the "state of the art" unless they are prohibitively expensive. A controller could be well advised to have proof that all the decisions relating to security of personal data were founded on professional expertise.

The directive also provides that the controller must, where processing is carried out on his behalf, choose a processor providing sufficient guarantees in respect of the technical securities measures and organisational measures governing the processing to be carried out and must ensure compliance with these measures. The carrying out of processing of personal data by another person must be governed by a contract or legal act, in writing or in other equivalent form, binding the processor to the controller and stipulating particularly that the processor shall only act on instructions from the controller and that the processor shall also be responsible for taking security measures in accordance with article 17 of the directive.

4.5.1.2   Notification (Article 18)

The controller has a last obligation which is that of notification of automated processing to a supervisory authority. The directive does however provide for the simplification or the exemption from notification for certain types of processing operations. It is not however clear how the national laws will transpose these measures. The general idea is to largely exempt controllers and to reserve the notification procedure for special categories of processing.

4.5.1.3   Liability (Article 23)

The Directive provides every person with a right to a judicial remedy for any breach of the rights guaranteed him by the national law applicable to the processing in question. In addition, any person who has suffered a damage as a result of an unlawful processing operation or of any act incompatible with the national provisions adopted is entitled to receive compensation from the controller for the damage suffered. The controller may be exempted from this liability, in whole or in part, if he proves that he is not responsible for the event giving rise to the damage.

4.6   Conclusion

The European Union directive on the protection of individuals with regard to the processing of personal data must transposed into the legislation of the Member States by October 24th 1998. From this date on, it will become a legally binding document.

The AIMedia user profile is 'personal data'. The directive adopts a broad definition of the term 'personal data', so as to include any information relating to an identified or identifiable person. In AIMedia personal data consists in collected data (the user has answered questionnaires) and extracted data (the AIMedia deduces user characteristics based on purchase history, and statistical comparisons). This data forms a user profile, which is directly related to the customer's identity. Thus all user related data in the AIMedia user profile is considered personal data.

The personal data is processed by the 'controller'. When considering simple home-shopping, the retailer (e.g. OTTO or Sainsbury) is the controller. In the case of a mall of retailers sharing user profiles, the consortium in itself, as a separate entity, would be the controller. On the other side, the customer is know as the 'data subject'.

5   Private International Law

5.1   Introduction

5.1.1   Introductory Remarks

The establishment of a web shop may create several advantages for the retailer. One is the simplification of reaching out to customers located in foreign countries. If a French retailer offers his products on the Internet, it will be equally easy for a Swede as for a French person to access the web page, find out what it has to offer, and eventually order some of the products. Consequently, it is easy to imagine that there may arise cross-border conflicts, that is, legal disputes which involves parties situated in different countries. An action, whether manually or computationally, committed on the Internet, whether in form of the collecting of personal data, advertisement of products etc., might be in accordance with the law of one country at the same time as it violates the law of another country. Which country's court shall have the competence to adjudicate, and which country's law shall form the basis for the solution of the material question? These are the issues that are going to be dealt with in the following chapters.

5.1.2 General Delimitation

The subject of this report is to sort out the questions of jurisdiction and choice of law. The framework of the project will not allow a profound analysis, whereas the report will have to concentrate upon identifying some of the more important questions, and try to point out possible solutions to these. Consequently, we will analyse three main fields which are relevant for AIMEDIA project, i.e. data protection, advertising and liability on the basis of loss suffered due to misleading information. Still, in this report one will have to operate with certain delimitation.

It is presumed that the legal disputes are of an international character, see under section 2. If the legal disputes are qualified to be a matter of public law, special questions arise in accordance with the application of the rules governing the questions of jurisdiction, choice of law and enforcement. In the following it will therefore be assumed that the legal disputes in question, are a matter of private law. However, this assumption will be suspended to some extent in discussing advertisements on the Internet. Questions of consumer rights and product liability will not be treated.

It is presumed that the legal disputes takes place between parties domiciled within the borders of the EC or the ECCA-states. It is presumed that the defendant of the legal dispute is the web shop's responsible institution. Third party conflicts (e.g. liability of intermediaries) fall outside the treatment. It is presumed that the objects, which are to be distributed, are assumed to be ordinary merchandise in the form of tangibles. The sale of services will not be considered.

5.2 Private International Law

5.2.1 The Problem

When two parties enter into a legal conflict, the usual step is to ask the courts for help. In a normal situation this does not cause any problems. Two neighbours will go to their local court, and this court will use its own rules. However, a problem arises when the two parties do not reside in the same country, or the problem has connections to more than one country.

The problem is defined by a "foreign element" [10], that is not the one of the court. It is in these cases one has to apply the rules of private international law. Private international law basically rules over matters between private parties and not when there is a public element involved.

5.2.2 The Main Questions

The judges in these cases must, before solving the material case itself, determine two major questions. First of all the court must decide whether it has jurisdiction over the case; i.e. if the parties in question can bring this case into the court. Secondly it must determine what rules to apply to this case. This is a choice of law, and not the application of certain rules to the case. The foreign element in this case gives the court the choice between more than one set of rules. A final question that has importance in interlegal law, is the question of recognition and enforcement. In this report we have chosen not to deal with this problem, mainly because it is often solved under the jurisdiction issue.

To be more practical, if two parties go to court to solve a legal problem that has a foreign element, the first task of the court is to determine if it has jurisdiction over the parties – which means whether they can render a valid decision with respect to the legal problem. If this is so, the next step will be to decide which law governs the case, i.e. the choice of law. This part consist of several elements. First of all there has to be a classification of the case. It is of great importance if the case is classified as contractual law rather than the law of procedure. When this is done, the court must see if there are some regulations dealing with this problem. If there are not, one has to apply the basic rules of private international law. The result of this will be to determine which country's substantive law governs the question. Once this law has been chosen, the court must primarily use this law to decide on the case. Unfortunately this is not always the end of the process. There may be mandatory rules in the country of the court, which collide with the *lex causae* (the law of the case). In some cases this leads to the use of *ordre public* (public policy of ethical and social character) which requires that other rules be applied. The rules may be either secondary rules of the *lex causae* that are not incompatible with the rules of the court, or rules of *lex fori* (the law of the court).

5.2.3   The Application to Cyberspace

Unfortunately it is a well-known fact that the courts often disregard private international law. First, the parties often do not have the means to get acquainted with a foreign law by hiring a specialist from a foreign country. Second, the court itself prefers to use its own *lex fori* because this is the law known and because the lack of time does not allow the judge to use more time than necessary on the case. Therefore the question for the future is how the courts in Europe will use the "instrument of private international law" on the legal questions that raises from the use of Internet as a commercial marketplace. It is at this point the interesting questions start.

5.2.4   The International Aspect of the Internet

What is considered to be an international case when it comes to cyberspace? When entering cyberspace things change because any contact made over the Internet can be "international". At no point is it sure that if you exchange email with your closest neighbour, this email will go directly to him – it may go across the world before reaching him. This is why the foreign element might be present at all times when using the Internet. Now, if you exchange emails with your neighbour about buying his Rolex, the court will most likely regard this as a national matter. On the other hand, if your neighbour places an advertisement offering his Rolex for sale on the Internet, it is not sure that you will be able to identify him. At this point the matters seems more international, and the court should consider if the case should be solved using private international law. We will not take this argument any further, but it may be a point to argue in front of a court.

5.2.5   Internet and Law

The laws applicable in the analogue world may not be the same as in the digital world. This is important to understand with respect to the question of applicable law. Not only is there is no direct contact between two contracting parties, but also the identification of these parties is not always possible. Many of the laws and acts related to international trade are based on the presumption of direct contact between the parties, and that the object of the trade is physical objects. When using the Internet this is not as obvious. What is contracted, may be sold and sent over the Internet. This again raises problems of intellectual property rights, which will not be addressed in this report.

In this report we will try to examine the main issues related to private international law and web-shops. This examination will mainly consist of looking at the present regulations, and whether they are applicable to the issues in question. For some issues there may be some regulations developed especially for a digital environment, which then will be applicable. On the other hand there might be issues where it will not be possible to apply current regulations. Here the question will be what alternative solutions can be found. The first solution is to consider if the traditional regulations can be adapted. This will in general mean to try to identify the parties in question and their places of attachment. If this is not possible, we will have to rely on the traditional private international law, and to explore the consequences of their possible application. However, at this point we will be arguing mainly on the basis of legal policies.

5.3　Jurisdiction

5.3.1　Introduction

When a legal dispute enters the court, the court will have to decide whether it has the competence to adjudicate in this specific case. Concerning courts within the area of the EC and the ECCA-area there are two conventions, which in many cases will provide a solution to the questions; the Brussels- and the Lugano Conventions. All the member states of the EC have become parties to the Brussels Convention of 27 September1968. Furthermore, all the ECCA-states (with the exception of Liechtenstein) have become parties to the Lugano Convention of 16 September1988, which for our purposes may be seen as identical to the Brussels Convention with respect the material content. The two conventions will be treated as one in the following.[2]

The conventions only provide solutions for cross-border disputes concerning "civil and commercial matters" (article 1(1)), that means legal disputes as part of *private law*. In the ruling of the EC-court *LTU v Eurocontrol*,[3] it is stated that essential for the qualification is the character of "the legal relationships between the parties to the action of the subject matter of the action". In other words, it is only in situations where a public authority has exercised public authority, that the provisions is inapplicable. The qualification of whether a legal relationship is to be deemed a matter of public or private law, is to be determined on the basis of an autonomous interpretation of the Convention, where respect shall be paid to the purpose and the

---

[2] Reference to articles in the following, will be based upon the provisions laid down in the Brussels Convention.

[3] Decision of October 14th, 1976 in Case 29/76, LTU v Eurocontrol [1976] ECR 1976; Concerning the Brussels Convention.

structure of the Convention, and also the shared principles that can be extracted from the legal systems of the parties to the Convention.

As concerning the enforcement of advertisement legislation, this typically will be considered a matter of public law, and thereby fall outside the scope of the conventions.

5.4   Choice of Law

5.4.1   Data Protection and Choice of Law

5.4.1.1   Introduction

Data protection will be in the future, as now, an important issue in a digital society. Increasingly personal data is being stored on computers that are connected to other computers. The possibility for people to access this information across jurisdictional borders is also increasing. This, in turn, increases in the potential for choice-of-law issues arising with respect to regulation of the information processing concerned.

The following analysis rests on several presumptions. First, we presume there is an issue involved which has a certain international, or foreign, element, thus allowing the issue to be considered a question of private international law. An example is a Web-shop, which collects data about customers who are not situated in the same country as the owner of the Web-shop. Second, we presume that the matter is of a private character. By this we mean that the parties presenting themselves to the court do not include government agencies. Third, we presume that the matter occurs within the geographical area of the EU/EFTA countries that have signed the Lugano and Brussels Conventions. Fourth, we presume that the parties have been identified, and that the transactions between the parties did not occur anonymously. Finally, we presume that the aim of this analysis is to allow the owner of the Web-shop to be able to predict more precisely which law will regulate the processing of data about his customers.

5.4.1.2   The Regulation of this Field Inside Certain Areas

Every EU/EFTA state has enacted data protection legislation. Furthermore, the EU has adopted a Directive on data protection (Directive 95/46/EC – hereinafter abbreviated "EC-DPD") which is aimed at harmonising data protection regimes inside the EU. This Directive will also be highly influential for the development of data protection law in EEA states that are not members of the EU – i.e., Norway and Iceland – especially once the Directive is formally incorporated in the EEA Agreement.

5.4.1.3   The Directive's Impact on Internet-Shopping

The EU DPD applies to "the processing of personal data wholly or partly automatic means, and to the processing otherwise than by automatic means of personal data which form part of a filing system or are intended to form part of a filing system" (art. 3(1)).

5.4.1.4   The Law Applicable to the Processing of Data

The next point is to identify the law applicable to the handling of the database and the data concerned (see section 4, Privacy Issues).

Of decisive importance for working out which law is to be applied to a given data-processing operation, especially in the present case of international private law, is the meaning of the term "establishment" in art. 4(1)(a) of the Directive. Some light is cast on the meaning of the term in recital 19, which states:

> 'Whereas establishment on the territory of a Member State implies the effective and real exercise of activity through stable arrangements; whereas the legal form of such an establishment, whether simply branch or subsidiary with a legal personality, is not the determining factor in this respect; whereas, when a single controller is established on territory of several Member States, particularly by means of subsidiaries, he must ensure, in order to avoid any circumvention of national rules, that each of the establishments fulfils the obligations imposed by the national law applicable to its activities; ...'

At this point, the principal rule must be said to be clear in the case where we have one controller with only one place of establishment: the applicable law will be the law of that place of establishment. This means that if a controller has headquarters in country A, the data protection law of country A will apply.

Problems arise when the controller is established in several jurisdictions. We will address these problems below.

5.4.1.5   Problems of the Directive

In this section, we will look at the problems resulting from a situation in which the controller is established in multiple jurisdictions. Second, we will consider the issue as to whether data mining can be considered as involving a contract between the controller and its counterpart. Finally we will look into the problem of *ordre public*.

Problem 1: The controller has more than one place of establishment.

As we have seen in sect. 4.2.4, it is quite clear that an "establishment" may include subsidiaries, branch offices, and perhaps also agents or similar representation. This means that if the controller has a main office in one country, and several branches in some other countries, different laws will be applicable to a single data-processing operation that extends across borders.

To be more specific, we can imagine one controller, A, situated in country A, exchanging information with its sub-branch, B, in country B. The collection (or mining) of this information can take place from almost any country. If there is no exchange of information, the data processing in country A will first have to comply with the data protection law of country A, and the data processing in country B will have to comply with the data protection law of country B. If B sends information to A, the situation changes. From the wording of art. 4(1)(a), the data protection law of country B will still be applicable to the case, even if the information now is in the hands of A. This rather complex situation could mean that A would have to separate all information according to where they come from, or comply with the strictest data protection law at the time. Inside a large community,[4] this means that one would at all times have to be looking at the possibility of new regulations and change internal routines.

But this problem has also another aspect: that is, a positive conflict of jurisdiction might arise [11].

Until now we have taken for granted that there is only one controller and that this controller has one or several sub-branches situated in different countries. But, as noted above, art. 2(d) of the Directive seems to presume that there may be more than one controller per data-processing operation. In cases where this occurs, we may again be faced with a situation in which one set of data or one data-processing operation is subject to different national laws. This will not be a problem if the laws are in harmony – which is the assumption of the Directive – but such harmony might not eventuate given that states are given a significant "margin of appreciation" in implementing the Directive.

Problem 2: Can data mining be considered a contract between the data subject and the controller? Can the contract derogate from the provisions of the Directive?

To the first question, it is quite clear that even a small web-wrap clause will be difficult to view as a contract. However, if the controller collects this information by, for example, a customer filling out a purchase, order or subscription form on the Internet, and the controller sends the customer a password to permit entry to the rest of the web-site, it is at least arguable that a contract has been made that is binding for the customer. It would be too speculative to attempt to draw any firm conclusions on this point, but it is probable that Continental-European conceptualisations of what constitutes a contract will be more restrictive than Anglo-American conceptualisations.

As for the second question, the Directive makes clear that one of its basic purposes is to protect human rights, in particular the right to privacy. This follows from art. 1(1):

'In accordance with this Directive, Member States, shall protect the fundamental rights and freedoms of natural persons, and in particular their right to privacy with respect to the processing of personal data ...'

It also follows from recitals 3, 7, 8 and 9 in the Directive's preamble. Accordingly, it could be argued that the Directive intends to set a "bottom-line" for protection of individual persons' fundamental rights. Thus, any contract which attempts to derogate from this bottom-line will probably not be tolerated, unless the controller "adduces adequate safeguards with respect to the protection of the privacy and fundamental rights and freedoms of individuals ..." (Art. 26(2)).

Problem 3: Can the rules of ordre public stop data mining?

It is possible to envisage a situation where the court has given the parties jurisdiction and made a choice of law that is not the law of the jurisdiction in which the court is established; i.e., *lex fori*. If the law chosen offers a level of data protection far below

---

[4] Now counting 18 countries, and we do not include the two non-EU EEA-countries.

that offered by the jurisdiction in which the court is established, there is a possibility that the court will refrain from applying the chosen law by reference to *ordre public* considerations. This possibility will increase the more the personal data concerned are sensitive and in need of stringent protection.

5.4.2 Advertising and Choice of Law

It is suggested above that the execution of advertisement legislation is part of public law. It is an acknowledged principle that a national court as a point of departure never shall apply foreign law when judging cases of public matters. The general rule therefore is that when it comes to public law, the jurisdiction is not governed by the ordinary collision norms of private international law, whereas it is left for each of the country's practical possibilities to apply their own legislation and determine which law is applicable. Typically possibilities of applying national law will exist if the court has been found competent to adjudicate, see above.

Exceptions from the general rule will principally only take place in cases where international agreements form a different solution, and the state of the court is a party to the agreement. The question therefore becomes whether there are international agreements in Europe which regulate the questions of choice of law concerning advertisement on the Internet.

For the time being, no such agreement exists which regulates the problem directly. However there are two EC-Directives and one European Council Convention concern-ing the questions of choice of law that concerns cross-border *broadcasting* [12]. Ad-vertising is one of the issues included, and it might be that the Directives and the Con-vention will be applied analogously to cross-border advertising disputes on the Internet.

5.5   Conclusion

Concluding with respect to issues where the uncertainties are as great as in private international law, can only be speculations. Trying to give clear answers might lead to further problems. Even so, we will try to give a short summary of this report as a sort of conclusion.

Considering the jurisdiction in Europe, the Lugano and Brussels Conventions will solve the problems of jurisdiction for private and commercial matters. For the parties addressing a court, these conventions give security as to always finding a jurisdiction. As for where this jurisdiction will be, there might be problems. And if it does, the European Court of Justice may be able to give a prejudicial judgement. Further problems arise in the field outside private law. In such cases, like advertising, public law causes problems in the digital world, mainly because they imply national jurisdiction. The location of an Internet web-site offering advertisement is not as certain as the location of the person accessing the web-site or the provider of the web-site. Any further conclusions can not be expected.

As for choice of law, there are different solutions for different issues. Unfortunately there are not too many international regulations available. The choice of law in data protection, is easy to solve for a simple case, but as quickly more controllers enter the stage, the problems abound. For advertising, the choice of law is not governed by any regulations and the only solutions would be to apply analogue regulations. If this is acceptable is not easy to say. The choice of law in the context of liability for loss suffered due to misleading information, the traditional rule of *lex loci delicti* must be said to compete with the method of the closest connection. This is how far we can dare to suggest a solution.

Finally this leads us to conclude that the digital world cannot be said to be completely compatible with analogue world. The traditional solutions given in the existing Directives or conventions, like the Brussels Convention, are not directly applicable to the digital world. The first cases dealing with these questions will therefore be very decisive. The EU may have to adopt new regulations directly applicable to the digital world. The latter solution would be welcome, implying a harmonisation of private international law in this field and offer increased predictability for the parties.

6   General Conclusion

From the analysis of the AIMedia scenarios and plans from a legal point of view, we drew a number of design conclusions.

The legal study was carried out from the very beginning of the project, based on the scenarios we presented in section 2. From this study we derived a number of conclusions, which were translated in the overall agent architecture, and security features.

When designing the two prototype applications, one for Otto Versand , one for J.Sainsbury's, we shall take special care of the user interface so that the Shopping Assistant provides the required level of information to the customer.

Users should be provided with tools for controlling their personal data, and especially their user's profile. This is taken care of in the architecture by the Personal Agent. It implements the P3P standard, a W3C proposed standard for secure profile exchange.

We further reviewed the legal issues of advertising, personal data protection and international private law in the case of the AIMedia agent framework. These questions often arise when designing personal user-centric agents for e-commerce applications, and this can serve as an example of how to bind legal requirements with agent development for e-commerce applications.

References

[1] M. J. Viamonte and C. Ramos, 'A model for an electronic marketplace', in present book.

[2] M. Dastani, N. Jacobs, C. M. Jonker and J. Treur, 'Modelling user preferences and mediating agents in electronic commerce', in present book.

[3] L. Ardissono et al., 'Agent technologies for the development of adaptive web stores', in present book.

[4] Directive 84/450 of 10 September 1984 relating to the approximation of the laws, regulations and administrative provisions of the Member States concerning misleading advertising, *O.J.E.C.* L. 250/17 of 19.09.1984.

[5] " propositions pour une loi générale sur la protection des consommateurs ", rapport de la Commission d'Etudes pour la Refonte du Droit de la Consommation (CERDC), Belgian Ministry of Economic Affairs, 1995, pp. 82-83.

[6] Directive 97/7/EC of 20 May 1997 concerning the protection of consumers with respect to distance contracts O.J.E.C. L.144/19 of 4.06.1997.

[7] Directive 95/46/EC of the European Parliament and of the Council of 24th October 1995 on the protection of individuals with regard to the processing of personal data and on the free movement of such data, OJ No L 281, 23.11.1995, p.31.

[8] Directive 97/55/EC of the European Parliament and the Council of 6 October 1997 concerning misleading advertising so as to include comparative advertising.

[9] COM (96) 192 final.

[10] Joachim Benno; *Consumer purchases through telecommunications in Europe*, Complex 4/93 Tano (Oslo 1993), p. 21

[11] Jon Bing: *The identification of applicable law and liability with the regard to the use of protected material in the digital context* (ECLIP draft report).

[12] "The Satellite and Cable Directive": Council Directive 3.10.1989 on the coordination of certain provisions laid down by law, regulation or administrative action in member states concerning the pursuit of television broadcasting activities (89/552/EEC OJ 17.10.1989 298:25), "The Broadcasting Directive": Council directive of 3 October 1989 on the coordination of certain provisions laid down by law, regulation or administrative action in member states concerning the pursuit of television broadcasting activities (89/552/EEC OJ 17.10.1989 298:25) as amended by the European Parliament and Council Directive 97/36/EC of 30.6.1997, and the European Convention on Transfrontier Television.

Energy Resellers – An Endangered Species?

Fredrik Ygge

EnerSearch AB
Chalmers Science Park
SE - 412 88 Gothenburg, Sweden
www.enersearch.se/ygge
ygge@enersearch.se

Abstract. Many markets, including the travel, music, and book markets, are undergoing dramatic changes due do the development of electronic commerce. Reseller margins often decrease significantly and sometimes even entire links in the supply chain are becoming completely superfluous.

Even though power markets have been deregulated already for some years in many countries, electronic commerce has not yet had a major impact on the business logic. This paper presents some of the major obstacles to electronic power trade, and presents promising solutions to these obstacles. In particular it is described how software agent mediated trade may enable medium and small size consumers and producers to trade directly from power pools, without the need of traditional energy resellers.

The conclusion that is there are good reasons to believe that energy resellers are as threatened in the new information era as, e.g., traditional travel agencies, and music and book-shops are.

1 Introduction

The recent development of electronic commerce has completely changed the possibilities for trade in a number of industries. The most striking trend in these different industries is the increasingly threatened position of resellers. As the Internet enables customers to directly purchase goods from importers or even producers, the volumes of the resellers definitely reduces. This change is depicted in Figure 1.

Examples of industries where this change is particularly evident is the travel, music, and book industries. From my own experience I know that it is only marginally more complicated to book a car (at almost any location in the world) directly from the car rental company than booking it from a travel agent.[1] Furthermore, the information at the web-site is likely to be more accurate, the services are sometimes better, there is typically less risk for misunderstanding,

---

[1] See for example www.hertz.com or www.avis.com.

A. Moukas, C. Sierra, and F. Ygge (Eds.): AMEC'99, LNAI 1788, pp. 68-93, 2000.
© Springer-Verlag Berlin Heidelberg 2000

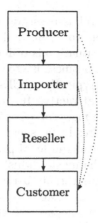

Fig. 1. The possible new business logic in the electronic commerce era. Customers are being able to purchase products directly from importers or producers without having to contact resellers.

and there are often on-line booking discounts. The same trends can be seen with hotel booking[2] and air-flight booking[3] Needless to say, this trend is devastating for the traditional travel agencies. However, there is a lot more to say about this. Bulk discounts, difficulties in comparing different packages etc. are good counter arguments in this discussion. These types of arguments should be carefully scrutinized though. For example, large companies could (and are already investigating) to get bulk deals with e.g. airlines and car rental firms, and at the trade occasion trade directly electronically with them. One could also envision totally new constellations, e.g. think of a Internet travel search engine that guarantees very low prices in order to attract many users, or specialized (Internet based) rental car brokers, such as holiday autos[4]. So, traditional arguments do not necessarily apply.

In the case of books and music, the change is in some respects even bigger. Not only can books now be bought from giant Internet bookstores[5] and even directly from publishers[6], but even the media itself is challenged. Though many persons still are reluctant and some even directly upset just by the thought, it is indeed conceivable that future lightweight reading pads can replace the book in the printed form, as we currently know it. Still, as long as there are significant shortcomings of reading pads – such as relatively low resolution, too limited

---

[2] See for example www.marriott.com or www.sheraton.com.
[3] See for example www.sas.se or www.lufthansa.co.uk.
[4] See www.holidayautos.uk.com.
[5] See for example www.amazon.com.
[6] See for example www.lonelyplanet.com

memory, high cost, insufficient robustness, too short battery run-time etc., there will still be bookshops for display of high quality books.

For the music industry the situation is different. It is already possible to buy CDs on the Internet[7], and this business is steadily growing. Here the product is even produced in digital form, typically as CDs or DATs, and there is no doubt that the Internet is a highly attractive future distribution channel. Furthermore, pre-listening also can be made possible over the Internet, and computer based listening stations can already be seen in semi-public places, e.g. gyms. Although there are some technical and legal problems (such as problems related to copyright) to solve before the music industry can be completely web-based, the current trends is an extreme threat to record stores as we currently know them. It is no exaggeration to say that it is hard to find any solid arguments for why there might exist record shops in 50 years in industrial countries. Also in the shorter perspective, say five to ten years, the profits for the record shops can be expected to decrease dramatically.

As seen from the above discussion, one can distinguish between two different levels of "IT-fication" of the industries:

- increased efficiency in more or less traditional business logic, and
- new structures in which resellers are completely eliminated.

As an example of the first level one can think of a travel agent that increases its services for example through increased information on the Internet. As an example of the second level we can again think of the case where a rental car is booked directly from the car rental company. A common denominator for all these industries is that the resellers were caught very much off guard. Whereas resellers have focused on measures on the first level, the second level has often been overlook, i.e. the focus has been on gaining competitive advantages over *other* traditional resellers when the real threat has been complete *bypass* of resellers.

The above examples constitute cases that are very often used as describing the possibilities (or threats depending on one's point of view) of electronic commerce. These examples are also studied in some detail in an article edited by Davis [10]. Interestingly, the article also mentions power utilities as being seriously threatened by the new possibilities electronic commerce. However, the properties of electronic power markets are much less understood, and they are not yet in use in their full potential. This paper describes the main principles of such markets and what impact on the business logic such markets bring, particularly from the perspective of energy resellers. In identifying the obstacles and possibilities, this paper very much serves as a position paper and pointer to relevant research questions for some of the activities in the Swedish research academy on IT in Energy.[8]

The paper is organized as follows. Section 2 describes the changing environment of power utilities in many countries, and what a bypass of resellers in

---

[7] See for example www.cdnow.com.
[8] See www.enersearch.se.

principle would look like. Then Section 3 describes the different design issues of an open electronic power market. The main obstacles for fine-grained markets are described together with some of the most promising solutions. Finally, Section 4 discusses what impact markets constructed along the lines of Section 3 would have on the situation for energy resellers. Appendix A gives a more technical description of what an agent for electronic power trade could look like.

2   The reregulation of the power industry

In many countries the power markets have been opened up for competition. There is no commonly agreed on term for this process. Early on, the term deregulation was used. After some time it however became apparent that the new markets had to be at least as regulated as the old ones (e.g. rules related to how network costs should be managed had to be constructed), and then the term *reregulated* markets came into use. In this paper the term reregulation refers to the process where competition is being brought into a market.

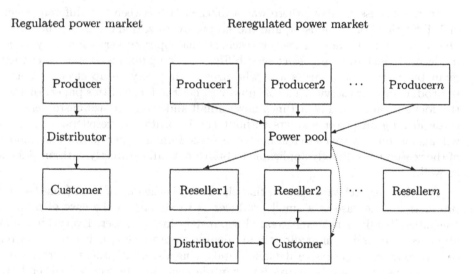

Fig. 2. The reregulation of the power industry. Can resellers be bypassed the same way here as they are starting to get bypassed in for example the travel industry?

The reregulation of the power markets in different countries (such as Norway, Sweden, Finland, UK, and USA) has taken somewhat different forms. In general, however, Figure 2 gives a quite adequate picture of the process. In the traditional regulated (monopolistic) setting the customer has no possibility to choose provider of power. As the power is purchased from a power utility, responsible for both production and transportation, there is generally no need to separate production from transportation, neither at the provider side nor at the consumer side.

In the reregulated setting there is typically some power pool through which most power is sold, though bilateral contracts are also commonly allowed. (Only some countries enforce by law that all production must be sold to a power pool.) The buyers from the power pool are power resellers and optionally very large customers. Transportation of the electricity is strictly separated from production at both the provider side as well as at the consumer side. Transportation costs are still a non-competitive business and will probably (for good reasons) remain so in the foreseeable future. The fee for transportation is often paid to the distributor by the reseller and the customer is charged for transportation when the power is charged for. Now the obvious question is: Can resellers be bypassed in power markets in a way similar to how resellers are bypassed in the travel, book, and music industries. That is, can smaller customers buy power directly from the power pool or even directly from the producers? As will be described in the coming sections, this is a non-trivial question.

In the discussion above there was a distinction between two different levels of "IT-fication" of an industry, and the same categorization can be applied here. One can think of slimmed energy resellers that operate very efficiently using modern IT, including, e.g. electronic billing, or companies who are doing their main business in other areas and who are offering very cheap electricity as a bi-product or extra service. This is, however, not the focus of this paper. Instead the focus is on if (and sometimes how) small and medium size customers can trade *directly* on power markets without the invocation of resellers. The focus will also be on how smaller customers can trade from a power pool, though most of the reasoning is directly applicable to bilateral trading directly with producers as well.

Another very relevant issue in this discussion is the one of local (small scale) production. The case of a small producer is so similar to the case of a small consumer that it is not even treated separately in the paper. Everything said about consumers is almost directly applicable to producers, it is only a matter of changing signs (negative demand) and using different process parameters, i.e. local decisions are based on for example generator properties rather than properties of walls and windows of houses.

3   The design of an open electronic power pool

There are critical design issues and potential difficulties when designing a power pool which allows for small and medium size customers to participate directly, and this section describes the major ones.

3.1 Software agents for managing the customer interests: HomeBots

In the case of electronic travel, book, and music purchase, tens or even hundreds of dollars can often be saved at each purchase occasion and/or service is significantly increased (e.g. differences in terms of selection of books between a giant Internet bookshop and a small local store). The case of trade in power pools is however fundamentally different. It is simply impossible to perfectly predict future consumption and therefore the purchase cannot be made for too long time periods at the time. At the same time the expected gain from trading directly from a power pool rather than through a reseller is small enough for making, e.g., daily manual purchase non-profitable for smaller customers. Therefore the power trade must clearly be managed by a software program representing the customer – a *software agent*. This type of agent mediated electronic commerce is thus a necessity for enabling small and medium size customers to trade directly from a power pool.

In previous work, e.g. [3, 28], we have described how software agents can be utilized for direct power load management, and - as argued before [28] - these agents can be relatively easily be extended for direct trade in power pools. An agent for energy management at the customer side, which we call a HomeBot, uses the

- customer preferences (e.g. how much the customer is prepared to pay for maintaining a certain indoor temperature),
- load model (e.g. how much energy it takes to heat a room to a certain temperature, and how much energy is dissipating to the environment through walls and windows),
- disturbance predictions (e.g. if people will be present during the period under consideration and what the weather will be like), and
- price predictions

to compute a *utility function*. The utility function expresses the valuation of the resource (i.e. electrical power). The techniques for doing this computation are by now well understood for a number of processes, both from theoretical investigations, e.g. [16, 28] as well as from practical field tests, e.g. [31]. Much works remains though to integrate these energy/optimization related issues with real-world market aspects, such as market strategies (e.g. risk management) and technical aspects, such as security, and payment transfer and accounting.

The fact that each customer is represented by a HomeBot does not imply that every customer needs to have the hardware required to run such an agent in its premises (though this is certainly conceivable if the proper infrastructure is in place). It suffices that there is some server on which the agent can reside, and the only important requirement is that there is a meter at the customer site, with which it is possible to communicate.[9]

---

[9] Currently not all customers have such a meter. However, it has recently been permitted in Sweden to utilize billing based on type curves, i.e. a meter that only measures accumulated consumption is used, and the consumption of the respective hours is

Clearly, the more sophisticated equipment the customer has (such as temperature sensors and actuators for loads), the more profitable it will be to participate on a dynamic market, but of course also the higher the investment costs. With only a communicating meter the benefit is limited to not having to pay the reseller any commission, and with more sophisticated equipment energy usage can be optimized against the power prices. That is, in the first case the task of the HOMEBOT is merely to purchase whatever the customer chooses to consume, in the latter case the task is extended to how much to purchase (and when) while taking prices into account. A somewhat more technical description of an example of the latter case is found in Appendix A.

3.2   Contract responsibility

In most reregulated electricity markets the time granularity is one hour, or possibly a half-hour. The trade is performed in advance of the time periods, and when the trade is closing the producer or consumer commits to the sold or purchased amount, called a contracted amount. Deviating from the contracted amount is penalized by substantial fees. For larger consumers and producers it is possible to predict the consumption very accurately (both because they have considerable resources for performing such prediction and because of statistical equalizing[10]). There are always also means to (at least partly) adjust consumption or production to meet the responsibility.

For a small consumer – say an individual household – this is a major problem, particularly when the HOMEBOT has no means to control the electricity use. Then even the unpredicted preparation of a meal (or vice versa – a predicted use does not occur) could completely ruin the prediction. However, the fact that this is a problem in current market structures is *not* an argument for that it is an inherent problem in all conceivable forms of power markets. The time resolution of hours or half hours is a very reasonable resolution for manual power trade, but with automated electronic trade, resolutions of minutes (and even seconds in extreme cases further described below) is definitely conceivable. This does on the other hand not imply that the resolution of the metering necessarily needs to increase – it could be an improvement in software only. The following example should clarify this.

> *Example 1.* A HOMEBOT which has no ability to control the loads of its consumer at some point in time commits to consume $1kWh$ during hour h_i. Then after 20 minutes into hour h_i the customer starts to prepare a meal. Now the estimated consumption increases to $1.5kWh$ and a substantial penalty is foreseen. Then the HOMEBOT may place a bid

---

estimated from typical consumption patterns for the specific type of consumer. Presumably such an approach could be used also for electronic trade. A detailed discussion is omitted from this paper though, as it is mainly a discussion on accounting and it adds little to the main message.

[10] That is, some loads are likely to increase, but as others are likely to decrease, the deviation is likely to be cancelled out for large number of loads.

in a power pool for an additional amount of $0.5kWh$ during hour h_i, at a price below the expected penalty. Exactly at what price the bid should be given and at exactly by what amount (it may for example be profitable to take some penalty for a small deviation and buy only parts of the $0.5kWh$ from the pool) is determined by the HOMEBOT's market information and customer preferences (such as risk aversion/liking).

Then one or more other HOMEBOTs who have either overestimated their consumption, or HOMEBOTs that are able to control (some of) their loads may sell (parts of) the $0.5kWh$ for hour h_i.

Thus, the meter needs not be more complicated (one hour measurement is still sufficient) for enabling more flexible agent mediated power markets.

As seen from the above example, the responsibility to contracted amounts becomes much less of a problem if trade is made more frequently. If the time between successive trades approaches zero, the deviation from the contracted amount also approaches zero (given that there always are buyers and sellers). As an extreme example, if trade is being made every second, and a household has a fuse of $16A$, it can deviate at most $0.001kWh$ from the contracted amount.[11] If the metering resolution is one hour, contracted amounts are probably in the order of one kWh and the deviation of $0.001kWh$ is then completely negligible.

In terms of prices, the introduction of large numbers of automated trading agents able to trade on short term markets and representing controllable loads, will definitely decrease the difference between spot prices (determined in advance) and regulating prices (momentarily determined on-line).[12]

There are currently markets with some of these properties in the Nordic countries. However, the market is not yet as developed as the one described in this section. The current short-term market is managed by the grid operator. Only producers can place bids (for increase or decrease of production) on the market, and the grid operator selects bids if there is apparent mismatch between supply and demand.

3.3 Grid operation

Whereas the production is being reregulated in many countries, the network operation is still a monopolistic, highly regulated business.

Grid stability and security is an extremely important issue in power systems. All possible consumption and production combinations are simply not allowed

---

[11] The number is based on a voltage of $230V$ at the customer's side (the standard voltage in Sweden). The maximum power of the household is then $16 \cdot 230 = 3.68kW$. Hence the maximum energy that can be consumed during the last second of the hour is $3.68 \cdot \frac{1}{3600} kWh \approx 0.001kWh$. The maximum deviation (predicting zero and consuming the maximum amount or vice versa) is then this maximum amount.

[12] A typical current difference between spot and regulating prices in the Nordic countries is shown in Figure 7. Also confer the discussion on regulating prices in Appendix A.

due to constraints of the power grid. Furthermore, too drastic and rapid *changes* in allocation may cause severe problems, even if the initial and final allocations are possible. As there are losses on the power line, there are transportation costs other than the ones stemming from investment costs. The magnitude of these problems varies significantly from country to country. For example, the constraints and losses are significantly more critical in the US than in the Nordic countries Norway, Denmark, Sweden, and Finland. Still it is an important (and probably the single most complicated) issue in all countries, and the aspects of grid stability and security as well as cost management must be carefully taken into consideration when designing a power market. The difficulties of integrating grid operation into competitive markets are probably the most important reasons for that electronic power markets are not already in use at a larger scale (including smaller customers). It is not the aim of this paper to describe all relevant problems and possible solutions to grid operation, not least because it is a very complicated issue with many delicate aspects, but also because good and pragmatic solutions, by necessity, are highly region dependent. Therefore this paper focuses on giving an overview of some quite general issues.

The cost management for transportation of electricity is performed in a variety of ways. Though there are strong couplings between the transportation markets and the power markets, they truly represent different commodities. Some transport cost management schemes are based on very complicated cost computations performed by Optimal Power Flow software in a quite centralized fashion, others are based on more decentralized auctions for transport rights. An important distinction is also whether costs are made available to the buyers of transportation services before or after they have already committed to production (or consumption) amounts. A good, detailed discussion (including pointers to a lot of relevant work) on transportation cost management is given by Imparatio [11].

From the grid stability and security point of view, Example 1 seems like a nightmare at a first glance. If the stability of the network is dependent on that allocations do not change too drastically, particularly between regions, how can any stability guarantees be made if there are agents trading very rapidly on-line?

This question is a fundamental misconception. Customers are already able to change their allocation in an arbitrary manner. If, for example, all inhabitants in Los Angeles would switch off all their lights at exactly the same moment as all inhabitants in New York would switch on their microwave ovens, the result would be a disaster, probably threatening the power supply of the entire US.[13] The resellers would be able to do nothing to save the situation, despite their responsibilities. Hence, the relevant question is whether a more fine-grained market would increase or decrease the random perturbations. Even though more research and actual field tests are required to give an unambiguous answer to this

---

[13] Similar examples exists in all disciplines. Consider, for example, what would happen if all toilet bowls in the Empire State Building were flushed at exactly the same moment. (This actually happened once as a student practical joke during the opening ceremony of a Swedish dormitory, and it had a catastrophic outcome.)

question, the most qualified guess is that they will decrease. The main argument for this position is that as more customers will be able to trade directly against dynamic prices, their incentives to control some loads will increase, and as there will always be some fee for performing a transaction, it will become more common to compensate for variations locally. It also seems reasonable that costs will be lower for transactions between agents close to each other, e.g. ones that are able to communicate with each other on a common power line, than for transaction between geographically dispersed agents. This would encourage variation compensation from neighbors before compensation from agents of other areas. The above example of electricity use in Los Angeles and New York would of course still be extremely difficult, but the risk for a disaster would probably be significantly reduced if the disconnection of many New York indoor climate systems very rapidly compensated the microwave oven use. Hence, the new system would most likely be significantly *better*.

Another interesting question is whether or not agent mediated electronic markets could be of interest for network security management in emergency situations. The current strategy varies from country to country, but a common pattern is that an independent operator is responsible for the network security, and the operator is authorized to take very dramatic measures, such as disconnecting a town or a county when there is an emergency. In such a situation there is actually no distinction between the treatment of for example a water heater and a respirator.[14] It is an interesting question whether or not very fast markets could serve as an instrument to prioritize loads in a more proper way in emergency situations. We intend to investigate this issue in depth in upcoming projects.

3.4 Market mechanism design

A market mechanism is the way that agents are allowed to interact and how resources are reallocated as a consequence of those bids. An example of a market mechanism is the Dutch auction. In the Dutch auction an auctioneer announces prices in decreasing order, and as soon as some bidder accepts the price, he notifies the auctioneer and the good bid for is assigned to the bidder at the price of the announcement.

When constructing a market mechanism for power markets it is necessary to decide *what commodities should be traded*. One important issue is what the time resolution should be. In most countries one hour is considered reasonable. This is very much predetermined by the resolution of the electricity meters. Another issue is if there should be a distinction between different production methods of the electricity, i.e. if it should be possible to construct bids including conditions like "I prefer hydropower to nuclear power if the price-difference is below 0.04SEK/kWh". Of course, the finer the time granularity and the more expressiveness of the bids, the more flexible markets can be constructed. At the

---

[14] There is of course local generation at critical places, such as hospitals, where keeping critical equipment on-line is top priority.

other hand, fine time granularity implies increased metering and administrative costs, and very expressive bids gives more complicated market mechanisms.

Once the commodities have been defined it has to be decided *how bids should be given*. Examples of considerations are if bids should be given as discrete amounts or if demand curves – giving relations between prices and demanded/offered amounts – should be submitted, and whether or not it should be possible to express dependencies between different commodities. This issue is not only related to complexity (again more complex bids implies more complex mechanisms), but also to agents' privacy. For example, in the current Nordic electricity market, the correlation between the prices on the financial (long term) market and the day-before spot market is very high [26]. Then the agents essentially bid for how they like to change their production/consumption for *small deviations* from the prices on the financial markets. Then the approach of revealing only desired responses to prices for each time period separately (i.e. without expressing any dependencies between commodities) may work fine and may be preferred by the agents as it reveals a very small amount of private information. A strongly related aspect is whether bids should be open (i.e. visible for other bidders) or closed.

In parallel with deciding what the commodities are and how bids are to be constructed, rules must be set up that defines *how the resource should be (re)allocated as a consequence of the bids*, and how this computation can be efficiently performed on a computer (or set of computers). Examples of issues are how accepted/winning bids are determined, how prices are set (e.g. first price vs. second price mechanisms), and what algorithms to use for computing the outcome.

The next issue is *when the trades should be performed*. Alternatives are continuous auctions – like the stock markets – or auctions at specific points in time – which is often the case when for example expensive art is sold. Combinations of the two are also conceivable. As discussed in Section 3.2 it is possible to perform trades more frequently than the rate of registration of consumption. This is illustrated in Figure 3

The above design parameters affect the following mechanism properties:

- **Communication requirements.** The communication requirements is one of the most important issues, as communication is often a more limiting factor than computation [4]. As argued before [8, 4], the number of messages is typically the critical property and message size is somewhat less important.
- **Computational efficiency.** Even though communication requirements are crucial, computational aspects can by no means be overlooked. Bids including complex relations between different commodities can result in allocation computations that cannot be performed in reasonable time. However, for many application areas, a number of assumptions about the properties of supply and demand can be made, and then very efficient algorithms can be used, e.g. [28–30].

  As discussed above (Section 3.3) it is conceivable to use agent-based markets also for grid-operation with very short time frames. Thus, it is impor-

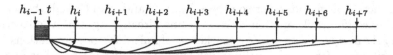

h_{i-1} t h_i h_{i+1} h_{i+2} h_{i+3} h_{i+4} h_{i+5} h_{i+6} h_{i+7}

Fig. 3. Illustration of the difference between the frequency of trade and the frequency of registration of consumption. t is the current time, and at t each HOMEBOT has committed to a consumption at h_i, and optionally also to one or several future time periods, e.g. h_4. The issue of when the trade should be performed relates to when the trades for the commitments of the different time points, h_j, should be performed, but it does not change the points of the measurements. If, for example, an error in the prediction leading to a deviation from the committed amount of h_i is detected at t and a continuous auction is used, the HOMEBOT might immediately place a bid for a change of the committed amount and directly receive a matching offer.

tant to define the *real-time demands* on the market. The communication requirements (together with the communication capabilities of the utilized communication infrastructure) and the computational efficiency determines whether or not the real-time demands can be met.

– **Allocation efficiency.** An example of a market mechanism with excellent communication and computation properties is the mechanism of doing nothing. Of course, this mechanism is nonsense, as it does not give any surplus. The total surplus of a system is often used as a measurement of the allocation efficiency of a mechanism. Clearly, a high efficiency is a very desirable property.

– **Allocation fairness.** The total efficiency is not the single interesting property of an allocation. It may for example be unacceptable to some that a mechanism has the form of a lottery where all surplus is given to one agent. There might hence also be some minimal fairness requirements on the mechanism.

– **Vulnerability to speculation.** In a market where the agents represent self-interested real-world parties, the agents can be expected to try to maximize their utility in many different ways, including giving false bids to fool others. It is therefore desirable that the mechanism does not encourage speculation that, by making the speculator somewhat better off, makes the other agents significantly worse off. In previous work we have investigated some important speculation issues related to market mechanisms that are very promising for electronic power markets [21, 20].

– etc.

As has been described in this section, there is a large number of interrelated design issues to take into account when selecting a market mechanism. Even though there is a vast literature on the subject[15], and even though there already are highly configurable auction servers on-line already, e.g. the AUCTIONBOT[16] it is clearly non-trivial to select a market mechanism for power auctions. There is also still room for significant improvements of existing mechanisms and introduction of new ones. Historically, mechanism design has mainly been performed by economists, but as the trades are now often electronic, there is a growing interest in the subject in computer science. This common interest point of two different disciplines has already generated new interesting results, and more are to be expected. It should be remembered though that real progress in electronic commerce requires substantial knowledge in both disciplines.

4   Discussion and conclusions

This paper described the threatened position of resellers in many industries due to the new possibilities of electronic commerce, and asked the question if the corresponding development can be expected in the energy sector as well. As described in this paper, the main necessary concept for enabling fine-grained markets is agent mediated electronic commerce. The main obstacles for constructing such markets, together with some of the most promising solutions, were described in Section 3. Weighting the obstacles against the potential solutions, the answer to the question of whether energy resellers are severely threatened becomes *yes* with rather big certainty.

If the direct trading with power pools or producers is enabled for medium and small size consumers and producers, the charge of a reseller cannot drastically exceed the economical (and technical) barrier preventing customers to trade directly through power pools. The economical barrier is interest rate of the investments in equipment required at the consumer's or producer's side plus the running costs associated with this equipment. In the minimal version, the only required equipment is a piece of software on some server. The cost for such software can be expected to be very small in large series. In such basic settings also the technical barriers are indeed low. Thus, the development of electronic commerce is a serious threat for today's energy resellers.

It is of vital importance for the resellers to thoroughly understand the development of the agent mediated electronic commerce technology in order to take advantage of the possibilities. Whereas it is true that for example many record stores has lost shares and margins in the new era, it is also true that others have profited enormously during the same time. The challenge for the energy resellers is to adapt their business to be on the winning side as the setting changes.

Then, how should the current resellers make money in the future? The uniform answer by the power industry seems to be to focus on value added services. The hard question is however what services should be considered. The most

---

[15] For general discussions and/or discussions of mechanisms originally designed for other application areas, see e.g. [17, 15, 14, 25, 1, 19, 8, 24], and for discussions on mechanisms particularly aimed at power markets see e.g. [23, 26, 6, 22, 7].

[16] See auction.eecs.umich.edu and [27].

discussed services are services related to communication and information management, such as different types of alarms, energy management, and different smart home services. One topic that has received a lot of recent attention in conjunction with communication and information services is power line communication, e.g. [2, 13]. As the technology already provides communication possibilities comparable to yesterday's telephone modems and as the technology is under rapid development, high hopes are on utilities' possibilities to compete with telecommunication companies. Indeed systems with bit rates in the order of Mb/s are being used in field tests to offer customers Internet access through the power grid. The main advantage of power line communication is that the communication network is already in place, and hereby power line communication is (apart for costs for transceivers) for free. However, it is not yet clear that energy resellers will have any privileges compared to other players. In the monopolistic setting, the reseller was also the grid owner, and then the privilege was clear, but now it is an open question whether the resellers or the distributor should have the right of selling communication services on the power line. Nor is it clear how customers are allowed to communicate within their premises if noise is dissipating out from the household and disturbs the communication of other parties.

Furthermore, it should be carefully remembered that energy resellers by no means are the only actors interested in offering these type of services to the customers. In the area of home systems there are major efforts such as the Open Service Gateway Initiative[17] and Microsoft's initiative together with 3COM[18]. It does not seem too far-fetched that these actors also will offer value-added services in order for customers to use their hardware, communication technology or operating systems. Hoping that offering for example a burglar alarm will be seen as a major competitive advantage does not seem realistic.

The main remaining area where it seems that energy resellers have a true competitive advantage is energy management. Though it may seem paradoxical, energy utilities have already for years helped customers to better use their energy and actually even to reduce their energy costs significantly, see e.g. [9, 12]. The need for this type of services will not decrease in the future. Someone also needs to provide the software of the trading agents, and here (former) energy resellers have valuable knowledge about energy trading. One can also envision interesting new merges between utilities and e.g. software and/or telecommunication companies. (In fact, it has already started to happen.)

Summing all the above arguments, the conclusion of the paper is:

- The role of energy resellers will most likely change drastically in the coming years.

---

[17] The OSG Initiative (OSGi) is an open industry effort lead by Alcatel, Cable and Wireless, Electricité de France, Enron Communications, Ericsson, IBM, Lucent Technologies, Motorola, NCI, Nortel Networks, Oracle, Philips Electronics, Sun Microsystems, Sybase and Toshiba. See www.osgi.org.

[18] See www.microsoft.com/presspass/press/1999/Mar99/3COMpr.htm

- There are good reasons to believe that the trends seen in the travel, book and music markets will also be seen in the energy market, as a consequence of the development of agent mediated electronic commerce. Furthermore, the competition from non-traditional energy resellers will increase. For example, we already now see how gasoline companies offer cheap electricity to loyal customers. The conclusion from all this is that it will be very hard to make money on selling electricity alone.
- As a consequence of the previous item, resellers must focus on value-added services. However, the services chosen must be very carefully selected. It was argued in this paper that it seems more reasonable to focus on services such as selling comfort (rather than power) and other energy related services, than to focus on e.g. burglar alarms.

An important final note is that the consequence of doing nothing is not that the current situation will prevail, but that the change will take place anyway and that the resellers then will be left with nothing.

A   A HomeBot Trading Example

In this appendix a more technical presentation of the construction of a software agent for electricity trade in a power pool is given. The presentation is started with a basic design of an electronic spot power market. Then, a HomeBot for managing the electricity of a heating system for a house is presented together with some generalizations.

A.1   A basic market design for electronic power markets - an equilibrium market

One of the most reasonable market mechanisms for electronic power markets is an *equilibrium market*. In this section a short presentation of such a market mechanism is given.[19] In an equilibrium market agents send *demand functions* telling how much they like to consume or produce at different prices.

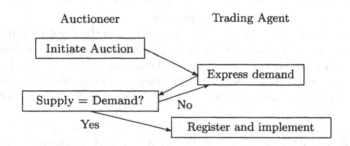

Fig. 4. *High-level view of an equilibrium market mechanism.*

Without loss of generality, one commodity (let its index be the highest one, k) is regarded as a numeraire whose price per unit is one, i.e. $p_k = 1$, so the prices of all other commodities are expressed in terms of this commodity. For example, we can use US dollars as this commodity and then say that the price of something else is, e.g., \$7 per unit. When participating in an equilibrium market each agent submits (parts of and/or samples of) a net demand function, denoted $z_i(p)$, $z_i : \Re^{k-1} \mapsto \Re^{k-1}$, where i denotes an agent. [20] Thus, the net demand function describes the demand for $k-1$ commodities at $k-1$ prices (the remaining price being fixed). For example, $z_i([1,2,1]) = [-1,3,0]$ means that at the prices 1, 2, and 1 for commodities 1, 2, and 3 respectively, agent i

---

[19] The overview presentation of the section is essentially from given by the introduction Sandholm & Ygge [21].

[20] In a market with k commodities, it is possible to regard the net demand function as a mapping $\Re^k \mapsto \Re^k$. However, if one price is fixed (which can always be done without loss of generality) and the demand of the kth commodity is given by the budget constraint (see further Equation (1) and below) treating $k-1$ dimensions is always sufficient.

wants to sell 1 unit of commodity 1 and buy 3 units of commodity 2 for 5 units of commodity 4 ($-1 \cdot 1 + 2 \cdot 3 = 5$). Maybe the agent wants to sell one gallon of gas and buy three gallons of milk for \$5. This example describes a consumer exchanging some commodities for some others, but z can be used for denoting production as well – a produced unit is a negative demand of one.

The process of submitting parts of the demand function may be iterated if an equilibrium price is outside the region captured by the submitted demand functions. One such process is the basic price tâtonnement process (cf. e.g. [8]) in which demand functions, $z_{ig}(p_g)$, $z_{ig} : \Re \mapsto \Re$, for the respective commodities, g, are sent to an auctioneer. Each of those demands are based on *expected prices* of the other commodities. That is, if those other prices change, a set of new demand functions may need to be submitted.

Once the auctioneer has established an equilibrium price, say $\mathbf{p}^*$, defined by

$$\sum_i z_{ig}(\mathbf{p}^*) = 0, \ g = [1..k-1],\tag{1}$$

each agent will receive (or deliver) $z_{ig}(p_g^*)$ of each of the $k-1$ commodities, g, and $\sum_{g=0}^{k-1} -z_{ig}(p_g^*)p_g^*$ of the k:th commodity.

The spot market of the main electricity market in the Nordic countries, Nord-Pool, is based on quite similar principles [18]. At noon each day each agent sends in its demand function for each of the 24 hours the following day. The demand functions for each hour are declared independently of prices of the other hours, and no iterations are allowed. Hence, it can be seen as 24 independent markets rather than one 24 commodity market.

As described in Section 3.1 the HOMEBOT of a customer can either be very simple and buy what is (expected to be) demanded at the different hours or plan the resource need while taking prices into account. In the former case the demand function $\mathbf{z}(\mathbf{p})$ is simply a constant for each period, independent of price. Computing the optimal demand function for the case where the HOMEBOT can plan the consumption is somewhat more involved and is described in detail in Section A.2 and Section A.3.

In this type of markets, the behavior of each agent will affect the market price, and hereby there is a potential gain by speculating about the demand of the other agents and utilize the market power. However, the agents investigated in this example, representing a household in a system with thousands or millions of large agents, this effect is completely negligible, and the risk for losses in the case of speculation under biased information is significant. Therefore, ignoring its own effect on prices is the most reasonable strategy for each agent. For a detailed analysis of the gains and losses in this type of setting, see the investigation by Sandholm & Ygge [21].

A.2   Planning the resource use at different price levels

The basic steps of computing the demand for resource at different price levels is shown in Figure A.2. The different symbols in the figure are described in detail below.

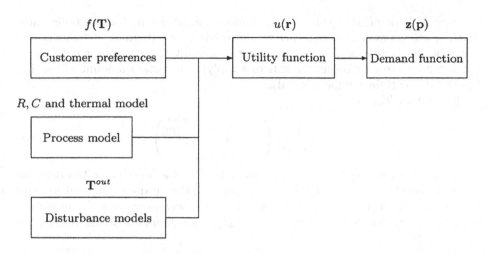

Fig. 5. The process of computing the demand function for the resource (power/energy) as a function of energy prices, given customer preferences and other important inputs. The symbols of the figure are for the case when the HOMEBOT under investigation is representing an electrically heated household. Obtaining the demand function however involves the above steps for all types of loads, though the quantities are somewhat different.

In the case of a HOMEBOT for buying the power for an electrically heated house, we start from a customer preference function, $f(\mathbf{T})$, giving the customer's valuation (in monetary units) of different temperatures, $\mathbf{T}$, $\mathbf{T} = [T_0, T_1, \ldots, T_k]$, where T_i is the temperature at time i. k is the total number of samples for which the computation is performed. k needs to be selected sufficiently large so that time periods that the HOMEBOT commits to do not significantly affect the time periods with index larger than k, see further [28, p. 153].

The next thing to do is to derive an expression for the temperature as a function of the resource. In doing this we need a model of how the temperature of the house can be derived from inputs and disturbances. Disturbances are all non-controllable inputs that affect the temperature. In this example we only take outdoor temperature into account, though many other things could be considered, e.g. wind, number of persons present, etc. We use a standard thermal model for the house, e.g. [28], as described by

$$
T_i = T_{i-1} + \underbrace{\frac{r_i - \overbrace{\frac{T_i - T_i^{out}}{R}}^{\text{dissipating heat}}}{C}}_{\text{total heating power}}, \tag{2}
$$

where T_i is the indoor temperature of the house at time i, T_i^{out} is the outdoor temperature at time i, r_i is the allocated resource (i.e. the power used by the radiators) at time i, R is a thermal isolation constant, i.e. a constant telling how much heating power is dissipating to the environment because o temperature difference, C is a thermal heat capacitivity constant, i.e. a constant telling how the temperature changes as a result of supplying a certain amount of heating power (at a certain sample interval).

Solving for T_i gives

$$T_i = \frac{1}{1 + \frac{1}{RC}} \left(T_{i-1} + \frac{r_i - \frac{T_i^{out}}{R}}{C} \right). \tag{3}$$

Hence, we have obtained an expression for T_i as a function of the resource of the different hours (and the thermal constants, the outdoor temperature, and the initial indoor temperature). Thus, there is a way to express the monetary valuation of resource $\mathbf{r}$ ($\mathbf{r} = [r_0, r_1, \ldots, r_k]$). This function of the resource is denoted $u(\mathbf{r})$.[21]

Then the demand function is the solution to the following optimization problem:

$$\arg\max_{\mathbf{z}} \quad u(\mathbf{z} + \mathbf{e}) - \mathbf{p} \cdot \mathbf{z}, \tag{4}$$

where $\mathbf{z}$ is (as before) the *change* in allocation, and $\mathbf{e}$ is the endowment (i.e. initial allocation).

A.3   A specific example

To make the above presentation more concrete, a specific example is now presented.[22] We investigate the heating of a large villa, and take all rooms except the sleeping room into account because the sleeping room has different hours of utilization. It is assumed that the villa is a private residence (with $8kW$ installed power, and that the customer's valuation of the temperature is given by a simple quadratic function (though this is not at all necessary for the system to work)

$$f(\mathbf{T}) = \sum_{i=0}^{k} a_i + b_i (T_i - T_i^{set})^2, \tag{5}$$

where T_i^{set} is the set point temperature of time interval i. a_i is an offset and b_i is a slope. As a_i only adds a constant to the valuation it does not affect the optimal choice and can hence be set to zero independently of its actual value. The slope, b_i, of this example is given by

$$b_i = \begin{cases} 0, & 1 \leq i \leq 5, 9 \leq i \leq 17, i = 24 \\ 5 \cdot 10^{-3}, & 6 \leq i \leq 8, 18 \leq i \leq 23 \end{cases}. \tag{6}$$

---

[21] One can either assume the function $u(\cdot)$ to implicitly be given in monetary units, or add a linear term m representing the money explicitly, i.e. let $u(\cdot)$ be described by $u(\mathbf{r}, m) = g(\mathbf{r}) + m$.

[22] The numbers of this example are mainly values from a specific test site; Villa Wega in Ronneby in the South-East of Sweden. In this Villa a number of HOMEBOT are installed communicating over the electricity power line. Some descriptions are given by Ygge et al. [31] and some more publication is in preparation.

That is, during the morning hours, $6-8$, and during the evening hours, $18-23$, the slope is $5 \cdot 10^{-3}$. For the rest it is zero. The slope is in Euro[23] and T is in degrees Celsius[24], and hence a slope of $5 \cdot 10^{-3}$ for example means that the customer is indifferent between a deviation of one degree from the set point during one hour and earning $5 \cdot 10^{-3}$ Euro.

Furthermore, $R = 7kW/°C$ and $C = 4.5°C/kW$ (at sample period $1h$). The outdoor temperature is shown in Figure 6. The set point is chosen to $20°C$ for all hours (though it is irrelevant for $b_i = 0$).

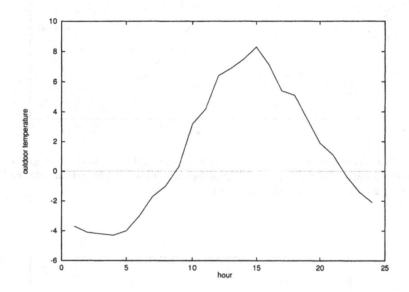

Fig. 6. The outdoor temperature.

The energy prices of the $24h$ under observation is shown in Figure 7. The figure shows both the spot price (which is the price we use for the computations of this section) as well as the (up) regulating price (further described below).

Given the customer preferences, the thermal model, and the outdoor temperature, the optimal resource for different price levels use can be computed by the HOMEBOT using the steps above. Under the (*very* reasonable) assumption that the HOMEBOT under investigation does not affect the electricity price of the Nordic countries, the resulting resource usage as is shown in Figure 8 where it is also compared to the result of using a simple thermostat which does not take prices into account.[25]

---

[23] One Euro is approximately equal to one US dollar.

[24] $x°C = 9x/5 + 32°F$.

[25] In the computations, $k = 48$ has been used. That is, the optimization has been done over $48h$, though only $24h$ are presented here. As discussed before, it is important to optimize over more hours than the ones being of main interest, as the last hours

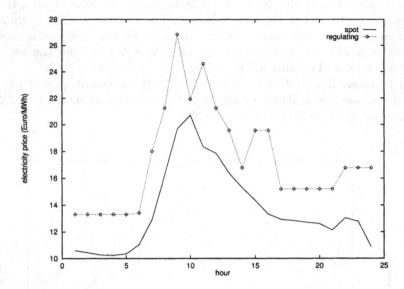

Fig. 7. The electricity price in Euro per MWh. The spot price is shown together with the (up) regulating price (further described below). This was the actual price of Nord-Pool (www.nordpool.no) on May 11, 1999.

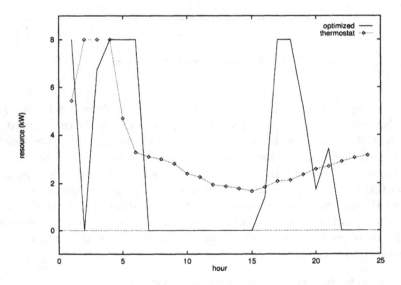

Fig. 8. The resource usage of the example. The optimal choice is compared to the result of using a simple thermostat, which does not take prices into account.

The temperature resulting from the optimal resource usage is shown in Figure 9. As seen from the figure, the deviation from the set point is typically less than $0.5°C$, during the interesting hours $(6 - 8$ and $18 - 23)$.

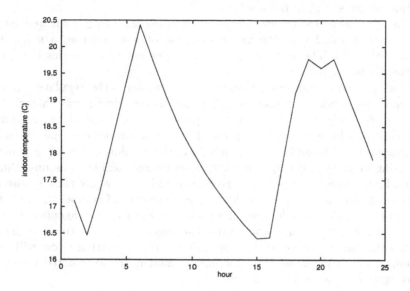

Fig. 9. The temperature resulting from optimal energy usage.

As discussed above one can consider different levels of sophistication of the involved HOMEBOTS. The difference between the most simple (the thermostat) and the most advanced (a HOMEBOT making optimal choices based on perfect estimates of thermal constants and outdoor temperatures) is significant as seen from Figure 8. In numbers, the energy usage is reduced from $81kWh$ to $66kWh$ (i.e. an improvement by approximately 18%), by using a more advanced HOMEBOT. The cost is reduced from 1.03 to 0.76 Euro (i.e. an improvement by approximately 26%). Under the assumption that this is an average day, this means that approximately 97 Euro can be gained yearly by using the more advanced HOMEBOT. (This result is essentially in-line with the results of others, e.g. [5].) Accordingly, with current technology and electricity costs it can hardly be motivated to use the more advanced technology. However, technology prices are continuously dropping, and more and more vendors are considering to market equipment with communication and computation capabilities. What will happen to electricity prices on a deregulated European market is hard to say, but many

of the optimization "sacrifices" future hours. Again, see [28, p. 153]. An interesting side note is that we have developed very efficient algorithms for the optimal resource selection. This enables optimal energy choice to be computed in some $100ms$ on a $300MHz$ uni-processor computer and in a few seconds on simple embedded systems processors. This will be presented in some detail in forthcoming publications.

experts claim that they will rise significantly compared to the current prices in the Nordic countries [12]. (The reader might like to compare the extremely low prices of Figure 7 to his own electricity bill if living outside the Nordic countries. Also for citizens of the Nordic countries the comparison is interesting as it clearly tells how much is paid to the resellers.)

When discussing the potential benefits of advanced energy management, one should keep in mind that the above example only constitutes a single large private household. The gains of energy management in industries is typically significantly larger [12].

Another issue further complicating the discussion is the regulating market. The regulating market is a market with much shorter time frame than the spot market. Essentially, the (up) regulating price in Figure 7 is the price that an agent must pay for extra units of power if it consumes more (or produces less) than it committed to on the spot market. As the regulating market is generally fluctuating more than the spot market, it seems reasonable to assume that on potential future electronic power markets, it could be very profitable to also plan energy usage to enable trade on short term markets. Of course, the gain from trade on this market will decrease if a large number software agents act on the short term markets, as that would push the regulating prices towards the spot prices. Thus, the difference between spot prices and regulating prices will reflect the magnitude of technical and economical barriers for automated trade with locally optimizing agents in large scale.

References

1. Agorics, Inc. Bibliography for the series Going, going, gone! (Available at http://www.agorics.com/agorics/auctions/bibliography.html), 1996.
2. J. M. Akkermans, D. Healey, and H. Ottosson. *The ISES Project Book*, chapter 10—The Transmission of Data over the Electricity Power Lines, pages 175–216. EnerSearch AB, Malmö, Sweden, 1998. (Available from http://www.enersearch.se).
3. J. M. Akkermans and F. Ygge. Smart software as customer assistant in large-scale distributed load management. In *Proceedings of Distribution Automation/Demand Side Management (DA/DSM) '97*. PenWell Conferences and Exhibitions, October 1997. (Available from http://www.enersearch.se/ygge).
4. A. Andersson and F. Ygge. Managing large scale computational markets. In H. El-Rewini, editor, *Proceedings of the Software Technology track of the 31th Hawaiian International Conference on System Sciences (HICSS31)*, volume VII, pages 4–14. IEEE Computer Society, Los Alamos, January 1998. ISBN 0-8186-8251-5, ISSN 1060-3425, IEEE Catalog Number 98TB100216. (Available from http://www.enersearch.se/ygge).
5. U. Bergström. Optimized energy systems and new customer services - the deregulated electricity market and the ronneby case. Technical report, Division of Energy Systems, Department of Mechanical Engineering, Linköping University, 1999. Lic. Thesis. (Available from http://www.enersearch.se).
6. J. C. Bernard, R. Zimmerman, W. Schulze, R. J. Thomas, T. Mount, and R. Schuler. Alternative auction institutions for purchasing electric power: An experimental examination. In *Proceedings of Bulk Power Systems Dynamics and Control - IV Restructuring*, August 1998. (Available from http://www.power.ntua.gr/bulkIV/technicalprogram.htm).
7. S. Borenstein and J. Bushnell. An empirical analysis of the potential for market power in California's electricity industry. (Available at http://nberws.nber.org/papers/W6463), 1998.
8. J. Cheng and M. P. Wellman. The WALRAS algorithm—a convergent distributed implementation of general equilibrium outcomes. *Computational Economics*, 12:1–24, 1998. (Available from http://ai.eecs.umich.edu/people/wellman).
9. S. Dag. A model for cost-efficient co-operation between Göteborg Energi and Volvo Car Corporation. Lic. thesis. No. 605, Division of Energy Systems, Department of Mechanical Engineering, Linköping Institute of Technology, 1997.
10. Davis (ed.). Are you next? 20 industries that must change. *Business 2.0*, pages 44–54, March 1999.
11. C. F. Imparatio. Self-management of ATC by the marketplace. In *Proceedings of the 32nd Hawaiian International Conference on System Sciences (HICSS32)*. IEEE Computer Society, January 1999.
12. B. Karlsson and S. Dag. *The ISES Project Book*, chapter 2—European Industries on a Deregulated Energy Market - The Volvo Case, pages 11–29. EnerSearch AB, Malmö, Sweden, 1998. (Available from http://www.enersearch.se).
13. G. Lindell. *The ISES Project Book*, chapter 7—Power Line Communications, pages 123–135. EnerSearch AB, Malmö, Sweden, 1998. (Available from http://www.enersearch.se).
14. Eric S Maskin and John Riley. Optimal auctions with risk-averse buyers. *Econometrica*, 52(6):1473–1518, 1984.
15. R. P. McAfee and J. McMillan. Auctions and bidding. *Journal of Economic Literature*, 25:699–738, 1987.

16. C. R. Melbourne and D. T. G. Strong. Celect–dynamic load control. EA Technology, Capenhurst, Chester, CH1 6ES, United Kingdom, 1996.
17. P. R. Milgrom. Auction theory. In T Bewley, editor, *Advances in Economic Theory: Fifth World Conference*. Cambridge University Press, 1987.
18. NordPool.   The elspot market—the spot market.   (Available from www.nordpool.no.), October 1998.
19. T. W. Sandholm. *Negotiation among Self-Interested Computationally Limited Agents*. PhD thesis, University of Massachusetts, Amherst, 1996. (Available at http://www.cs.wustl.edu/~sandholm/dissertation.ps.).
20. T. W. Sandholm and F. Ygge. On the gains and losses of speculation in equilibrium markets. In *Proceeding of the Fifteenth International Joint Conference on Artificial Intelligence, IJCAI 97*, pages 632–638, August 23–29, 1997. (Available from http://www.enersearch.se/ygge).
21. T. W. Sandholm and F. Ygge.   Constructing speculative demand functions in equilibrium markets.   Technical Report WUCS-99-26, Department of Computer Science, Washington University, October 1999.   (Available from www.enersearch.se/ygge).
22. S. Stoft. Analysis of the california WEPEX applications to FERC. (Available from http://www.path.berkeley.edu/~ucenergy/x/index.html), 1996.
23. Wepex Review Team. Ad hoc bidding options: Review team report. (Available from http://www.energyonline.com/wepex/reports/reports2.html), 1996.
24. W. E. Walsh, M. P. Wellman, P. R. Wurman, and J. K. MacKie-Mason. Some economics of market-based distributed scheduling. In *Proceedings of the Eighteenth International Conference on Distributed Computing Systems*, pages 612–621, 1998. (Available from http://ai.eecs.umich.edu/people/wellman/Publications.html).
25. M. P. Wellman. A market-oriented programming environment and its application to distributed multicommodity flow problems. *Journal of Artificial Intelligence Research (http://www.jair.org/)*, (1):1–23, 1993.
26. F. A. Wolak.   Market design and the behavior of prices in restructured electricity markets: An international comparison.   (Available from http://www.stanford.edu/~wolak/), 1998.
27. P. R. Wurman, M. P. Wellman, and W. E. Walsh.   The Michigan Internet AuctionBot: A configurable auction server for human and software agents. In *Proceedings of the Second International Conference on Autonomous Agents (AGENTS)*, pages 301–308, Minneapolis/St. Paul, MN, May 1998.   (Available from http://ai.eecs.umich.edu/people/wellman/Publications.html).
28. F. Ygge. *Market-Oriented Programming and its Application to Power Load Management*. PhD thesis, Department of Computer Science, Lund University, 1998. ISBN 91-628-3055-4, CODEN LUNFD6/(NFCS-1012)/1-224/(1998) (Available from http://www.enersearch.se/ygge).
29. F. Ygge and J. M. Akkermans. Duality in multi-commodity equilibrium computations and any-time algorithms. In C. Zhang and D. Lukose, editors, *Proceedings of the Third Australian Workshop on DAI*, pages pp. 65–78, Perth, Australia, December 1997. (Available from http://www.enersearch.se/ygge).
30. F. Ygge and J. M. Akkermans. On resource-oriented multi-commodity market computations. In Y. Demazeau, editor, *Proceedings of the Third International Conference on Multi-Agent Systems ICMAS'98*, pages 365–371. IEEE Computer Society, July 4–7 1998. (An extended version is available from http://www.enersearch.se/ygge).

31. F. Ygge, J. M. Akkermans, A. Andersson, M. Krejic, and E. Boertjes. The Home-Bots system and field tests: A multi-commodity market for predictive load management. In *Proceedings of the Fourth International Conference and Exhibition on The Practical Application of Intelligent Agents and Multi-Agents (PAAM99)*, pages 363–382, April 19–21 1999. (Available from http://www.enersearch.se/ygge).

Modeling Supply Chain Formation in Multiagent Systems*

William E. Walsh and Michael P. Wellman

Artificial Intelligence Laboratory
University of Michigan
1101 Beal Avenue, Ann Arbor, MI 48109-2110 USA
{wew,wellman}@umich.edu

Abstract. Supply chain formation is an important problem in the commercial world, and can be improved by greater automated support. Hence, the multiagent systems community should work to develop new solutions to the problem. The problem is complex and challenging, and a complete model must encompass a number of issues. In this paper we highlight some issues that must be understood to make progress in modeling supply chain formation.

1 Introduction

Much of the popular coverage of electronic commerce has focused on technology for facilitating bilateral exchange between customers and merchants. However, complex economic activity often involves interrelated exchange relationships among multiple levels of production, often referred to as a *supply chain*. Whereas a great deal of current commercial effort is being devoted to technology to support and manage supply chains, much of it is oriented toward maintaining pre-existing relationships in the chain. To achieve the oft-expressed visions of dynamically forming and dissolving business interactions (e.g., the rhetoric of "virtual corporations") requires automated support for *supply chain formation*, the process of bottom-up assembly of complex production and exchange relationships.

Automated support can extend beyond speeding the communications, calculations, and routine computation in the supply chain formation process. The artificial intelligence and multiagent system (MAS) communities are well-positioned to develop technology that will increasingly automate the decision making in business interactions. However, we must recognize that merely describing computational entities as "agents" will not immediately solve the problem. Institutions and modes of interaction must be carefully designed to achieve desirable behavior. Supply chain formation is a complex and challenging problem, and a complete model would encompass a number of issues. We focus on the issue of resource contention, which has not been well addressed in most models relevant to supply chain formation.

A. Moukas, C. Sierra, and F. Ygge (Eds.): AMEC'99, LNAI 1788, pp. 94–101, 2000.
© Springer-Verlag Berlin Heidelberg 2000

In this paper we highlight some issues that must be understood to make progress in modeling supply chain formation. We outline these issues broadly in Section 2. In Section 3 we discuss several relevant models in multiagent systems, and highlight task dependency networks for representing resource contention. In Section 4 we describe some difficulties that arise from resource contention, and suggest that market-based approaches can be effective in solving them. In Section 5 we identify some open problems in supply chain formation, and conclude in Section 6.

2   Aspects of Supply Chain Formation

The defining characteristic of supply chain formation is *hierarchical subtask decomposition*. Agents have specialized capabilities and can perform only certain combinations of tasks, or produce certain resources. In order to complete a complex task, an agent may delegate subtasks to other agents, which may in turn delegate further subtasks.

Resource contention constrains the set of feasible supply chains. When agents require a common resource (e.g., a subtask achievement, or something tangible like a piece of equipment) to complete their own tasks, resource scarcity may exclude these agents from jointly operating in the supply chain.

Agents aim to maximize their *value* in a supply chain. The model should account for values over multiple attributes such as monetary cost, time, and quality.

In a MAS containing autonomous, self-interested agents with private information, no entity has all information necessary to centrally form supply chains. This *decentralization* constraint implies that we should distribute decision making throughout the supply chain. Ideally, agents would be able to form supply chains in a strictly bottom-up manner, requiring only local communications and limited knowledge of the rest of the system.

Even when distributed, agent interactions during supply chain formation can be complex. Agents do not generally have the incentive to truthfully reveal information, hence we must analyze *strategic interactions* between agents.

Uncertainty introduces many complications in a model of supply chain formation. The constructed supply chain can be disrupted by failures in agents, failure in communications, and intentional fraud. Agents may be allowed to legally decommit from their contracts for a cost (e.g. to take advantage of better opportunities). The negotiation process itself may be affected by uncertain events. Bounds on rationality, variations in knowledge across agents, and multiplicity of equilibria make an agent's negotiation strategy uncertain. Failures in agents, negotiation mediators, and communications channels can occur during negotiation. Even if we know the full negotiation protocol and agent strategies and no failures occur, asynchronous communications introduces random elements into negotiation.

3 Models of Task Allocation and Supply Chains

Several existing models from the MAS research literature capture some, but not all, elements of supply chain formation. We review some of the dominant models of relevance here.

Rosenschein and Zlotkin [6] study a class of problems they call Task Oriented Domains (TODs). A TOD consists of a set of tasks that must be accomplished, and a (generally non-additive) cost function over sets of tasks. Sandholm [7] examines a generalization of TODs to include agent-dependent costs and constraints on task achievement. Agents are initially allocated a set of tasks, and may negotiate mutually beneficial exchanges of tasks to lower their costs. Andersson and Sandholm extend the model to allow agents to pay to decommit from contracts when better contracts become available [1]. These models address strategic interactions and increasing value via bilateral and multilateral task exchange, but do not incorporate the subtasking relationships characteristic of supply chains.

Hierarchical subtask decomposition is a core feature of the model underlying the CONTRACT NET protocol [2]. Subtasking proceeds in a distributed manner, in that agents communicate only with potential and actual subtasking partners. The protocol can flexibly accommodate multiattribute optimization criteria. However, these optimization criteria are applied locally within a level, in a greedy fashion, and do not reflect negotiation at other levels in the evolving supply chain.

Joshi et al. [3] consider issues arising from simultaneous negotiation of multiple subtasking issues at various levels of a supply chain. In their asynchronous model, agents may have the opportunity to finalize a contract while other negotiations are still pending. This uncertainty induces a complex decision problem for agents that do not wish to overextend their commitments.

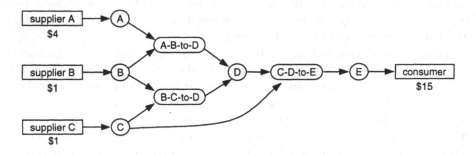

Fig. 1. A task dependency network.

Balancing interacting subtask commitments at multiple levels is especially important in the presence of resource contention. We represent resource contention in a supply chain with a **task dependency network** [8]. The nodes of a network represent agents and goods. We use the term **good** to refer to any task or discrete resource provided or needed by agents. The edges in the network represent input/output relationships between agents and goods. An edge from good to an agent indicates that the agent can make use of one unit of the good, and an edge from an agent to a good indicates that the agent can provide one unit of the good. A *consumer* is an agent that obtains some value from acquiring a good. A *producer* can provide one unit of one output good, contingent on acquiring each of a set of input goods. A *supplier* can provide a good, at some cost, without requiring any inputs.

Figure 1 shows an example task dependency network. The goods are indicated by circles, the consumer and suppliers by boxes, and the producers by curved boxes. The consumer value and supplier costs are indicated under the respective agents.

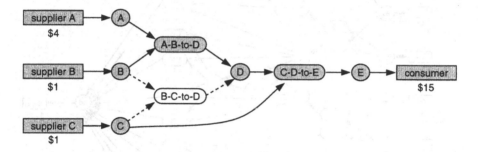

Fig. 2. The optimum allocation (and only solution) in the network.

An *allocation* is a subgraph containing all agents that acquire or provide goods, all goods that are acquired or provided, and all edges corresponding to the acquiring/providing relationships between the goods and agents in the allocation. A *feasible allocation* is one in which: 1) producers that provide their outputs also acquire all necessary inputs, and 2) all goods are in material balance (the number of edges into a good equals the number of edges out of a good). An *optimal allocation* is a feasible allocation that maximizes the difference between the sum of consumer value, and sum of supplier cost in the allocation. A *solution* is a feasible allocation in which one or more consumers acquire a desired good. Figure 2 shows the optimum allocation (and only solution) for the network from Figure 1. The allocation includes the shaded agents and goods and the solid edges.

4   Problems with Resource Contention

Consider a simple greedy allocation protocol, whereby subtask requests flow from consumers to suppliers, and subtask offers flow back to the consumer in a single pass. At each point in the offer flow, an agent sends offers as a function of the best offers it receives. Figures 1 and 2 show an example of how such a greedy

policy could run into trouble with resource contention. Locally, it appears that
B-C-to-D could provide D cheaper than A-B-to-D. However, the only solution
includes C-D-to-E, which requires the one available unit of C. This necessarily
excludes B-C-to-D from the solution.

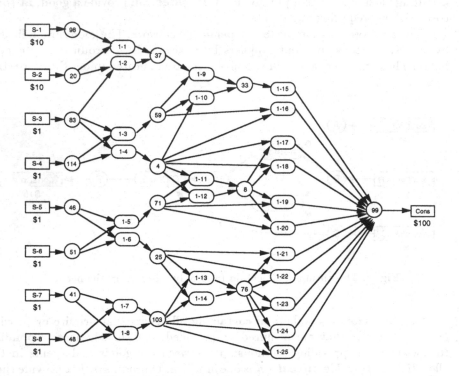

Fig. 3. A harder task dependency network.

We might address this problem by augmenting a greedy protocol with looka-
head or backtracking capabilities to identify these constraints. However, we argue that even with these capabilities, the protocol would flounder when faced
with more complicated networks such as the one in Figure 3. Any solution must
include suppliers S-1 and S-2 (the optimum is shown in Figure 4). However, because these suppliers have the highest costs, the network would severely mislead
a greedy protocol.

We can show that the problem of finding solutions is NP-complete, hence it
should not be surprising that greedy approaches would have difficulty. Indeed,
we should not expect any decentralized protocol to always form optimal supply
chains.

We identify a market-based protocol that, while not uniformly optimal, performs well on task dependency networks [8]. Markets utilize *price systems*

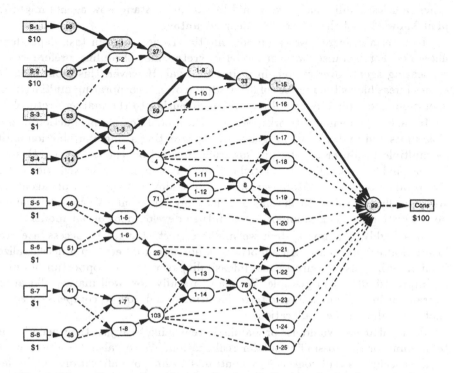

Fig. 4. The optimum allocation (and only solution) to the harder network.

to guide agent decisions in a decentralized manner. Agents negotiate through simultaneous, ascending auctions, one for each good. We examine simple, non-strategic agent bidding policies, requiring only local information. The protocol quickly finds solutions for the example problems shown in this paper. Experiments suggest that the protocol reliably converges to solutions (when they exist, and when the consumers have sufficiently high value) [10]. When combined with contract decommitment to remove dead ends in the supply chain, the protocol produces high value allocations on average [9].

5 Open Problems

Task dependency networks account for resource contention in supply chain formation, which has not been adequately addressed in other models. We have identified a market-based protocol that performs well on task dependency networks, but there remain many open problems to be addressed.

Strategic interactions are extremely complicated in any reasonable model of supply chain formation. In our work we have assumed simple agent bidding policies that work well from a system perspective. We must perform a strategic analysis to determine the plausibility of the policies, and how they fare against other policies. Additionally, we would like to understand how agents might exploit knowledge of the network to their advantage.

To a certain degree, we can model multiattribute value in task dependency networks. For instance, we can model discrete-time scheduling preferences by replicating agents over periods in a time interval. However, this replication becomes infeasible as the number of attributes grows. Incorporating multiattribute valuations more directly would require an extension to the market protocol.

In task dependency networks, we can also model flexible production of multiple units and multiple output goods by representing a single production entity as multiple producer agents, one for each production choice. Again, this can be reasonable for small-scale multiplication, but may not scale well with extensive production choices. Moreover, we cannot claim that the multiple agents are strategically equivalent to the single entity they represent. We consider these to be interesting challenges, important to future development of our model.

In a highly dynamic system we might expect changes to necessitate reallocation after quiescence. An adaptive system would detect—in a decentralized fashion—when lost resources cause infeasibility or when new opportunities make an improved allocation possible. We plan to study how well market allocations degrade or improve in response to reallocations, and how to compensate agents that lose value in the reallocation.

Rational agents would use probabilistic reasoning to adjust their negotiations to account for the possibility of later reallocation. We can also introduce devices such as securities and contingency contracts to improve allocations in the face of uncertainty.

Although we have presented the task dependency networks as pre-defined entities, in a dynamic system we would expect the goods of interest and the available auctions to change over time. Mullen and Wellman [4] studied mechanisms and policies for starting and maintaining auctions, and others [5, 11] are working to design *goods description languages* to allow agents to communicate their needs.

6   Conclusion

Supply chain formation is an important problem in the commercial world, and can be improved by greater automated support. The problem is salient to the MAS community and deserving of continued research.

Acknowledgments

This work was supported by a NASA/Jet Propulsion Laboratory Graduate Student Researcher fellowship and DARPA grant F30602-97-1-0228 from the Information Survivability program.

References

[1] Martin R. Andersson and Tuomas W. Sandholm. Leveled commitment contracting among myopic individually rational agents. In *Third International Conference on Multi-Agent Systems*, pages 26–33, 1998.

[2] Randall Davis and Reid G. Smith. Negotiation as a metaphor for distributed problem solving. *Artificial Intelligence*, 20:63–109, 1983.

[3] Pawan Joshi, Mayuresh Oke, Vivek Sharma, and Dharmaraj Veeramani. Issues in dynamic and highly-distributed configuration of supply webs. In *First IAC Workshop on Internet-Based Negotiation Technologies*, 1999.

[4] Tracy Mullen and Michael P. Wellman. The auction manager: Market middleware for large-scale electronic commerce. In *Third USENIX Workshop on Electronic Commerce*, pages 37–47, Boston, 1998.

[5] Daniel M. Reeves, Benjamin N. Grosof, Michael P. Wellman, and Hoi Y. Chan. Automated negotiations from formal contract descriptions (work-in-progress report). In *First IAC Workshop on Internet-Based negotiation Technologies*, March 1999.

[6] Jeffrey S. Rosenschein and Gilad Zlotkin. *Rules of Encounter*. MIT Press, 1994.

[7] Tuomas W. Sandholm. An implementation of the CONTRACT NET protocol based on marginal cost calculations. In *Eleventh National Conference on Artificial Intelligence*, pages 256–262, 1993.

[8] William E. Walsh and Michael P. Wellman. A market protocol for decentralized task allocation. In *Third International Conference on Multi-Agent Systems*, pages 325–332, 1998.

[9] William E. Walsh and Michael P. Wellman. Efficiency and equilibrium in task allocation economies with hierarchical dependencies. In *Sixteenth International Joint Conference on Artificial Intelligence*, 1999.

[10] William E. Walsh, Michael P. Wellman, Peter R. Wurman, and Jeffrey K. MacKie-Mason. Some economics of market-based distributed scheduling. In *Eighteenth International Conference on Distributed Computing Systems*, pages 612–621, 1998.

[11] Peter Weinstein and William P. Birmingham. Service classification in a proto-organic society of agents. In *IJCAI-97 Workshop on Artificial Intelligence in Digital Libraries*, 1997.

Jangter: A Novel Agent-Based Electronic Marketplace

Shim Yoon, JuYoung Yun, SooWoong Kim, and Juneha Kim

Information Technology R&D Center
Samsung SDS CO., LTD.
707-19, Yoksam-Dong, Kangnam-Gu
Seoul, Korea, 135-080
{syoon,jeffyun,soowoong,kjh}@sds.samsung.co.kr

Abstract. Electronic commerce makes it easier to trade goods between individuals. Classified ad or electronic auctions are examples of this consumer to consumer commerce. This paper proposes an agent-based electronic marketplace called "Jangter"[1] with mechanisms including "Matching", "Negotiation", and "Reputation".
The Matching mechanism using Floor and Room concept makes it possible to build a totally scalable marketplace. There are several benefits to use this mechanism. The first one is to solve the ontology problem. When creating category floor, ontology describing the category floor is defined. The second is that the computational complexity can be reduced with minimized search space. The third advantage is extensibility to the distributed system because it is natural to create each category floors on different hosts.
We suggest the automated negotiation mechanism reacting on the various types of user's commerce taste. With this mechanism, the user can control rate of successful deal and select various price strategies freely. And it considers product's non-price conditions such as delivery and quality option.
One of the problems in electronic commerce is how can people trust one who is now trading with me. And much of the dissatisfactions after trading occur when one cannot get proper products and services in time. Our reputation mechanism provides helpful ratings of the user's counterparts.
Keywords: *Electronic commerce, Software agent, Electronic marketplace, Mobile agent, Electronic auction.*

1   Introduction

Rapidly growing electronic commerce has caused changes in commerce model in comparison with the conventional commerce model. The most important one is that everyone could be a buyer or a seller in the cyber commerce world, i.e., the consumer-to-consumer commerce can be done easily. Classified ads and electronic auctions are examples of this kind of commerce. Several researches and commercial services have tried to enhance the usability of this kind of commerce.

---

[1] 'Jangter' means a marketplace in Korean.

A. Moukas, C. Sierra, and F. Ygge (Eds.): AMEC'99, LNAI 1788, pp. 102–112, 2000.
© Springer-Verlag Berlin Heidelberg 2000

For example, some electronic auction services provide proxy-bidding services in order to eliminate auction tediousness. Proxy bidding service will bid on the customer's behalf as necessary by increasing the bid by the current bid increment up until their maximum is reached. Nowadays electronic marketplace models using agents are proposed by several researchers. Among them, Kasbah model [1] is an innovative approach in the sense that artificial agents are forming the marketplace for buying and selling goods.

We propose a novel agent-based electronic marketplace called "Jangter" which is equipped with concrete and efficient components needed in doing inter-customers commerce. These components largely consist of a personal agent manager running on the customer side and an agent mart. The philosophy embedded in our model is to save the time that human being could spend for buying and selling something so that they gain time for more luxurious leisure. Saving time means many things. First, our model is simple from the user's viewpoint so that the user does not need complicated thinking for choosing a merchant or a product. Second, our model pursuits the totally distributed infrastructure. It allows the user to order and personalize the strategy on his desktop not necessarily connected to the server. Hence the network traffic problem and the commerce server overload can be avoided. Third, Jangter marketplace does most of user's commerce processes so that the user does not need to keep track of whole on-going processes.

This paper consists of following sections. In the section 2, we describe the Jangter model and its process flow. Section 3 presents the matching process called room algorithm; and, section 4 shows the negotiation mechanism. Trust issues, the most critical factor for boosting electronic commerce, are discussed in section 5. We give a simple sketch on the implementation of Jangter model in section 6; and, we conclude this paper in section 7.

2   The Jangter Model

The Jangter model is divided into two major parts that are an agent mart and a personal agent manager. Agent mart is a marketplace where agents meet each other for buying and selling goods on behalf of a user. Personal agent manager could create as many agents as the user wishes. Fig. 1 shows how agents created by users go through the overall marketplace and what they do. The commerce flow in Jangter goes as follows.

1. Agents can be created at the users' will by incorporating enough information and intention such as description of goods, maximum or minimum price, due date for the deal and negotiation strategy. Most of these personalized profile parameters can be reused later for other goods if the users keep all other options except goods description. As soon as agents are created, they move to the agent mart. This step is called "Listen and Depart".
2. When agents arrive to the agent mart, they are dispatched to the appropriate meeting rooms where they meet agent companions who have similar goods to buy or sell. The category manager and room managers do dispatching. This step is called "Match and Dispatch".

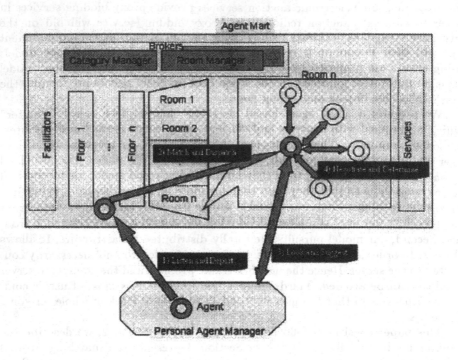

Fig. 1. Agent Flow in Jangter

3. In the meeting room, agents can start the negotiation with other agents or can suggest the list of potential agents valuable to negotiation to their user. This step depends on the user's intention that is set initially to the agent. If users wanted to have suggestion list, the agent notify the list to their user. This is called "Look and Suggest".

4. The negotiation starts among the agents in the room or the agents selected by the user from the suggestion list. If the successful negotiation takes place, the next step is to make a deal and notify the users. The user can interact at this time also in order to confirm the final decision. We discuss this mechanism called "Negotiate and Determine" in detail in Section 5.

5. Through the commerce flow in Jangter, the reputation mechanism is used for providing users more safe transaction and for attracting more users who may be hesitating because of the trust problems.

3   Matching Process

For supporting "Match and Dispatch" step in which agents find their counterpart easily, Jangter provides the following components as seen in Fig. 2.

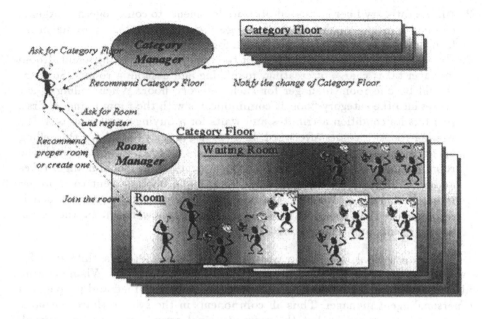

Fig. 2. Conceptual Design for Matching-Agent Module

Category floor is the logical workplace for agents to trade the special type of products. One category floor is composed of several rooms. Each category floor has attributes to describe the product. Room is the actual trading place. Agents who want to trade create rooms. The room has some attributes describing the trading conditions. Therefore room means candidate filtering. There is a special type of room named 'waiting room' in which selling agents wait for matched buying agents. Category manager has the ability to guide the coming agent to the proper category floor. Category manager manages a list of Category floors. Room manager has a list of rooms and sends agents to proper rooms. If there is no proper room for an agent, it creates a new one. Attributes can be classified into 'category attributes' and 'condition attributes'. Category attributes describe the product type traded by agents in the category floor. Condition attributes specify the product that agents want to buy or sell.

To select the candidate agents, the system takes the following steps.

1. Before the trade starts, a market should be created. In Jangter model, the market is represented by the category floor. Thus category manager creates new category floor to start trading. Attribute notations - category attributes and condition attributes - are defined when the category floor is created. These attributes are the ontology for agents. After the category floor is created, it registers the category attributes to the category manager and propagete these attributes to personal agents managers.

2. After a category floor is created, it waits for agents to come together. Agents can find a proper market through category manager. Category manager informs the agent of the category floor information.
3. For real trade, a room is created as for the request of the buying agent. Room manager takes charge of creating, managing and assigning rooms. So there should be one room manager for each category floor. When selling agent comes into the category floor, it communicates with the room manager first, registers its condition attributes and waits for a buying agent who is in the waiting room or comes afterward. If there are already rooms for the selling agent, it comes into the rooms. Buying agents also communicates with the room manager when they come into the category floor. Room manger takes an action either to create new room or to guide buying agent to a proper room. If there is a room for the buying agent to trade products, then it recommends that room. Otherwise, it creates a new room. In the room, buying agents and selling agents start trading.

There are several benefits to use the above room system architecture for matching agents. The first one is to solve the ontology problem. When creating category floor, ontology describing the category floor is defined and propagated to personal agent manager. Thus all components in the system share the same ontologies. The second is that the computational complexity can be reduced. Search space for each agent to find its counterparts and make a deal can be minimized by using category floor and rooms. In the room, there are all agents in the system concerning the product. The third advantage is easy extensibility to the distributed system because it is natural to create each category floors on different hosts. When the category manager is requested for new room, it finds a host which has less system load and creates category floor on that host. If the host has many category floors or high system load, some category floor on that host move to another and notify the category manager of the change. With this architecture, the system can use resources efficiently.

4   Negotiation

Price negotiation is a primary concern on agent-mediated electronic commerce. This section proposes a model for price negotiation between agents. The model describes what is input parameters, how to generate a negotiation plan and how to do negotiation process. Before delegation of price negotiation to an agent, user has to set some parameters. The followings are input parameters in our model.

- Minimum desired price, Maximum desired price, Desired date to sell or buy the item by:
- Exploration period: Deal is not allowed but price investigation is allowed during the period. For example, 30% of desired date or more than 20 times price query with another agents could be the exploration period.
- Desired successful deal rate: A internal price line is a proper price range generated by the agent. The inclination of this line can be changed depending on the desired successful deal rate.

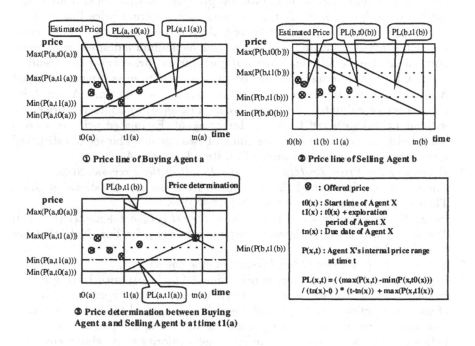

Fig. 3. Price Determination Process

- A ratio of price to condition: This parameter permits to consider not only the price but also product's other conditions in negotiation. Agent can convert degree of satisfaction on optional condition to a value. The value influences price strategy by moving internal price line up or down in parallel.
- Mandatory conditions: Conditions to be filtered by a room manager before negotiation. (e.g. more than 30 MB Hard Disk, used within 3 years, need high reputation).
- Optional conditions: User can enter some optional conditions (e.g. more than 1DiskDrive, High quality product).
- Auction allowed: If answer is 'Yes' then agent can join the possible auction deal with a lowest price extracted during exploration period.

Buying agent A determines price as follows:

1. *Investigate Market Price.*
   Agent A generates price line $PL(a, t_0(a))$ using minimum desired price, maximum desired price and deadline which are entered by owner of agent A at $t_0(a)$. Agent A collects public price information which contains current price at time t0(a) and slope of internal price line at time t0(a) from selling agents. In addition, agent A reconstructs each 'internal price line without any bound' from information gathered. At the time, agent A doesn't know any selling agent's private information such as minimum desired price, maximum desired price and dead line but just current price and price trend at time t0. Because internal price line of any agents change as time goes, Agent A doesn't predict buyer agent's internal price line at any time. Agent A induces a set of estimated price from own PL(a,t0(a)) and internal price line without bound gathered from any buyer agent. Estimated price is a cross point between each internal price lines of two agents. The set of estimated price represents the market price of an item for agent A.
2. *Determine the Price Strategy Using the Result of the Previous Step.*
   Choose the minimum and the maximum from the set of estimated price. Then compute internal price line $PL(a, t_1(a))$ as
   $(\max(P(a,t) - \min(P(a,t_0(a)))/(t_n(a) - t)) * (t - t_n(a)) + \max(P(a,t_1(a))$
   The first graph in Fig. 3 shows a shape of internal price line. Note that the price line depends on time.
3. *Select the Lowest Price Offered from Buying Agents.*
   Begin negotiation using internal price line $PL(a, t_1(a))$ with buying agents in turn by increasing sorted price. At that time, a value representing degree of user satisfaction about optional conditions is applied to the $PL(a, t_1(a))$. The value varies by each buying agent. If another agent give a better price before contract with an agent, the agent gets priority at making a contract. The third graph in Fig. 3 shows point of price determination.

Selling Agent can determine the price as Buying agent does. You can find an example of internal price shape of a selling agent B at the second graph in Fig. 3.

In the view of user, the user can control rate of successful deal and select various price strategies freely. And the user can apply both price and condition to own price strategy intuitively. Also agent can recommend new strategy using user preference and user feedback to make agent more smart. On the point of market, this proposed price model unifies price models of auction market, classified ad market and stock market. This means user can access to any kind of market with just same input parameters. Using this price model, users can change their price strategy dynamically according to market status.

5   Reputation Mechanism

One of the problems in electronic commerce is how they can trust each other who are participating in the trade. And much of the dissatisfactions after trading occur when one cannot get proper products and services in time. In real trading systems, there are post-operations that one can cancel the trade or send it back to the seller if he has proper reason. But it is essential to know the exact degree of trust of the sellers/buyers who are the candidate of trade to make a satisfactory trade. Nowadays user can rate his counterparts in commercial auction system such as 'eBay' [2] or 'onSale' [9]. But there can be problems in the above systems. First, one can easily change or renew one's identity in the system. Second there can be fake transactions between two participants who promise to rate each other highly in advance.

In Jangter system, we will show the considering conditions for electronic commerce and propose the reputation mechanism. We add the new property, reputation, in order to rate counterparts correctly. Reputation is a measure of trust of participant. We can believe that one who has high reputation will deliver the proper products and service in proper time. The following conditions must be considered for new reputation mechanism

1. *The reputation of non-trusted agent can be lower than that of beginner. And one should not change his identity or renew it.*
2. *Rating of the one whose reputation is high should be considered much importantly than that of the one whose reputation is low.*
3. *The value of the product in trading is an important factor in reputation.*
4. *For a number of ratings between each pair, the last rating is the real rating (It prevents fake transaction).*
5. *Recent rating should be treated importantly.*
6. *Buyer will purchase the products and service to get as much profit as possible. And buyer will not purchase them with a loss.*
7. *There should be a reputation administrator (RA) in the system that manages reputations of all agents in the system.*

In Jangter system, we propose a reputation mechanism as Fig 4 in order to solve the above 7 problems.

Considering the above reputation mechanism, we have selected the utility of agent. The utility function is used in Economics and can be adapted to check the benefit of the trade. The system administrator should set 3 system constants, which are decreasing factor (Df), α and β. Decreasing factor is used to reduce the effect of the previous rating so that system can count for the recent rating. Users only rate the trading whether they are satisfied with the trade. The other variables are determined by the system, which are evaluation of trade products and services, utility, and the reputation of each joining the trade. Buyers and sellers rate each other for each pair. So there can be an n by m matrix for n buyers and m sellers (personal reputation matrix). If there is no trade between buyer k and seller p, the value of row k and column p should be n/a. RA also keeps this matrix and updates it. α and β are the weight factors of general and personal reputations.

To evaluate the proposed reputation mechanism, we simulate it. The result of the simulation can be found in [12]. In that simulation, we make some portion of non-trusted agents. (0.5%, 1%,5%,10%) After lots of trades, reputations of those

Utility of Agent for each transaction (U_i)
= F(reasonable price, trading price)
= reasonable price(P_r) - trading price(P_t)
    // Utility = difference between worth of achieving a goal
    // and the price paid in achieving it

Rating(W_i) = the rating value which the counterpart evaluates the trade
= { -1, -0.5, 0, 0.5, 1}

Df = decreasing factor $(0 < Df \leq 1)$
$\theta(R_i^{other})$ = projection of reputation of the rating agent
        (M : the mean, δ : the standard variation)
    0.1 if $R_i^{other} < M - 2\delta$
    0.2 if $R_i^{other} < M - \delta$
    0.4 if $R_i^{other} < M$
    0.5 if $R_i^{other} = M$
    0.6 if $R_i^{other} < M + \delta$
    0.8 if $R_i^{other} < M + 2\delta$
    0.9 otherwise

R_t = reputation value for one identity, public reputation
= $\sum (R_i * Df) + R_c$
        // join the decreasing factor to the reputation mechanism
$R_c = W_i * U_i * \theta(R_i^{other})$
        // join the rating agent's reputation to reputation mechanism
$(R_t = R_c,$ if t=1)

if $U_i < 0$ then   stop trading
        // making utility function
else
    if $W_i \geq 0$ then // rating = 1, 0.5, -0.5, -1 and 0 for no response
        $U_i = (P_r - P_t) * W_i = F * W_i$
    else
        $U_i = P_t * W_i$

Reputation of Agent = $\alpha * R_t + \beta * R_p$
        $(R_p$: personal reputation, $0 \leq \alpha, \beta \leq 1)$

Fig. 4. Reputation algorithm

agents are below zero. Below zero means the sign of non-trusted participant. As we know from the result of the simulation, the proposed reputation mechanism can represent the real world very well. Therefore we can use this reputation value in matching, negotiation and recommendation steps.

6 Implementation

In this chapter, we will show the implementation architecture for Jangter system, agent marketplace. To satisfy the proposing agent market model, agent should have the structure in Fig 5.

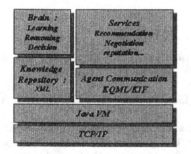 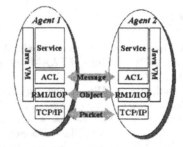

Fig. 5. Agent Architecture   **Fig. 6.** Inter Agent communication

Agent is composed of user interface, brain and knowledge repository, services, agent communication module and agent platform. Using user interface, agents interacts with user. Its Brain and knowledge repository replace human intelligence. Services replace human actions. Agent can communicates with other agents using agent communication module. Agents work on agent platform. You can see the inter-agent communication diagram in Fig. 6. Agents communicate to achieve their objects on the service level. Using JavaVM, we distribute agents in real time. Agents operate in meeting room, facilitator office and broker office [12]. This distributed agent marketplace architecture ensures the extensibility and the security. For example, control agent creates sub markets dynamically according to the number of agents

7 Conclusion

We have proposed an agent-based marketplace model, Jangter, having concrete architecture and performable mechanisms including matching, negotiation, and reputation. The main contribution of this research can be summarized as follows: First, we proposed a sophisticated agent-based marketplace model where the agents are able to interact with other agents. They can perform their user's order for getting the best deal. Second, the matching mechanism using floor and room concept makes it possible to build a totally scalable marketplace depending on the market size. Third, we suggested the automated negotiation mechanism and various strategies applicable. This mechanism contains various types of user's commerce tastes and the methods serving as a strategic gauge when doing automated negotiation. Fourth, the users hesitation of the electronic commerce due to the unsafe trust could be solved by using the reputation mechanism proposed in Jangter.

We are currently implementing Jangter prototype on top of JVM. We need to experiment on the real world's system with this model in order to prove the effectiveness and the adaptability. While the Jangter model is designed in the context of consumer to consumer electronic commerce model, we believe that it can be applied in business to consumer model with a slight extension.

References

1. A.Chavez and P.Maes. Kasbah: An Agent Marketplace for Buying and Selling Goods. Proceedings of PAAM' 96, p.75-90. London, UK, April 1996
2. http://www.ebay.com
3. Guanhao Yan, Wee-Keong Ng, Ee-Peng Lim. Toolkits for a Distributed, Agent-Based Web Commerce System.
   http://www.WebDevelopersJournal.com/articles/ecommerce/yan01.html
4. R. Guttman and P. Maes. Cooperative vs. Competitive Multi-Agent Negotiations in Retail Electronic Commerce. To appear, Proceedings of the Second International Workshop on Cooperative Information Agents (CIA'98). Paris, France, July 1998
5. Robert H. Guttman, Alexandros G. Moukas, and Pattie Maes. Agent-mediated Electronic Commerce: A Survey, 1999
6. Y.Labrou and T.Finin. A Semantics Approach For KQML: A General Purpose Communication Language for Software Agents. Proceedings of CIKM'94, New York, 1994
7. P. Maes, R. Guttman and A. Moukas. Agents that Buy and Sell: Transforming Commerce as we Know It. To appear, Communications of the ACM, March 1999 Issue.
8. A. Moukas, R. Guttman, and P. Maes. Agent-mediated Electronic Commerce: An MIT Media Laboratory Perspective. Proceedings of the First International Conference on Electronic Commerce (ICEC'98), Seoul, Korea, April 1998.
9. OnSale: Live Online Auction House. http://www.onsale.com/
10. J.Rosenschein and G.Zlotkin. Rules of Encounter: Designing Conventions for Automated Negotiatio among Computers. MIT Press, 1994
11. Shaw Green, Fergal Somers. Software Agent: A review. May 1997.
12. JuYoung Yun, SooWoong Kim, Shim Yoon, Juneha Kim. Consumer-oriented agent-based electric marketplace. Technical paper. Samsung SDS. Feb 1999
13. G. Zacharia, A. Moukas, R. Guttman, and P. Maes. An agent system for comparative shopping at the point of sale. Proceedings of the European Conference on MM & E-Commerce, Bordeaux, France, September 1998.
14. G. Zacharia, A. Moukas, and P. Maes. Collaborative Reputation Mechanisms in Electronic Marketplacesm, Proceedings of Electronic Commerce Technology Minitrack, HICSS-32, Wailea Maui, Hawaii, January 1999.

Bid Selection Strategies
for Multi-agent Contracting
in the Presence of Scheduling Constraints

John Collins[1], Rashmi Sundareswara[1], Maria Gini[1], and Bamshad Mobasher[2]

[1] Department of Computer Science and Engineering
University of Minnesota
[2] School of Computer Science, Telecommunications, and Information Systems
DePaul University

Abstract. Bid evaluation in a multi-agent automated contracting environment presents a challenging search problem. We introduce a multi-criterion, anytime bid evaluation strategy that incorporates cost, task coverage, temporal feasibility, and risk estimation into a simulated annealing framework. We report on an experimental evaluation using a set of increasingly informed search heuristics within simulated annealing. The results show that excess focus on improvement leads to faster improvement early on, at the cost of a lower likelihood of finding a solution that satisfies all the constraints. The most successful approach used a combination of random and focused bid selection methods, along with pruning and repeated restarts.

1 Introduction

The University of Minnesota's MAGNET (Multi-Agent Negotiation Testbed) system is an innovative agent-based approach to complex contracting and supply-chain management problems. The MAGNET system [7] comprises a set of agents who negotiate with each other through a market infrastructure using a finite, leveled-commitment protocol [22]. It is designed to support the execution of complex plans among a population of independent, autonomous, heterogeneous, self-interested agents. We call this activity *Plan Execution By Contracting*.

Plan Execution by Contracting is designed to extend the applicability of agent negotiation to new domains, where schedules for production and delivery affect the cost and feasibility of services and products, and where monitoring the performance of task execution is an essential part of the process. This is especially important for domains such as logistics, dynamic planning and scheduling, and coordination of supply-chain management with production scheduling, where what is important is flexibility, ease of use, quality, performance, as opposed to just cost [13].

In general, a MAGNET agent has three basic functions: planning, negotiation, and execution monitoring. Within the scope of a negotiation, we distinguish between two agent *roles*, the *Customer* and the *Supplier*. A Customer is an agent

A. Moukas, C. Sierra, and F. Ygge (Eds.): AMEC'99, LNAI 1788, pp. 113–130, 2000.

who has a goal to satisfy, and needs resources outside its direct control in order to achieve its goal. The goal may have a *value* that varies over time. A Supplier is an agent who has resources and who, in response to a *Request for Quotes (RFQ)*, may offer to provide resources or services, for specified prices, over specified time periods. Once the Customer agent receives bids, it must decide which bids to select by solving both bid-allocation and temporal feasibility constraints, while attempting to minimize cost and risk.

We have developed a highly tunable anytime search [2], based on a simulated annealing [18] framework with a set of modular selectors and evaluators. Given that the time allocated to search will seldom be sufficient to explore a significant fraction of the search space, we must find an appropriate tradeoff between systematic optimization and random exploratory behavior. We describe here a set of experiments using our bid selection algorithm and characterize its performance on a variety of problems.

This paper is organized as follows. We describe our study on bid selection in Section 2, and the experimental setup in Section 3. In Section 4 we present our empirical results on the performance of the various bid-selection strategies. Section 5 covers the background and related work. Section 6 describes our conclusions and suggestions for future work related to this problem.

2   Agent Interactions and Time Allocation

The negotiation portion of the MAGNET protocol is a finite 3-step process that begins when a Customer agent issues a RFQ. The RFQ specifies a set of tasks that must be performed, along with time and precedence constraints. Suppliers may reply with bids, and the Customer accepts the bids it chooses with bid-accept messages.

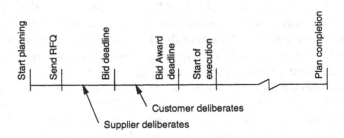

Fig. 1. Agent Interaction Timeline

The timeline in Figure 1 shows an abstract view of the progress of a single negotiation. At the beginning of the process, the Customer agent must allocate time to deliberation for its own planning, for supplier bid preparation, and for its own bid evaluation. In general, it is expected that bid prices will be lower if suppliers have more time to prepare bids, and more time and schedule flexibility in the execution phase. On the other hand, the Customer's ability to find a good set of bids is dependent on the time allocated to bid evaluation, as we shall see. Since the Customer's goal is time-sensitive, the negotiation process requires Customer and Suppliers to agree on the times for execution of tasks, and time factors can affect the cost of execution.

For each task listed in the RFQ the following must be specified:

- a time window, consisting of an earliest start time $t_{es}(s)$ and a latest finish time $t_{lf}(s)$, for each task s,
- a set of precedence relationships for the task.

Our contracting protocol allows Supplier agents to bid on combinations of items (possibly including a discount or a premium for accepting the whole bid), and assumes exclusive OR bids, which means that when multiple bids on combinations of tasks are submitted by the same agent, at most one of them can be accepted. Each bid represents an offer to execute some subset of the tasks specified in the RFQ. Each bid b includes:

- the overall bid price,
- the set of tasks. For each task s it includes:
  - the time window, that consists of early start $t^b_{es}(s)$, and late finish $t^b_{lf}(s)$,
  - the duration $duration^b(s)$,
  - the individual price $price^b(s)$ for the task.

The difference between the overall bid price and the sum of the individual task prices is referred to as the *discount* or the *premium* of the combination.

The semantics of a bid is that the Supplier agent is willing to perform task s for the bid price $price^b(s)$ starting at any time $t_s(s)$ within the time window specified in the bid as long as the task is completed before the late finish, i.e. $t^b_{es}(s) \leq t_s(s) \leq t^b_{lf}(s) - duration^b(s)$, and finishing at time $t_s(s) + duration^b(s)$. It is a requirement of the protocol that the time parameters in a bid are within the time windows specified in the RFQ.

The Customer agent's objective is to maximize utility, which requires minimizing cost and risk of not accomplishing the goal. To determine which bids (or parts of bids) to accept, the Customer agent considers coverage (we assume that there is no point in accomplishing only a part of the goal), temporal feasibility (the time windows for tasks must allow to compose them in a feasible schedule), cost, and risk. Risk factors include elements such as availability of suppliers, supplier reliability, profit margin, expected cost of recovering from supplier decommitment or delay, loss of value if the end date is delayed, cost of plan failure. MAGNET agents have to assess their own preferences and risk tolerance, as described more in detail in [5].

Once the Customer has selected the optimal set of bids (or parts thereof) the resulting *task assignment* forms the basis of an initial schedule for the execution of the tasks. The execution may involve additional negotiations over schedule adjustments, and in some cases may require repeating the bidding cycle if a supplier decommits or if a delay in completing some task forces other tasks to go outside the time windows agreed between Customer and Supplier. We will not cover the execution process here, we will limit our presentation to the selection of bids.

3   Experimental Setup

The experimental setup includes three main components: a MAGNET Server as described in [7], a Customer agent that requests and evaluates bids, and a Supplier agent that generates and submits bids. The bid evaluation process is instrumented to measure the rate of improvement for various search strategies. Random variable seeds are controlled to ensure that different search strategies are presented with exactly the same problems.

3.1   Customer Agent: Construct and Issue a Request for Quotes

The Customer agent starts with a set of tasks with their precedence relations, and constructs and issues a RFQ.

We assume the agent has general knowledge of normal durations of tasks, which can be obtained from the MAGNET market infrastructure [7]. The Customer agent schedules tasks using expected durations, and computes early start and late finish times using the Critical Path (CPM) algorithm [14].

The Critical Path algorithm walks the directed graph of tasks and precedence constraints, forward from the start time t_0 to compute the earliest start $t_{es}(s)$ and finish $t_{ef}(s)$ times for each task s, and then backward from time t_{goal} to compute the latest finish $t_{lf}(s)$ and start $t_{ls}(s)$ times for each task s. The minimum duration of the entire plan, defined as $max(t_{ef}(s)) - t_0$, is called the *makespan* of the plan.

The difference between t_{goal} and the latest early finish time is called the *total slack* of the plan. If t_{goal} is set equal to $t_0 + makespan$, then the total slack is 0, and all tasks for which $t_{ef}(s) = t_{lf}(s)$ are called *critical* tasks. Paths in the graph through critical tasks are called *critical paths*.

The tradeoff between minimizing plan duration and attracting usable bids from suppliers affects how slack should be set. Slack is important in determining the expected schedule risk, which is associated, among other things, with constraint-tightness.

In order to allow for variability in actual task durations, to allow suppliers some degree of flexibility in their resource scheduling, and to take advantage of lower-than-expected task durations, the specified start and finish times are relaxed from their expected values. For example, in the set of experiments described in Section 4.1, we relax the time windows by 40%. This amount has been shown to give a good balance between supplier flexibility and the need of the Customer agent to be able to compose feasible plans [6]. We do this by setting t_{goal} as discussed above, reducing the task durations to 60% of their expected values, and re-running the CPM algorithm on the task graph.

Figure 2 shows in Gantt chart form how such a plan would be specified by a Customer. In the example, each of the tasks has an expected duration of 1.0, and the plan has an overall slack of 10%, giving a target finish time of 3.3. The time windows in the RFQ are specified with task durations of 0.6. The arrows show precedence relationships, and the extension bars show per-task slack. Task 2 is labeled to show the early start, early finish, and late finish times.

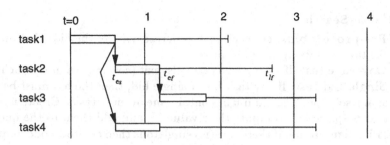

Fig. 2. Plan as specified by Customer

3.2 Supplier Agent: Generate Bids

The Supplier agent is a test agent that masquerades as an entire community of suppliers. Each time a new RFQ is announced, the Supplier agent attempts to generate some number of bids.

Bids are generated for random sets of contiguous tasks within the RFQ. Task durations are randomly distributed around the expected value used by the Customer, and the time windows are randomly set to be smaller than the time windows specified in the RFQ and larger than the computed durations. Because of this, arbitrary combinations of bids frequently generate infeasible schedules. Full details on the bid generation process are given in [6].

3.3 Customer Agent: Evaluate Bids

Once the bidding deadline is past, the Customer evaluates the set of bids in an attempt to find a combination that provides coverage of all tasks, allows for a feasible schedule, and minimizes a combination of cost and risk. Since bids are exclusive OR (when multiple bids are submitted by the same agent, only one of them can be accepted) for each bid the Customer has the option of selecting which parts of the bid (if any) to accept.

The evaluator uses a generalized simulated annealing [18] search as described below. Nodes are kept in an ordered queue of fixed maximum length (the *beam width*), sorted by the node's value. The node value is computed as shown in step 2.4 in the algorithm. The value is a combination of factors and includes a risk component. Intuitively, whenever accepting a task from a bid will increase the probability of missing the goal deadline, or of missing the latest start time $t_{ls}i(s)$ for tasks already selected, the risk increases.

The simulated-annealing framework is characterized by two elements, the annealing temperature T which is periodically reduced by a factor ε, and the stochastic node-selection procedure. The algorithm is outlined here below.

1. **Initialize Search:**

   1.1 **Pre-process bids:** For each task generate a list of the bids that include the task and its average bid price.

   1.2 **Coverage test:** If any task has no bids, exit (coverage cannot be achieved).

   1.3 **Single bid test:** If any task has a single bid, then the bid must be part of any solution. The bid might contain one or more tasks. Create node(s) that map the bid, compute their value V, and add them to the queue.

   1.4 **Initialize queue:** If there were no singletons then create a node mapping all tasks to no bids, and add it to the queue.

   1.5 **Set initial annealing temperature.**

2. **While not** timeout **and** improving **do:**

   2.1 **Select a node N for expansion:**
   Select a random number $R = V_{min} - T \ln(1 - r)(V_{max} - V_{min})$, where
   - r is a random number uniformly distributed between 0 and 1,
   - T is the current annealing temperature, and
   - V_i is the value of node i in the queue. Nodes in the queue are sorted by increasing values, V_{min} is the value of the first node.

   Choose node N as the last node in the queue such that $V_N \leq R$

   2.2 **Select a bid B:**
   Discard all bids that appear on the tabu list of N.
   Discard all bids that have already been used to expand N.
   Choose a bid according to the current bid selection policy.

   2.3 **Expand node N with bid B, producing node N':**
   For each task mapped by bid B that was already mapped to bid B', remove bid B'.
   If B' was a singleton bid, abandon the expansion.
   Add B to the expansions-tried list of node N.
   Copy the tabu list of node N into node N' and add bid B in front.
   Truncate the tabu list in node N' to the tabu size limit.

   2.4 **Evaluate node N':**
   $V_N = Cost_N + Risk_N + Feas_N + Cov_N$. where
   - $Cost_N$ is the sum of bid prices (uncovered tasks are assigned an average price),
   - $Risk_N$ is the expected cost of recovering from plan failure, times a weighting factor.
   - $Feas_N$ is the weighted sum of schedule overlaps.
   - Cov_N is the number of tasks that are not mapped to a bid, times a weighting factor.

   2.5 **Update best-node statistics.**

   2.6 **Adjust the annealing temperature T.**

3. **Return** the best node found.

The following bid-selection methods, used in Step 2.2 of the algorithm, have been implemented and tested. Note that the feasibility and cost improvement methods have significant complexity costs associated with them.

Random Bid, Random Bid Component: Choose a bid or a bid component at random, and attempt to add it to the node. The ratio of bids to bid components is adjustable. This method is fast ($O(1)$) and promotes general exploration of the search space.

Coverage Improvement: Choose a bid or bid component that covers a task that is not mapped in the node. The probability of choosing a bid component is equal to the coverage factor of the node. This method is also $O(1)$ if the set of unmapped tasks and the set of bids per task is stored.

Feasibility Improvement: The mapping is scanned to find tasks s that have negative slack, i.e. tasks such that $t^b_{es}(s) + duration(s) > t^b_{lf}(s)$. Of those, the tasks that are constrained by their bids rather than by predecessors or successors could be moved in a direction that would relieve the negative slack. They are sorted by their potential to reduce infeasibility, and saved. The untried bid or bid component with the highest potential to reduce infeasibility is chosen. Note that when a bid is chosen, there is no guarantee that it will not introduce other infeasibilities. The complexity of this method is $O(xy)$, where x is the total number of tasks and y is the number of tasks in the mapping that meet the above improvement criteria, incurred once the first time a node is subjected to feasibility improvement, and $O(z)$, where z is the number of bids that could potentially be mapped to a task, each time a feasibility improvement is attempted on a node.

Cost Improvement: Choose the (untried) bid or bid component that is responsible for the maximum positive deviation from the average price, and replace it with a lower-priced bid that covers at least the task with the highest positive cost deviation. The first time this method is applied to a node, it has a complexity of $O(xy + z)$, where x is the number of bids mapped to a node, y is the number of tasks in a bid, and z is the number of potential bids per task. Subsequent expansions of the same node by this method incur a complexity of only $O(z)$.

These selectors can be composed together and used to generate focused improvement for a given node. The following selectors were used in our experiments:

Random: The random selector described above.

FeasCov: If the node is infeasible, use the feasibility improvement selector; otherwise if it is not fully covered, use the coverage improvement selector; otherwise use the random selector.

CostFeasCov: If the cost of the covered portion of the node is above average, attempt to reduce its cost; otherwise use the *FeasCov* selector.

Combined: Run the *Random* selector as long as it produces improvement, then switch to *Feasibility Improvement* until that fails to produce improvement, then switch back to *Random*, then to *Coverage Improvement*, then back to *Random*, then to *CostFeasCov*, and finally back to *Random*.

4   Experimental Results

We describe three different experiments that we have carried out in the process of developing and characterizing the bid evaluation search. The results give us confidence that the bid evaluation problem can be solved for reasonably large problems using the simulated annealing approach.

4.1   Comparing Systematic and Stochastic Search

Our first experimental goal was to determine how well the simulated annealing search performed with respect to a known optimal reference. For that purpose, we constructed an alternate search engine that generates all feasible combinations of bids and bid components in order to be guaranteed of finding optimal solutions. Because of bid overlap and feasibility issues, no more efficient method is known that will provide such a guarantee. Its structure is similar to the method reported in [23] with the addition of a feasibility test.

The test problem for this experiment is necessarily small, because of the long run times of the systematic search engine. We generated 20 random problems with 10 tasks and 11 bids each. The "branch factor" that controls the density of precedence relationships was 2.4, and the average bid size was 2.72 tasks. Overall schedule slack was set to 1.4, and task durations were set to 70% of expected values to open up the time windows in the RFQ.

The summary data for this experiment is in Table 1. Solutions (feasible mappings that covered all tasks) were found for 9 out of the 20 problems. The others either lacked coverage (in 7 of the 20 runs there was at least one task for which no bid was submitted) or no feasible combinations existed (4 cases). The node counts and solution evaluations are the mean for the cases where solutions were found. The data for the Stochastic 1 and Stochastic 3 trials are normalized to account for the missing solution. The four trials used identical plans and bid sets.

Table 1. Systematic and Stochastic Results

	Systematic	Stochastic 1	Stochastic 2	Stochastic 3
Nodes Generated	115480	2171	2205	1323
Covered & Feasible	46916	435	448	219
Best Solution Eval.	7960	8073	7998	8073
Solutions Found	9	8	9	8
Run Time (min.)	242	9.8	9.4	6.2

The search engine parameters were set up as follows:

Systematic: Systematic search with problem setup as described above.
Stochastic 1: Simulated-annealing search, initial temperature 0.35, reduced by 0.95 every 100 iterations, *patience factor* (number of iterations without

improvement) 100. The stopping criterion for the stochastic search is either timeout (no timeout was used in this trial) or failure to improve for a number of iterations

$$n \geq patienceFactor \ln(taskCount) \ln(bidCount)$$

where *taskCount* is the number of tasks in the plan, and *bidCount* is the number of bids being considered. The bid selector is the Combined selector, as described in the previous section.

Stochastic 2: Setup as in Stochastic 1, except that a uniqueness test is added to prevent identical nodes from being evaluated and added to the search queue.

Stochastic 3: Setup as in Stochastic 2, except that the patience factor was reduced to 50.

The conclusion is that the simulated-annealing search engine performs well, with solution quality within 2% of the systematic search at radically reduced run times. It is also clear that it needs to be tuned to avoid missing solutions.

4.2   Comparing Bid Selectors

In the second study, we are comparing the random bid selector with the more "focused" bid selectors. We are interested in both the ability to find solutions, and in the rate of improvement. The latter attribute is important for setting time limits in an anytime search. The results show that the more focused methods alone are ineffective, even if used with high annealing temperatures. The best results were obtained by combining random and focused methods. The *Combined* selector outperforms all the others. It seems that excess focus on improvement leads to faster improvement early on, at the cost of a lower likelihood of finding a solution that satisfies all constraints.

In order to probe a range of problem complexity factors, we ran the *Random*, *Cov*, *FeasCov*, and *Combined* selectors against two different problem types of the same size but different levels of complexity. Both of them contain 50 tasks and 100 bidders, and all are generated with the same random number sequences. Total slack is 10%, and task durations are set to 60% of their expected values to relax time windows in the RFQ. In the *small-bid* problem, the average bid size (number of tasks included in a discounted bid) is 5, and in the *large-bid* problem, the average bid size is 15. Earlier work [23] has shown that this difference has a significant impact on the search difficulty due to the greater probability of overlap among bids.

Figure 3 shows the improvement curves for the four bid selectors on the *small-bid* problem, and Figure 4 shows improvement curves for the same selectors on the *large-bid* problem. Error bars show $\frac{\sigma}{\sqrt{n}}$ where σ is the standard deviation across runs, and n is the number of runs. The *Combined* selector clearly gives the best overall performance, both in terms of solution quality and in terms of consistency.

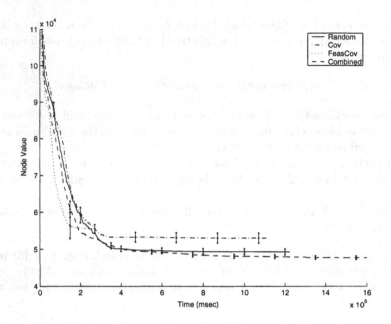

Fig. 3. Improvement curves for the *small-bid* problem. Averages are shown for 20 runs.

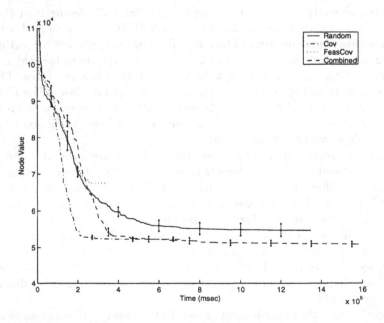

Fig. 4. Improvement curves for the *large-bid* problem. Averages are shown for 20 runs.

Table 2 shows the number of acceptable assignments found for the *small-bid* and *large-bid* problems. The table shows how effective the four selectors were at finding solutions that satisfied all constraints. The actual number of such solutions is not known. Again, we see the advantage of the *Combined* selector, which uses random selection to generate sets of candidates, and then switches to more focused selectors to clean up.

Table 2. Solutions Found

Selector	small-bid problem	large-bid problem
Random	2	2
Cov	3	0
FeasCov	2	0
Combined	6	1

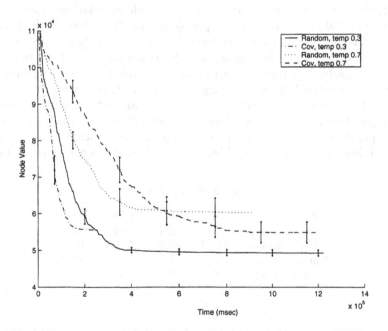

Fig. 5. Improvement curves for two different annealing temperatures.

In Figure 5, we explore the effect of raising the annealing temperature on the performance of the selectors. The experiments described earlier were all run with an initial annealing temperature of 0.3. We see that raising the annealing temperature does not improve performance, and the focused selectors do not perform any better at higher temperatures.

4.3   Improving Search Results

The third series of experiments is an attempt to improve the performance of the Simulated Annealing search in terms of its ability to find solutions. In the previous experiment we were concerned with the rate of improvement, but only a few of the problems were actually solved. This happened because the problems generated by the given test conditions had few solutions, but could also indicate that the search method was ineffective. In this experiment, we modify the problem parameters to increase the number of problems that have solutions, and we try several modifications to the search procedure in an attempt to find a combination that performs well across a range of problem characteristics.

In this experiment we use four problem sets that vary in two dimensions. The *branch factor* is the average number of precedence relationships per task in the plan. The *bid size* is the average number of tasks per bid. In the problem setup, the branch factor is controlled directly, while the bid size is controlled indirectly through the probability that the bidder will follow a precedence link when composing a bid. This behavior produces bids that are primarily composed of tasks that are *contiguous*, connected by precedence relations. Each problem set consists of 50 problems, 40 tasks/problem, and 90 bidders. Overall schedule slack is set to 40%, and task durations are set to 80% of their expected values.

Because of the way resource availability is simulated, not all bidders will bid on each problem. Because of our random approach to bid generation, there is no guarantee that bids will be generated for all tasks in a particular plan. Problems for which a full set of bids is generated are called *covered*. Among the covered problems, it is not known how many actually have feasible solutions. We call the problems sets *p-b-*, *p-b+*, *p+b-*, and *p+b+*, to indicate low-precedence – small-bid, low-precedence – large-bid, etc. Their statistics are given in Table 3.

Table 3. Problem Sets

Problem type	p-b-	p-b+	p+b-	p+b+
Branch factor	2.4	2.4	4.0	4.0
Mean bid size	11.79	20.93	11.95	19.62
Number of bids	88.68	88.62	87.72	87.92
Number covered	29	37	45	49

Preliminary experiments showed that four specific modifications to the search procedure had the potential to improve the ability to find solutions. We will show that, under the stated experimental conditions, the combination of all four performed better than any three of them. The modifications are:

1. A "variable-temperature" bid selector uses the current annealing temperature to adjust the amount of randomness in bid selection. At the initial temperature T_0, bid selection is completely random. As the temperature changes, coverage improvement is attempted with a probability of $(1 - \frac{T}{T_0})$.

2. Infeasible nodes are pruned from the search space rather than being left in for improvement. The intent is to improve the probability that a given node can be extended into a solution. Since feasibility checking is part of the node evaluation process, there is essentially no extra cost for this test.

3. Non-unique nodes are pruned from the search space. Because of the exclusive-or nature of bid combination, non-unique nodes can be produced by many paths, and the standard method of using tabu lists and preventing repeated identical expansions to a given node are not strong enough to prevent non-unique nodes from being produced. The cost for uniqueness checking is linear in the number of tasks in the plan.

4. The search is repeated multiple times, each time clearing out the queue and increasing the "patience factor" by some amount (10% in these tests). A maximum of 9 restarts is allowed. Once a solution is found, one additional restart is permitted in an attempt to further optimize the result.

We ran 5 tests on each of four problem sets, 50 runs per test, for a total of 2000 runs. In each test, we are interested in the following:

- significant differences in search effort as evidenced by the number of nodes generated,
- significant differences in the number of problems solved, and
- significant differences in the evaluation scores of the solutions found.

The criterion for significant difference will be a probability of the null hypothesis (no difference, or in some cases no improvement) of less than 5% using a paired-sample t-test. Note that the normal-distribution assumption of the t-test may not be satisfied. We will evaluate the criteria on each problem type, and on the composite of all four types. When looking for difference, we use the 2-tail criterion, and when looking for specific improvement we use the 1-tail criterion

The tests conditions are:

1. **Baseline:** The "variable-temp, adaptive restart" baseline, containing all the elements described above.

2. **Random:** As 1, but replace the variable-temp selector with a purely random selector. We expect to see higher search effort.

3. **Infeasible:** As 1, but do not filter out infeasible nodes. We expect to find fewer solutions.

4. **Non-unique:** As 1, but do not filter out non-unique nodes. We expect to find fewer solutions.

5. **Early Stop:** As 1, but do not run the extra restart after a solution is found. We expect to see lower search effort and poorer optimization performance.

The next three tables give the mean results for search effort, problem-solving ability, and optimization performance for each of the five test conditions and for each of the problem types. We also combine the results from the four problem types into a "composite" problem type. Where a significant difference is found, we give the probability of the null hypothesis and indicate whether it is a one-tail or two-tail probability.

Table 4. Search Effort (mean number of nodes generated)

	p-b-	p-b+	p+b-	p+b+	composite
baseline	4803	4827	7195	6600	6036
random	8237	6850	10172	9779	8933
	$p_{1T} < .01$	$p_{1T} < .01$	$p_{1T} < .01$	$p_{1T} < .01$	$p_{1T} < .01$
infeasible	8751	6697	4898	4899	5999
	$p_{2T} < .01$	$p_{2T} < .01$	$p_{2T} < .01$	$p_{2T} < .01$	–
non-unique	5974	3510	7822	6466	6491
	–	–	–	–	–
early stop	4864	3713	5794	5385	5019
	–	$p_{1T} < .05$	$p_{1T} < .05$	$p_{1T} < .05$	$p_{1T} < .01$

We see from Table 4 that the use of the random selector drives up search effort, while the elimination of the extra restart drives search effort down. This is what we expected.

In Table 5 the first row is simply the number of problems for which bid coverage is achieved. There is no guarantee that all covered problems actually have feasible solutions, although only one problem, in the *p-b-* set, was not solved by any method. This data set shows that the pruning of infeasible nodes has a dramatic impact on the problem-solving capability of the search, while the pruning of non-unique nodes has a small but significant impact. The use of the purely random bid selector also had a negative impact on problem-solving, but it is only significant when the results of all four problem sets is combined.

Table 5. Problem Solving (number of problems solved)

	p-b-	p-b+	p+b-	p+b+	composite
maximum	29	37	45	49	160
baseline	28	37	44	49	158
random	26	37	39	47	149
	–	–	–	–	$p_{2T} < .01$
infeasible	15	24	23	22	84
	$p_{1T} < .01$	$p_{1T} < .01$	$p_{1T} < .01$	$p_{1T} < .01$	$p_{1T} < .01$
non-unique	27	37	39	48	151
	–	–	$p_{1T} < .05$	–	$p_{1T} < .01$
early stop	28	37	43	49	157
	–	–	–	–	–

Finally, in Table 6 we see the results for the optimization performance of the various approaches. The improvement afforded by running an extra round of search is surprisingly small; the reduction in solution quality for the "early stop" case is only significant when data from all problem types is combined. The use of the purely random selector yields a slight improvement in quality, and the pruning of non-unique nodes is shown to improve quality slightly.

Table 6. Solution Quality (mean evaluation score)

	p-b-	p-b+	p+b-	p+b+	composite
baseline	35236	31886	27691	25902	29539
random	32683	30729	26524	24569	28032
	$p_{2T} < .05$	–	–	–	$p_{2T} < .01$
infeasible	32326	31318	29318	24740	29280
	–	–	–	$p_{2T} < .05$	–
non-unique	34878	32564	30237	26982	30593
	–	–	$p_{2T} < .05$	–	$p_{2T} < .05$
early stop	34758	32654	29510	27299	30503
	–	–	–	–	$p_{2T} < .05$

All hypotheses are confirmed, at least in the composite case. Note that the evaluation score data in Table 6 are only approximately comparable, since for each comparison the analysis must compare scores only for problems that both methods solved. Some interesting results can be observed:

- The random method is clearly more costly, and is a poorer solver, but when it succeeds it produces slightly better solutions.
- The extra restart appears to have a rather high cost in terms of search effort for a small but significant improvement in solution quality.
- The filtering of infeasible nodes appears to have a positive impact on search effort when the density of precedence relations is low, but a negative impact when the density is high. On the other hand, this is the factor that appears to have the largest impact on problem-solving ability.

5 Related Work

Markets play an essential role in the economy [1], and market-based architectures are a popular choice for multiple agents (see, for instance, [4, 19, 24, 26] and our own MAGMA architecture [25]). Most market architectures limit the interactions of agents to manual negotiations, direct agent-to-agent negotiation [22, 8], or some form of auction [27].

Auctions are becoming the predominant mechanism for agent-mediated electronic commerce [11]. AuctionBot [27] and eMEDIATOR [21] are among the most well known examples of multi-agent auction systems. They use economics principles to model the interactions of multiple agents. Auctions are not the most appropriate mechanism for the business-to-business transactions we are interested in, where scheduling plays a major role, and where reputation and maintaining long term business relations are often more important than cost.

The determination of winners of combinatorial auctions [16] is hard. Dynamic programming [20] works well for small sets of bids, but does not scale and imposes significant restrictions on the bids. Shoham [9] produces optimal allocations for OR-bids with dummy items by cleverly pruning the search space. Sandholm [21] uses an anytime algorithm to produce optimal allocations for a more general class of bids, that includes XOR and OR-XOR bids. The major difference is that in the cases studied for combinatorial auctions bid allocation is determined solely by cost. Our setting is more general, MAGNET agents have the ensure the scheduling feasibility of the bids they accept. Finding a set of bids that has minimal cost but is not feasible (i.e. no feasible schedule for the bids exists) is of no use.

We have chosen to use a simulated annealing framework for bid evaluation. Since the introduction of iterative sampling [15], a strategy that randomly explores different paths in a search tree, there have been numerous attempts to improve search performance by using randomization. Randomization has been shown to be useful in reducing the unpredictability in the running time of complete search algorithms [10].

A variety of methods that combine randomization with heuristics have been proposed, such as Least Discrepancy Search [12], heuristic-biased stochastic sampling [3], and stochastic procedures for generating feasible schedules [17], just to name a few. The algorithm we presented is based on simulated annealing, and as such combines the advantages of heuristically guided search with some random search. Our experimental results show that additional benefit can be obtained by using domain-specific heuristics when deciding how to expand a node. This combined with the basic simulated annealing framework produces good results in a short time frame.

6   Conclusions and Future Work

Bid evaluation in the MAGNET automated contracting environment is a difficult optimizing search problem that must be performed within a predetermined amount of time. Ignoring the use of individual bid components, in our experiment there are approximately 10^{14} bid combinations that could be tested.

We have chosen a simulated annealing framework to drive broad exploration of the search space. For this to be effective, it is necessary to set a number of parameters, including the beam width, annealing temperature and rate, and penalty factors, to avoid placing large potential barriers around the solutions. Eventually, we hope to be able to use problem metrics to set these parameters on the fly.

We have presented a bid evaluation process for automated contracting that incorporates cost, task coverage, temporal feasibility, and risk estimation, and we have provided, using this evaluation process, an empirical study of the tradeoffs between focus and ultimate success on this large, multicriterion search problem. Time constraints dictate that only a tiny fraction of the search space can be explored, and local minima abound. The best results were obtained with a combination of random and informed bid selection methods, along with pruning of infeasible and duplicate nodes and repeated restarts of the search.

This work raises several interesting questions for future research. Work is required to develop a clear understanding of how the various tuning parameters should be adjusted in accordance with problem parameters. An ideal tuning would reduce the incidence and size of local minima, and minimize potential barriers around usable solutions. At a higher level, the scheduling of planning time, bid preparation time, bid evaluation time, and execution time needs to be driven by knowledge of the relative contributions of each of those components to overall solution quality.

References

1. Yannis Bakos. The emerging role of electronic marketplaces on the Internet. *Comm. of the ACM*, 41(8):33–42, August 1998.
2. Mark Boddy and Thomas Dean. Solving time-dependent planning problems. In *Proc. of the 11th Joint Conf. on Artificial Intelligence*, volume 2, pages 979–984, Detroit, MI USA, August 1989.
3. John L. Bresina. Heuristic-biased stochastic sampling. In *Proc. of the Thirteenth Nat'l Conf. on Artificial Intelligence*, 1996.
4. Anthony Chavez and Pattie Maes. Kasbah: An agent marketplace for buying and selling goods. In *Proc. of the First Int'l Conf. on the Practical Application of Intelligent Agents and Multi-Agent Technology*, London, UK, April 1996.
5. John Collins, Corey Bilot, Maria Gini, and Bamshad Mobasher. Mixed-initiative decision support in agent-based automated contracting. In *Proc. of the Fourth Int'l Conf. on Autonomous Agents*, June 2000. (to appear).
6. John Collins, Maksim Tsvetovat, Rashmi Sundareswara, Joshua Van Tonder, Maria Gini, and Bamshad Mobasher. Evaluating risk: Flexibility and feasibility in multi-agent contracting. Technical Report 99-001, University of Minnesota, Department of Computer Science and Engineering, Minneapolis, Minnesota, February 1999.
7. John Collins, Ben Youngdahl, Scott Jamison, Bamshad Mobasher, and Maria Gini. A market architecture for multi-agent contracting. In *Proc. of the Second Int'l Conf. on Autonomous Agents*, pages 285–292, May 1998.
8. Peyman Faratin, Carles Sierra, and Nick R. Jennings. Negotiation decision functions for autonomous agents. *Int. Journal of Robotics and Autonomous Systems*, 24(3-4):159–182, 1997.
9. Yuzo Fujishima, Kevin Leyton-Brown, and Yoav Shoham. Taming the computational complexity of combinatorial auctions. In *Proc. of the 16th Joint Conf. on Artificial Intelligence*, 1999.
10. Carla Gomes, Bart Selman, and Henry Kautz. Boosting combinatorial search through randomization. In *Proc. of the Fifteen Nat'l Conf. on Artificial Intelligence*, pages 431–437, 1998.
11. Robert H. Guttman, Alexandros G. Moukas, and Pattie Maes. Agent-mediated electronic commerce: a survey. *Knowledge Engineering Review*, 13(2):143–152, June 1998.
12. William D. Harvey and Matthew L. Ginsberg. Limited discrepancy search. In *Proc. of the 14th Joint Conf. on Artificial Intelligence*, pages 607–613, 1995.
13. S. Helper. How much has really changed between us manufacturers and their suppliers. *Sloan Management Review*, 32(4):15–28, 1991.

14. Frederick S. Hillier and Gerald J. Lieberman. *Introduction to Operations Research.* McGraw-Hill, 1990.
15. Pat Langley. Systematic and nonsystematic search strategies. In *Proc. Int'l Conf. on AI Planning Systems*, pages 145–152, College Park, Md, 1992.
16. R. McAfee and P. J. McMillan. Auctions and bidding. *Journal of Economic Literature*, 25:699–738, 1987.
17. Angelo Oddi and Stephen F. Smith. Stochastic procedures for generating feasible schedules. In *Proc. of the Fourteenth Nat'l Conf. on Artificial Intelligence*, pages 308–314, 1997.
18. Colin R. Reeves. *Modern Heuristic Techniques for Combinatorial Problems.* John Wiley & Sons, New York, NY, 1993.
19. J. A. Rodriguez, P. Noriega, C. Sierra, and J. Padget. FM96.5 - a Java-based electronic auction house. In *Second Int'l Conf on The Practical Application of Intelligent Agents and Multi-Agent Technology (PAAM'97)*, London, April 1997.
20. Michael H. Rothkopf, Alexander Pekeč, and Ronald M. Harstad. Computationally manageable combinatorial auctions. *Management Science*, 44(8):1131–1147, 1998.
21. Tuomas Sandholm. An algorithm for winner determination in combinatorial auctions. In *Proc. of the 16th Joint Conf. on Artificial Intelligence*, pages 524–547, 1999.
22. Tuomas W. Sandholm. *Negotiation Among Self-Interested Computationally Limited Agents.* PhD thesis, University of Massachusetts, 1996.
23. Erik Steinmetz, John Collins, Maria Gini, and Bamshad Mobasher. An efficient algorithm for multiple-component bid selection in automated contracting. In *Agent Mediated Electronic Trading*, volume LNAI1571, pages 105–125. Springer-Verlag, 1998.
24. Katia Sycara and Anandeep S. Pannu. The RETSINA multiagent system: towards integrating planning, execution, and information gathering. In *Proc. of the Second Int'l Conf. on Autonomous Agents*, pages 350–351, 1998.
25. Maxsim Tsvetovatyy, Maria Gini, Bamshad Mobasher, and Zbigniew Wieckowski. MAGMA: An agent-based virtual market for electronic commerce. *Journal of Applied Artificial Intelligence*, 11(6):501–524, 1997.
26. Michael P. Wellman and Peter R. Wurman. Market-aware agents for a multiagent world. *Robotics and Autonomous Systems*, 24:115–125, 1998.
27. Peter R. Wurman, Michael P. Wellman, and William E. Walsh. The Michigan Internet AuctionBot: A configurable auction server for human and software agents. In *Second Int'l Conf. on Autonomous Agents*, May 1998.

Resource Allocation Using Sequential Auctions*

Craig Boutilier[1], Moisés Goldszmidt[2], Claire Monteleoni[2], and Bikash Sabata[2]

[1] Dept. of Computer Science University of Toronto
Toronto, ON, M5S 3H5, Canada
cebly@cs.utoronto.ca
[2] Dept. of Computer Science Stanford University
Stanford, CA 94305
{moises,cmontel,sabata}@robotics.stanford.edu

Abstract. Market-based mechanisms such as auctions are being studied as an appropriate means for resource allocation in distributed and multiagent decision problems. When agents value resources in combination rather than in isolation, one generally relies on *combinatorial auctions* where agents bid for resource bundles, or *simultaneous auctions* for all resources. We develop a different model, where agents bid for required resources *sequentially*. This model has the advantage that it can be applied in settings where combinatorial and simultaneous models are infeasible (e.g., when resources are made available at different points in time by different parties), as well as certain benefits in settings where combinatorial models are applicable. We develop a dynamic programming model for agents to compute *bidding policies* based on estimated distributions over prices. We also describe how these distributions are updated to provide a learning model for bidding behavior.

1 Introduction

A great deal of attention has been paid to the development of appropriate models and protocols for the interaction of agents in distributed and multiagent systems (MASs). Often agents need access to specific resources to pursue their objectives, but the needs of one agent may conflict with those of another. A number of market-based approaches have been proposed as a means to deal with the resource allocation and related problems in MASs [5, 21].

Of particular interest are *auction mechanisms*, where each agent bids for a resource according to some protocol, and the allocation and price for the resource are determined by specific rules [13]. Auctions have a number of desirable properties as a means for coordinating activities, including minimizing the communication between agents and, in some cases, guaranteeing Pareto efficient outcomes [13, 21].

An agent often requires several resources before pursuing a particular course of action. Obtaining one resource without another—for example, being allocated trucks without fuel or drivers, or processing time on a machine without skilled labor to operate

---

* Parts of this paper appeared in C. Boutilier, M. Goldszmidt, B. Sabata, "Sequential Auctions for the Allocation of Resources with Complementarities," Proc. Sixteenth Intl. Joint Conf. on AI, Stockholm, pp.527–534 (1999).

A. Moukas, C. Sierra, and F. Ygge (Eds.): AMEC'99, LNAI 1788, pp. 131–152, 2000.
© Springer-Verlag Berlin Heidelberg 2000

it—makes that resource worthless. When resources exhibit such *complementarities*, it is unknown whether simple selling mechanisms can lead to efficient outcomes [21, 1]. Moreover, groups of resources are often *substitutable*: obtaining the bundle needed to pursue one course of action can lower the value of obtaining another, or render it worthless. For instance, once trucks and drivers are obtained for transporting material in an optimal fashion, helicopters and pilots lose any value they may have had.

Two methods for dealing with complementarities have been studied: simultaneous auctions for multiple goods [1, 17]; and *combinatorial auctions* in which agents submit bids for *resource bundles* [16, 18, 19, 9, 21]. Specific models sometimes deal (possibly implicitly) with substitution effects, and sometimes not. In this paper, we explore a model that combines features of both simultaneous and combinatorial auctions. Our *sequential auctions model* supposes that the set of resources of interest are auctioned in sequence. Agents bid for resources in a specific, known order, and can choose how much (and whether) to bid for a resource depending on past successes, failures, prices, and so on.

Our model has several advantages over standard combinatorial and simultaneous models. The chief benefit of such a model is that it can be applied in situations where combinatorial and simultaneous models cannot. Specifically, when multiple sellers offer various resources of interest, or when the resources are sold at different points in time, one does not have the luxury of setting up either combinatorial or simultaneous auctions. As such, our model is suitable for agents who are required to interact with multiple suppliers over time. Even in settings where combinatorial models can be applied, there may be some advantages to using a sequential model. Unlike combinatorial models, our model relieves the (computational) burden of determining a final allocation from the seller, effectively distributing computation among the buyers (as in the simultaneous case); note that determining an optimal allocation that maximizes the seller's revenue is NP-hard [18]. Our sequential model also has the advantage that buyers are not required to reveal information about their valuations for specific resource bundles that they do not obtain. Furthermore, it has greater flexibility in that agents can enter and leave the market without forcing recomputation of entire allocations. In contrast to simultaneous models, agents in the sequential model may lessen their exposure. If an agent does not obtain a certain resource early in the sequence, it need not expose itself by bidding on complementary resources occurring later in the sequence. Agents are typically bidding in a state of greater knowledge in the sequential model, at least in later stages; however, in earlier stages agents may have lesser information than they would in a simultaneous model.

One difficulty that arises in the sequential model is how an agent computes bids for individual resources (the same difficulty arises in simultaneous models). An agent has a valuation for a particular resource bundle $b = \{r_1, \cdots, r_k\}$, but has no independent assignment of value to the individual resources.[1] While auction theory can tell us how an agent should bid as a function of its valuation of resource r_i for specific auction mechanisms, in our setting no such valuation exists. If b is worth $v(b)$, how is an agent to "distribute the value" among the resources r_i in order to compute bids?

---

[1] In fact, we will assume that several bundles can be valued, with possible overlap. This accounts for possible substitution effects.

In this paper, we develop a dynamic programming algorithm for doing just this. We assume that each agent has a probabilistic estimate of the size of the maximum bids for each resource (excluding its own). It can then compute a *bidding policy* that maximizes its expected utility, and apply this policy as dictated by its initial endowment. Bids for resources early in the sequence are computed as a function of the odds of being able to obtain their complements and substitutes, while bids for later resources are conditioned on the resources obtained early in the sequence.

We also interested in adaptive bidding behavior, and to this end investigate a *repeated sequential auction model* in which agents repeatedly bid for the same resources over time. We consider the problem of estimating the probability distributions over maximal bids in this repeated scenario. If agents persistently find themselves requiring resources to pursue their aims, we want them to learn which resources they will be able to obtain and which they will not. This is related to recently proposed learning models for auctions [11, 12], though our focus is on learning prices and the effect this has on the valuation of individual resources in bundles.

The problem we study is part of a more general research program designed to study the impact of specific resource allocation schemes on the solution of sequential multiagent decision problems. We motivate the problem studied here as follows. We suppose that a number of agents have certain tasks and objectives to pursue, and for any objective there may exist a number of potential courses of action that are more or less suitable. For instance, an agent may construct a policy for a Markov decision process [15, 2], from which it can determine the value of various courses of action, their likelihood of success, and so on. Any specific course of action will require certain resources, say, bundle b^k, whose value can be determined as a function of the expected value of that course of action (and the expected value of alternative courses of action). As such, we suppose each bundle b^k has an associated value $v(b^k)$ and that the agent will use only one bundle (the one associated with the highest-valued course of action among those bundles it possesses). It is from these valuations that the agent must determine its bidding policy for individual resources. This is the problem considered here.

Ultimately, the decision problem we hope to study is far more complex. Determining appropriate courses of action will depend on perceived probability of obtaining requisite resources, uncertainty in that course of action, alternatives available and so on. We envision very sophisticated reasoning emerging regarding the interaction bidding behavior and "base-level" action choice (in the MDP), such as taking a few critical steps along a specific course of action before deciding to enter the market for the corresponding resources (e.g., perhaps because this policy is fraught with uncertainty). We also foresee interesting interactions with other coordination and communication protocols.

In Section 2 we describe the basic sequential bidding model. We note a number of dimensions along which our basic model can vary, though we will focus only on specific instantiations of the model for expository reasons. We describe our dynamic programming model for constructing bidding policies in Section 3. We also describe the motivation for using the specific model proposed here instead of using explicit equilibrium computation. We discuss *repeated* sequential auctions in Section 4, focusing on the problem of highest-bid estimation. In Section 5 we describe some preliminary experimental results. These reflect the impact that different prior beliefs and different degrees of contention have on the dynamics of multi-round auctions and the quality of the resulting allocations over time. We conclude in Section 6 with discussion of future research directions.

While bidding strategies for sequential auctions would seem to be an issue worthy of study, there appears to have been little research focused on this issue. What work exists (see, e.g., [8, 10]) tends to focus on the seller's point of view—for example, will simultaneous or sequential sales maximize revenue—and does not address the types of complementarities we consider here. Generally, existing work assumes that single items are of interest to the buyer.

2   Basic Model

We assume we have a finite collection of agents, all of whom require resources from a pool of n resources $R = \{r_1, \cdots, r_n\}$. We denote by R^t the subset $\{r_1, \cdots, r_t\}, t \leq n$, with $R^0 = \emptyset$ by convention. We describe the quantities relevant to a specific agent a below, assuming that these quantities are defined for each agent. Agent a can use exactly one bundle $b^i = \{r^i_1, \cdots, r^i_{|b^i|}\}$ of resources from a set of k *possible bundles*: $B = \{b^1, \cdots, b^k\}$. We denote by $U(a) = \cup B$ the set of *useful resources* for our agent.

Agent a has a positive valuation $v(b^i)$ for each resource bundle $b^i \in B$. Suppose the *holdings* of a, $H(a) \subseteq U(a)$, are those resources it is able to obtain. The value of these holdings is given by $v(H(a)) = \max\{v(b^i) : b^i \subseteq H(a)\}$; that is, the agent will be able to use the resource bundle with maximal value from among those it holds in entirety, with the others going unused. This is consistent with our interpretation given in Section 1 where resource bundles correspond to alternative plans for achieving some objective (though other value combinators can be accommodated).

The resources will be auctioned sequentially in a commonly known order: without loss of generality, we assume that this ordering is $r_1, r_2, \cdots, r_n$. We use A_i to denote the auction for r_i. We refer to the sequence of auctions $A_1, A_2, \cdots, A_n$ as a *round* of auctions. There may be a single round, some (definite or indefinite) finite numbers of rounds, or an infinite number of rounds.

Supposing for the moment only one round, we assume that agent a is given an initial endowment e which it can use to obtain resources. At the end of the round, a has holdings $H(a)$ and d dollars remaining from its endowment.[2] We assume that the utility of being in such a state at the end of the round is given by $v(H(a)) + f(d)$, where f is some function attaching utility to the unused portion of the endowment. Other utility functions could be considered within this framework.

There are a wide range of options one could consider when instantiating this framework. We define a specific model here, but list the options that could be explored. We develop the algorithms in this paper for the specific model, but where appropriate, indicate how they should be modified for other design choices. The main design choices are:

---

[2] If speculation or reselling is allowed, there is the possibility that $d > e$, depending on the interaction protocols we allow. We will mention this possibility below, but we will examine only protocols that disallow it.

- What auction mechanism is used for the auctions A_i?
- What rules are instituted for reselling or speculation?
- What information is revealed to the agents? When?
- What information do agents have when a round begins?

We assume that the individual auctions will be first-price, sealed-bid—each agent will provide a single bid and the highest bidder will be awarded the resource for the price bid. We adopt this model because of the ease with which it fits with our approach to bid computation; however, we believe our model could be adapted for other auction protocols. We also assume that bids are discrete (integer-valued); but we do describe the appropriate amendments to deal with continuous bids. Agents, once obtaining a resource, cannot resell that resource to another agent. This, of course, means that an agent may obtain one resource r_i, but later be unable to obtain a complementary resource r_{i+k}, essentially being "stuck" with a useless resource r_i. We do this primarily for simplicity, though in certain settings this assumption may be realistic. We are currently exploring more sophisticated models where agents can "put back" resources for re-auctioning, or possibly resell resources directly to other agents.

Each agent is told the winning price at the end of the each auction (and whether it was the winner). We could suppose that no information (other than winning or losing) is provided, that the distribution over bids is announced, or that the bids of specific individuals are made public; our assumption seems compatible with the first-price, sealed-bid model. However, different information about possible bids would influence the belief update method we describe in Section 4.

Finally, agent a believes that the highest bid that will be made for resource r_i, excluding any bid that a might itself offer, is drawn from some unknown distribution $\overline{Pr}^i$. Because bids are integer-valued, this unknown distribution is a multinomial over a non-negative, bounded range of integers.[3] To represent a's uncertainty over the parameters of this distribution, we assume a has a prior probability distribution Pr^i over the space of bid distributions. Agent a models Pr^i as a Dirichlet distribution with parameters $\beta_0^i, \cdots, \beta_{m_i}^i$ [6], where m_i is the (estimated) maximum possible bid for r_i. We elaborate on this probability model in Sections 3 and 4.

We make two remarks on this model. First, if the space of possible bids is continuous, a suitable continuous PDF (e.g., Gaussian) could be used to model bid distributions and the uncertainty about the parameters of this PDF. More questionable is the implicit assumption that bids for different resources are uncorrelated. By having distributions Pr^i rather than a joint distribution over *all* bids, agent a is reasoning as if the bids for different resources are independent. When resources exhibit complementarities, this is unlikely to be the case. For instance, if someone bids up the price of some resource r_i (e.g., trucks), they may subsequently bid up the price of complementary resource r_j (e.g., fuel or drivers). If agent a does not admit a model that can capture such correlations, it may make poor bids for certain resources. Again, we make this assumption primarily for ease of exposition. Admitting correlations does not fundamentally change the nature of the algorithms to follow, though it does raise interesting modeling and computational issues (see Section 4).

---

[3] We assume that a bound can be placed on the highest bid.

3 Computing Bids by Dynamic Programming

In this section we focus on the decisions facing an agent in a single round of auctions. A key decision facing an agent at the start of a round is how much to bid for each resource that makes up part of a useful bundle b_i. In standard single item auctions (e.g., first/second-price, sealed bid) rational agents with an assessment of the valuations of other agents can compute bids with maximum expected utility [13]. For example, in first-price, sealed bid auctions, an agent should bid an amount below its true valuation, where this amount is given by its beliefs about the valuations of others.

Unfortunately, the same reasoning cannot be applied to our sequential setting, since individual resources cannot be assessed a well-defined valuation. For instance, if bundle $b^i = \{r_1^i, r_2^i\}$ has valuation $v(b^i)$, how should agent a apportion this value over the two resources? Intuitively, if there is a greater demand for r_1^i, a larger "portion" of the value should be allotted for bidding in the first auction rather than the second. If the agent fails to obtain r_1^i, the value of r_2^i goes to zero (ignoring other bundles). In contrast, should a obtain r_1^i, it is likely that the agent should offer a substantial bid for r_2^i, approaching the valuation $v(b^i)$, since the price paid for r_1^i is essentially a "sunk cost." Of course, if the agent expects this high price to be required, it should probably not have bid for r_1^i in the first place. Finally, the interaction with other bundles requires the agent to reason about the relative likelihood of obtaining any specific bundle for an acceptable price, and to focus attention on the most promising bundles.

3.1 The Dynamic Programming Model

These considerations suggest that the process by which an agent computes bids should not be one of assigning value to individual resources, but rather one of constructing a *bidding policy* by which its bid for any resource is conditioned on the outcome of events earlier in the round. The sequential nature of the bidding process means that it can be viewed as a standard sequential decision problem under uncertainty. Specifically, the problem faced by agent a can be modeled as a fully observable Markov decision process (MDP) [15, 2]. The computation of an optimal *bidding policy* can be implemented using a standard stochastic dynamic programming algorithm such as value iteration.

We emphasize that agents are computing optimal *bids*, not true valuations for individual resources. Thus issues involving revelation of truthful values for resources are not directly relevant (but see Section 4 on multiple rounds).

We assume the decision problem is broken into $n + 1$ stages, n stages at which bidding decisions must be made, and a terminal stage at the end of the round. We use a time index $0 \leq t \leq n$ to refer to stages—time t refers to the point at which auction A_{t+1} for r_{t+1} is about to begin. The *state* of the decision problem for a specific agent a at time t is given by two variables: $H^t(a) \subseteq R^t$, the subset of resources R^t held by agent a; and d^t, the dollar amount (unspent endowment) available for future bidding. We write $\langle h, d \rangle^t$ to denote the state of a's decision problem at time t. Note that although we could distinguish the state further according to which agents obtained which resources, these distinctions are not relevant to the decision facing a.[4]

---

[4] This is true under the current assumptions, but may not be under different models; see below.

The dynamics of the decision process can be characterized by a's estimated transition distributions. Specifically, assuming that prices are drawn independently from the stationary distributions $\overline{Pr}^i$, agent a can predict the effect of any action (bid) z available to it. If agent a is in state $\langle h, d \rangle^t$ at stage t, it can bid for r_{t+1} with any amount $0 \leq z \leq d^t$ (for convenience we use a bid of 0 to denote nonparticipation). Letting w denote the highest bid of other agents, if a bids z at time t, it will transition to state $\langle h \cup \{r_{t+1}\}, d - z \rangle^{t+1}$ with probability $\overline{Pr}^{t+1}(w < z)$ and to $\langle h, d \rangle^{t+1}$ with $\overline{Pr}^{t+1}(w \geq z)$.[5]

This does not form an MDP *per se*, since a may be uncertain about the true distribution $\overline{Pr}^{t+1}$, having only a Dirichlet distribution $\langle \beta_1^{t+1}, \cdots, \beta_{m_{t+1}}^{t+1} \rangle$ over the possible parameters of $\overline{Pr}^{t+1}$. However, the expectation that the highest bid is w is given by the relative weight of parameter β_w^{t+1}; thus,

$$\mathrm{Pr}^{t+1}(w < z) = \frac{\sum_{i=0}^{z-1} \beta_i^{t+1}}{\sum_{i=0}^{m_{t+1}} \beta_{i+1}^t}$$

While the observation of the true winning bid can cause this estimated probability to change (properly making this a partially observable MDP), the change cannot impact *future* transition probability estimates or decisions: we have assumed that the high bid probabilities are independent. Thus, treating this as a fully observable MDP with transition probabilities given by *expected* transition probabilities is sound.

The final piece of the MDP is a reward function q. We simply associate a reward of zero with all states at stages 0 through $n - 1$, and assign reward $v(h) + f(d)$ to every terminal state $\langle h, d \rangle^n$. A *bidding policy* π is a mapping from states into actions: for each legal state $\langle h, d \rangle^t$, $\pi(\langle h, d \rangle^t) = z$ means that a will bid z for resource r_{t+1}. The *value* $V^\pi(\langle h, d \rangle^t)$ of policy π at any state $\langle h, d \rangle^t$ is the expected reward $E_\pi(q(\langle H(a), d \rangle^n) | \langle h, d \rangle^t)$ obtained by executing π. The expected value of π given the agent's initial state $\langle \emptyset, e \rangle^t$ is simply $V^\pi(\langle \emptyset, e \rangle^t)$. An *optimal bidding policy* is any π that has maximal expected reward at every state. We compute the optimal policy using value iteration [15], defining the value of states at stage t using the value of states at stage $t + 1$. Specifically, we set

$$V(\langle h, d \rangle^n) = v(h) + f(d)$$

and define, for each $t < n$:

$$Q(\langle h, d \rangle^t, z) = \mathrm{Pr}^{t+1}(w < z) \cdot V(\langle h \cup \{r_t\}, d - z \rangle^{t+1})$$
$$+ \mathrm{Pr}^{t+1}(w \geq z) \cdot V(\langle h, d \rangle^{t+1})$$
$$V(\langle h, d \rangle^t) = \max_{z \leq d} Q(\langle h, d \rangle^t, z)$$
$$\pi(\langle h, d \rangle^t) = \arg\max_{z \leq d} Q(\langle h, d \rangle^t, z)$$

---

[5] For expository purposes, the model assumes ties are won. Several rules can be used for ties; none complicate the analysis.

Given that V is defined for all stage $t + 1$ states, $Q(\langle h, d \rangle^t, z)$ denotes the value of bidding z at state $\langle h, d \rangle^t$ and acting optimally thereafter. $V(\langle h, d \rangle^t)$ denotes the optimal value at state $\langle h, d \rangle^t$, while $\pi(\langle h, d \rangle^t)$ is the optimal bid.

Implementing value iteration requires that we enumerate, for each t, all possible stage t states and compute the consequences of every feasible action at that state. This can require substantial computational effort. While linear in the state and action spaces (and in the number of stages n), the state and action spaces themselves are potentially quite large. The number of possible states at stage t could potentially consist of any subset of resources R^t together with any monetary component. The action set at a state with monetary component d has size $d + 1$. Fortunately, we can manage some of this complexity using the following observations: first, a never needs to bid for any resource outside the useful set $U(a)$, so its state space (at stage t) is restricted to subsets of $U^t(a)$; and second, if a resource r_t requires a complementary resource $r_{t'}$, $t' < t$, (that is, all bundles containing r_t also contain $r_{t'}$), then we need never consider a state where a has r_t but not $r_{t'}$.[6] Reducing the impact of the number of possible bids is more difficult. We can certainly restrict the state and action space to dollar values no greater than a's initial endowment e. If the PDF is well-behaved (e.g., concave), pruning is possible: e.g., once the expected value of a larger bids starts to decrease, search for a maximizing bid can be halted.[7]

This dynamic programming model deals with the complementarities and substitutability inherent in our resource model; no special devices are required. Furthermore, it automatically deals with issues such as uncertainty, dynamic valuation, "sunk costs," and so on. Given stationary, uncorrelated bid distributions, the computed policy is optimal.

3.2   Extensions of the Model

While the assumptions underlying our (single-round) model are often reasonable, there are two assumptions that must be relaxed in certain settings: the requirement for discrete bids and the prohibition of reselling or returning resources for resale. We are currently exploring these relaxations.

Continuous bidding models are important for computational reasons. Though money is not truly continuous, the increments that need to be considered generally render explicit value calculations for all discrete bids infeasible. Continuous function maximization and manipulation techniques are often considerably more efficient than discrete enumeration, and approximately optimal "integer" bids can usually be extracted. We are currently exploring certain continuous models, specifically using parameterized bid distributions (such as Gaussian and uniform distributions) and linear utility functions (as described above). The key difficulty in extending value iteration is determining an appropriate value function representation. While the maximization problem (over bids) for a specific state is not difficult, we must represent V^t as a function of the continuous

---

[6] This reasoning extends to arbitrary subset complementarities.

[7] If we move to a continuous action space, the value function representation and maximization problems may become easier to manage for certain well-behaved classes of probability distributions and utility functions (see Section 3.2 and [3]).

state space. This function is linear (in d) at all states where the remaining endowment d is greater than the maximal worthwhile bid. But a different function representation is needed for states with endowment less than the best bid. In [3], we present initial results using piecewise linear representations of continuous value functions. The model and algorithms explored in [3] allow various approximation schemes to be adopted as well, making the computation of policies much more efficient, with often little impact on the quality of the policies produced (and allowing error in expected value to be bounded.)

Reselling may be appropriate in many settings and can allow agents to bid more aggressively with less risk. We are currently developing a simple model in which agents are allowed, at the end of a round, to "put back" resources for re-auction that are not needed (e.g., are not part of the agent's max-valued complete bundle).[8] Several difficulties arise in this setting, including the fact that agents may need to estimate the probability that an unobtained resource may be returned for re-auction.

3.3 Equilibrium Computation

The model described above does not allow for strategic reasoning on the part of the bidding agent. The agent takes the expected prices as given and does not attempt to compute the impact of its bids on the behavior of other agents, how they might estimate its behavior and respond, and so on; that is, no form of equilibrium is computed. Standard models in auction theory generally prescribe bidding strategies that are in Bayes-Nash equilibrium: when each agent has beliefs about the *types* of other agents (i.e., how each agent values the good for sale), and these beliefs are common knowledge, then the agents' bidding policies can be prescribed so that no agent has incentive to change its policy.[9] This, for instance, is the basis for prescribing the well-known strategies for bidding in first and second-price auctions [20].

Our approach is much more "myopic." There are several reasons for adopting such a model rather than a full Bayes-Nash equilibrium model. First, equilibrium computation is often infeasible, especially in a nontrivial sequential, multi-resource setting like ours. Second, the information required on the part of each agent, namely a distribution over the possible types of other agents, is incredibly complex—an agent type in this setting is its set of valuations for *all* resource bundles, making the space of types unmanageable. Finally, the common knowledge assumptions usually required for equilibrium analysis are unlikely to hold in this setting.

We expect that the MDP model described here could be extended to allow for equilibrium computation. Rather than do this, we consider an alternative, adaptive model for bidding in which agents will adjust their estimates of prices—hence their bidding policies—over time. Implicitly, agents learn how others value different resources, and hopefully some type of "equilibrium" will emerge. We turn our attention to this process of adaptation.

---

[8] More complicated models that allow agents to put back resources during the round or resell directly are also possible.

[9] We use *type* here in the sense used in game theory for games with incomplete information [14].

4   Repeated Auctions and Value Estimation

In certain domains, agents will repeatedly need resources drawn from some pool to pursue ongoing objectives. We model this by assuming that the same resource collection is auctioned repeatedly in rounds. While agents could compute a single bidding policy and use it at every round, we would like agents to use the behavior they've observed at earlier rounds to update their policies. Specifically, observed winning prices for resource auctions A_i in the past can be used by an agent to update its estimate of the true distribution Pr^i of high bids for r_i. Its bidding strategy at the next round can be based on the updated distributions.

If each agent updates its bidding policy based on past price observations, the prices observed at earlier rounds may not be reflective of the prices that will obtain at the next round. This means that the agents are learning based on observations drawn from a nonstationary distribution. This setting is common in game theory, where agents react to each others past behavior. Myopic learning models such as *fictitious play* [4] (designed to learn strategy profiles) can be shown to converge to a stationary distribution despite the initial nonstationarity. This type of learning model has been applied to repeated (single-item) auctions and shown to converge [11]. Our model is based on similar intuitions—namely, that learning about prices will eventually converge to an acceptable steady state. Hu and Wellman [12] also develop a related model for price learning in a somewhat different context.

The advantage of a learning model is that agents can come to learn which resources they can realistically obtain and focus their bidding on those. If agents A and B have similar endowments and both equally value having either r_1 or r_2, they may learn over time not to compete for r_1 and r_2; instead they may learn to anticipate (implicitly, through pricing) each other's strategy and (implicitly) coordinate their activities, with one pursuing r_1 and the other r_2. If one agent has a greater endowment than another (e.g., it may have higher priority objectives in a distributed planning environment), the poorer agent should learn that it can't compete and focus on less contentious (and perhaps less valued) resources. Another important feature of learning models is that they can be used to overcome biased or weak prior price assessments.

Given the form of the probabilistic model described in Section 3, an agent can update its estimate of a bid distribution rather easily. Suppose agent a has parameters $\langle \beta_1^t, \cdots, \beta_{m_t}^t \rangle$ that characterize its distribution Pr^t over the true distribution $\overline{\mathrm{Pr}}^t$ of high bids for resource r_t. After auction A_t the winning bid w is announced to each agent.[10] If a fails to win the resource, it should update these Dirichlet parameters by setting β_w^t to $\beta_w^t + 1$; at the next round, its estimate that the highest bid will be w is thus increased. If a wins resource r_t for price z, the only information it gets about the highest bid (excluding its own) is that it is less than z. The Dirichlet parameters can then be updated with an algorithm such as EM [7]. Roughly, the expectation step computes an update of the parameters of the Dirichlet using current estimates to distribute the observation over the parameters $\beta_1^t, \cdots, \beta_{z-1}^t$: each β_j^t ($j < z$) is increased by $\beta_j^t / \sum_{i=0}^{z-1} \beta_i^t$. The maximization step corresponds to the actual update followed by the substitution of these

---

[10] Our model can accommodate both more (e.g., the bids of all agents) and less (e.g., only whether an agent won or lost) revealed information about the auction outcome rather easily.

parameters in Pr. Whereas the EM algorithm requires an iteration of these two steps until convergence, we performed this iteration about 10 times.[11]

In the specific probability model developed here, agents cannot profitably use this updated estimate during the current round. Because prices are assumed independent, learning about one price cannot influence an agent's bidding strategy for other resources.[12] Thus the agent continues to implement the bidding policy computed at the start of the round. The updated bid distributions are used prior to the start of the next round of auctions to compute an new bidding policy.

As mentioned above, the price-independence assumption may be unrealistic. If prices are correlated, the observed price of a resource can impact the estimated price of another resource that will be available later in the round. Agents in this case should revise their bidding policies to reflect this information. Two approaches can be used to deal with correlations. First, agents can simply recompute their bidding policies during a round based on earlier outcomes. An alternative is to model this directly within the MDP itself: this entails making the MDP partially observable, which can cause computational difficulties.

One thing we do not consider is agents acting strategically within a round to influence prices at subsequent rounds. Agents are reasoning "myopically" within a specific round. By formulating multi-round behavior as a sequential problem, we could have agents attempting to manipulate prices for future gain. Our current model does not allow this.

5   Results

We now describe the results of applying this model to some simple resource allocation problems. These illustrate interesting qualitative behavior such as adaptation and coordination. We also explain why such behavior arises. In most examples we describe the "performance" of the model under various initial conditions by measuring the *allocation value* or the *social welfare* of the outcome at a given auction round, and examining how the allocation quality varies as a function of the number of rounds played. Our aim is to show the dynamics of the adaptive bidding behavior in which agents engage.

As mentioned, we distinguish two measures of solution quality: by allocation value, we simply refer to the sum of the values of the complete bundles obtained by all agents; by social welfare, we refer to this allocation value plus the α-discounted value of remaining endowments for each agent. By an optimal allocation for a given problem, we mean the allocation of resources to agents with the highest allocation value. For a given allocation, social welfare will be higher if agents have paid less for their resources. α is set at 0.5 unless stated otherwise. Except in the experiments studying the effects of varying prior beliefs, agents beliefs about expected prices for any fixed good are set to

---

[11] Preliminary experiments showed this to be sufficient.

[12] With correlated prices, an agent could attempt to provide misleading information about its valuation of one resource in order to secure a later resource at a cheaper price. This type of deception, studied for identical item auctions in [10], cannot arise within a single round in our current model, even if strategic reasoning is used.

be a slightly increasing linear function of price (with slope $1/30$. We will refer to this later as "nearly-uniform priors."

We often show results for a specific problem instance to clearly illustrate the dynamics of the agents' behavior in repeated auctions; we also describe aggregate behavior over a set of randomly drawn problems occasionally as well. However, we sometimes describe the procedure by which a "random" problem is drawn when showing the results for one problem instance—in such cases, the instance described illustrates "typical" behavior for problems drawn from this class.[13]

5.1 Adaptation

In this section, we describe a series of examples demonstrating the adaptive nature of agent bidding behavior over multiple auction rounds. Agents will often learn to bid in such a way that good or optimal allocations are obtained, and tend to learn to increase social welfare by lowering the prices they pay.

Example 1. This simple, handcrafted, two-agent example illustrates the basic adaptation of the agents during the repeated rounds of the auction. There are two agents whose optimal bundles are disjoint: a_1 requires $b_1^1 = \{r_1, r_3\}$ (with value 20) or $b_2^1 = \{r_4, r_5, r_6\}$ (value 30), while a_2 requires $b_1^2 = \{r_2, r_3\}$ (value 20) or $b_2^2 = \{r_7, r_8, r_9\}$ (value 30). Initially, because of the ordering of the auctions, both agents focus on the smaller (and lower-valued) bundles. At the first round, a_1 obtains b_1^1, while a_2 gets "stuck" with r_2, since a_1 outbid it for r_3. The next round sees a_2 bid less for r_2, and more for r_3 (outbidding a_1). Since it obtains b_1^2, because of its prior belief about the bid needed to win b_2^2, it does not attempt to bid for b_2^2. But without b_1^1, and with its estimated prices for resources in b_2^1 lowered, a_1 now bids for and gets b_2^1 (its optimal bundle). Up to the fourteenth round, one of the agents gets its best bundle and the other its second best. At the fourteenth round, each gets its best bundle, and after the sixteenth round the optimal allocation (the one with maximal allocation value) is reached each time: the agents (more or less) "realize" that they need not compete. The agents do "hedge their bets" and still keep bidding for resources r_1, r_2 and r_3. They also offer fairly high bids for the nonconflicting resources, though these bids are reduced over time. Note that had the agents received more detailed information about the prices offered by the other agents for resources it won in a given round (e.g., if the auctions had been open-cry), the prices for nonconflicting resources would have been lower (and lowered more quickly).

This first example shows that optimal allocations will emerge when agents are not in direct competition. It also illustrates the following general behavioral phenomena that occur in almost all examples:

1. Agents tend to bid more aggressively (initially) for resources in bundles of smaller size, since the odds of getting all resources in a larger bundle are lower.
2. Agents tend to bid more aggressively for resources that occur later in the sequence. Once an agent obtains all resources in a bundle but one, the last resource is very

---

[13] The reason for focusing on individual instances is to illustrate phenomena that are present in individual instances that would be blurred by averaging a number of instances.

valuable (for example, in round 16 above, a_1 obtains b_2^1 by paying 1 for r_4 and r_5, and 27 for r_6).

3. Agents tend to initially offer high bids for certain resources, and gradually lower their bids over time (realizing slowly that there is no competition). For example, a_1 reduces its bid for r_6 to 26 only at round 36. This is a consequence of the simple priors and belief update rules we use, and the lack of information it obtains when it wins the resource consistently: it is not told what the next highest bid is (it is zero), and can only conclude that it was less than 27, making belief update slow. The equivalent sample size of our priors also makes adjustment somewhat slow. Domain-specific (more accurate) priors, or the use of exponential decay (or finite histories) in price-estimation, would alleviate much of this slowness of response.

Example 2. In this example, we illustrate adaptation under conditions of resource contention. There 100 resources and ten agents, each with one identical bundle and a randomly drawn number of additional bundles (drawn from the normal distribution $N(1,1)$ and rounded to the nearest non-negative integer). Each bundle, including that common to all agents, has two resources (with those in the extra bundles drawn uniformly from the set of resources). The problem exhibits extreme contention since the highest-valued bundle for each agent is the common bundle. Figure 1 illustrates the dynamics of a particular "typical" run, showing both allocation value and social welfare as a function of the auction round. The optimal allocation for the specific example has value 146: the agents very quickly reach an allocation value that is very near optimal. However, even once this allocation is reached, the agents will slowly lower the prices they bid for the resources they obtain, as illustrated by the fact that social welfare steadily increases. This is due to the fact that each agent, when it wins its good, adjusts its price estimate to reflect the fact that the highest bid among all other agents was lower than its own. Although this is not illustrated here, this behavior will typically result in deviation from the optimal allocation: once prices are lowered sufficiently, other agents can "sneak in" and win a resource they had given up on. However, the resulting cycles of behavior become exceedingly long, since agents' price beliefs are harder to overturn later in the sequence of rounds.

Example 3. Because agents are acting optimally with respect to their own value functions—and are not interested in contributing to an optimal allocation or performing any strategic reasoning—an agent may change its behavior once an optimal allocation is reached in order to further its own interests. Apart from generally leading the final allocation away from optimality, this behavior can often lead to a worse outcome for the deviating agent, since a change in bid can cause other agents to change their behavior at auctions occuring later in the round (this is a consequence of the lack of strategic reasoning). This can lead to cycling phenomenon as illustrated in this example, involving ten agents and 24 resources. Each agent has a single highest-valued bundle, determined as follows: the normal distribution $N(12, 2.5)$ is sampled four times, with the nearest "resource" (labeled 1–24) added to the bundle (hence the bundle has four resources). This procedure produces bundles for each of the ten agents that are likely to exhibit a fair amount of contention. The agents also receive a random number of additional bundles drawn from $N(2, 1)$ and a number of resources in each drawn from $N(4, 1)$ (with the specific resources drawn uniformly).

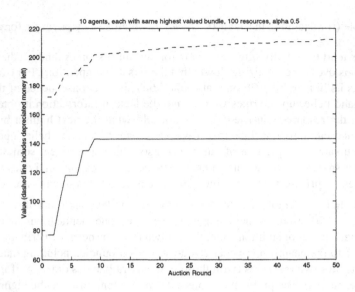

Fig. 1. Adaptive behavior over 50 auction rounds with direct competition for the highest-valued bundle (10 agents, 100 resources)

Figure 2 shows the behavior (with respect to allocation value) of one typical example produced by the above procedure. We see cycling occur for quite some time, until sometime after round 60 when the system seems to converge on the optimal allocation (with value 68). This example shows that, even if there is some contention, if agents have lower-valued bundles with resources that are less contentious, they will adapt their bidding behavior to obtain these bundles. As a consequence, good—or even optimal—allocations generally emerge eventually.

5.2 Prior Beliefs

The next series of examples explore the effects that prior beliefs have on the final allocations attained, how soon the system converges, and the value a single agent receives over auction rounds. Specifically, we wish to examine the effect of having some or all of the agents possess as prior beliefs those beliefs about prices they "would have learned" had they been given our nearly-uniform priors and allowed to learn these prices.

The examples in this section involve ten agents and 24 resources: each agent has a highest-valued bundle plus an average of two additional bundles; each bundle has an average of four resources; and the highest-valued bundle is drawn from a normal distribution of resources. Thus the set-up is much the same as in the preceding experiment. Each of the examples was run using two different normal distributions for producing the highest-valued bundles: a "more contentious" distribution with $\sigma = 1.5$, and a "less contentious" distribution with $\sigma = 2.5$. For all agents, we set $\alpha = 0.1$ as the discount rate for remaining endowment.

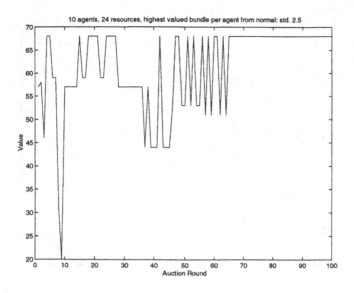

Fig. 2. Widely varying behavior over 100 auction rounds with high contention (10 agents, 24 resources)

Example 4. In the first experiment, we set the priors of all but one agent to be nearly uniform. The distinguished agent's priors were set by having its β-parameters set to reflect the same *relative weight* as those the agent reached by learning—starting from nearly-uniform priors—during a calibration run of 100 sequential auction rounds (in an otherwise identical setup). In other words, the distinguished agent has prior beliefs about expected prices that match those it would have learned had it been given the same priors as everyone else. One difference is that the magnitude of the distinguished agent's β-parameters are reduced so that its priors are of comparable equivalent sample size with the priors of the other (nearly uniform) agents. This ensures that all agents are "equally adaptive." The calibration run is also used as a control run against which to compare allocation quality.

For each of the two setups ($\sigma = 1.5$ and $\sigma = 2.5$), tens runs were performed, with each of the ten agents being the distinguished agent in one run. Over these 20 runs, the distinguished agent reached the value it obtained in the control run 55% of the time, doing worse 45% of the time. Hence the knowledge gained from the calibration run seems to have little positive impact on an agent's performance. This is hardly surprising for two reasons. First, though the agent's initial behavior is determined largely by its priors, these priors will be overwhelmed rather quickly by contrary evidence about actual bids. As a result, the effect on behavior of these priors is transient. Second, its priors change its behavior, which can influence the behavior of the other agents. This means that what it learned in the calibration run need not be relevant to the current run.

The allocation value (for all agents) was, on average, lower than in the corresponding control runs. Figure 3 shows behavior in one instance of the setup with $\sigma = 1.5$,

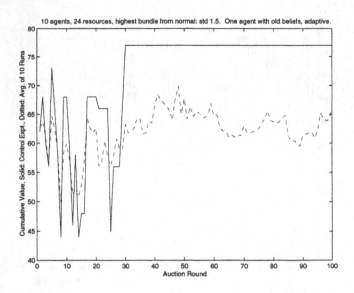

Fig. 3. The effect of fixing "previously learned" prior beliefs in a single highly-adaptive agent over 100 auction rounds with high contention (10 agents, 24 resources).

illustrating the average (over the ten runs) allocation value over time in both the control and experimental cases. The value obtained when a distinguished agent tries to "anticipate" learned prices is significantly lower than in the case where it retains a nearly-uniform prior. This is also true for $\sigma = 2.5$.

Example 5. This example is identical to the previous example with one exception: the distinguished agent's priors are *exactly* those beliefs it learned during the calibration run of 100 auction rounds. Specifically, the β-parameters are not reweighted to give the agent an equivalent sample size identical to the other agents; rather they reflect its experience over the 100 training rounds. This means that its beliefs are held quite strongly, and individual price observations will not have as strong an influence on its beliefs as in the earlier example; in other words, the distinguished agent is not very adaptive. In this setting, the distinguished agent reaches the same value 95% of the time. One reason for this may be that, since the agent's beliefs are strong, it will consistently offer the same bids, thus causing other agents to mold their behavior to its own.

Example 6. This example is similar to the previous one; in each run we have eight of the ten agents having prior beliefs dictated by an earlier calibration run of 100 rounds, while the remaining two agents have nearly-uniform priors. Ten runs were constructed for each of $\sigma = 1.5$ and $\sigma = 2.5$, with a different pair of agents starting with nearly-uniform priors in each run. In 95% of the runs, the agents that started with the nearly-uniform priors ended with the same value as in the corresponding control run, and generally reached this value more quickly. This would appear to be a result of the fact that the system is largely stable due to the majority of agents having stable beliefs. Hence, the two adaptive agents will quickly learn the prices that were "set" at the end of the control round and adapt their behavior. Though the adaptive agents might conceivably use the stationarity of the other agents to their advantage, the fact that the calibration run "converged" means that they can gain no advantage by deviating from their ealier behavior in the—otherwise they would have done so in the control round.

Since there are a large number of agents playing using the beliefs established in the calibration run (which reached an optimal allocation), it is not surprising that near-optimal allocations are reached much earlier than in the control run. Figure 4 shows the allocation value of the control experiment and the average allocation value attained in the ten runs using $\sigma = 1.5$.

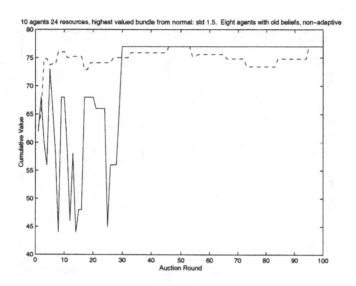

Fig. 4. The effect of fixing "previously learned" prior beliefs in a majority of highly-nonadaptive agents over 100 auction rounds with high contention (10 agents, 24 resources).

5.3 Contention

In this section we present several examples illustrating the impact of resource contention, including how endowment size (or relative value of money) impacts the resolution of resources, and how our approach behaves in a case where a price equilibrium fails to exist due to resource contention.

Example 7. To examine the impact of various levels of resource contention, we ran seven experiments in the expected level of contention was varied. We have ten agents, 30 resources, a mean of three bundles per agent, a mean of four resources per bundle, all resources drawn uniformly to be placed in all but the highest-valued bundle. The highest valued bundle was determined using a normal distribution over resources, as described above; but in each of the seven runs, σ varied, ranging from 1 (relatively high odds of contention) to 7 relatively low odds of contention (all other bundles were held constant throughout the experiment). Remaining endowment is valued at $0.1d$ ($\alpha = 0.1$). Figure 5 shows the average fraction of optimal allocation value attained during the previous ten rounds over 100 rounds. (with the average and error bars based on the seven different runs). After 70 rounds, the allocation attained is at least 82% of the optimal value. Even with the high variance across different levels of contention, the worst-case behavior is still quite good, with 73–75% of optimal being attained even at early stages. Thus, even across varying levels of contention, the system tends to see its performance improve over time.

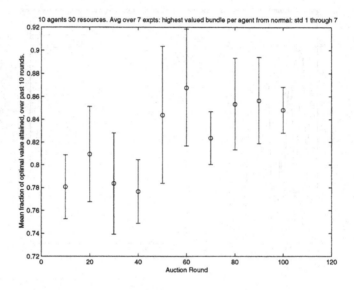

Fig. 5. Fraction of Optimal Value obtained in past 10 rounds: 10 agents, 30 resources. The error bars show the variance over the 7 experiments.

Example 8. An interesting phenomenon emerges in a two-agent example of [21] that has no price equilibrium: assume resources r_1, r_2, with a_1 valuing bundle $\{r_1, r_2\}$ at 6, and a_2 valuing either of r_1, r_2 at 4. The agents have equal endowments. Though there is no price equilibrium, in our adaptive protocol a_2 wins one of its bundles much more frequently than a_1. It bids for r_1, and if it wins it need not bid for r_2; if it loses it can outbid a_1 for r_2 (since a_1 has paid for r_1). a_2 experiments with r_1 and wins it occasionally. a_2 gradually lowers its bid for r_2 and, since it does not model correlations in prices, occasionally loses r_2, allowing a_1 to get both r_1 and r_2. When this occurs, a_2 will quickly raise its bids and win one of the resources again. By modeling price correlations, or estimating the requirements of a_1, agent a_2 *could* guarantee that it obtains one of its resources (see Section 6).

Example 9. To observe the impact of endowment on the agents behavior we performed the following experiment. We have 3 resources and 2 agents, each valuing $\{r_1, r_2\}$ at 10 and r_3 at 5, but differing in initial endowment: a_1 begins with 6, a_2 with 8. Initially, a_1 gets the first (higher-valued) bundle (at prices 2 and 5) and a_2 the second (at price 3). By the fourth round, a_2 realizes that it can win r_1 with bids of 3 and 5. It spends 8 on $\{r_1, r_2\}$, leaving a_1 to bid 4 for r_3. These prices persist, with a_2 not bidding on r_3 and a_2 eventually not bidding on r_1 or r_2. This illustrates that agents with larger endowments (or less relative value for money compared to bundles) have greater odds of obtaining their most important bundles, leaving "poorer" agents to get what is left.[14]

We also studied the bidding behavior on randomly generated allocation problems. Here we describe two sets of experiments. In problem set Ps1, five allocation problems were randomly generated with the following characteristics: four agents are competing for 12 resources with an initial endowment of 30 each; each agent has a random number of needed bundles (normally distributed with mean 4 and s.d. 1); each bundle contains a random number of resources (normally distributed with mean 3 and s.d. 1, where the resources are themselves drawn uniformly from the set of 12); and the value of each bundle is random (normally distributed with mean 16 and s.d. 3). Problem set Ps2 is identical except there are five agents and the mean number of resources per bundles is 4: hence problems in Ps2 are more constrained, with more competition among the agents. Typical behavior for one trial from Ps2 (the more constrained problem set) is shown

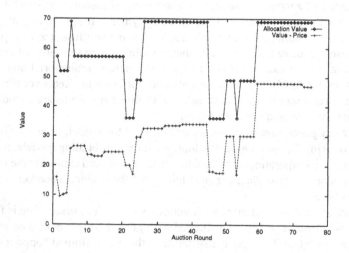

Fig. 6. Sample Behavior over 75 Auction Rounds: 5 agents (optimal allocation has value 69)

in Figure 6, which plots the the value of the allocations obtained at each round, as well as the collective surplus. The agents find good allocations in this problem, reaching the

---

[14] This last property is useful for teams if agents with higher priority objectives are given larger endowments.

(socially) optimal allocation (with value 69) at many of the rounds. On average, over the 75 rounds, the allocation obtained has value 59 (85% of optimal). Note that once the agents "find" a good allocation, they may not stick with it—generally such allocations are not in equilibrium in the sequential game induced by a round of auctions. At the very least, agents have a tendency to attempt to lower the prices they bid after consistently winning a good, due to the lack of information about what other agents bid and how they update their beliefs (as mentioned above). This itself can cause some instability. The greater cause of instability however is the fact that a socially optimal allocation does not generally make self-interested agents happy.

Other trials illustrate similar qualitative behavior. When comparing Ps1 (the less constrained problem set) to Ps2 (the more constrained), we find that the allocations in Ps1 have value that is, on average, within 87% of the optimal, while with Ps2, allocations are within 80% of optimal. This suggests that for less constrained problems, sequential auctions among self-interested agents can lead to allocations with higher social welfare value. Given that agents "discover" many different allocations, one might view sequential auctions as a heuristic search mechanism for combinatorial auctions. [15] However, we emphasize that the main goal of our model is to compute bidding policies when combinatorial and simultaneous auctions are not possible.

6   Concluding Remarks

We have described a model for sequential auctioning of resources that exhibit complementarities for different agents and described a dynamic programming algorithm for the computation of optimal bidding policies. We have also illustrated how price learning can be used to allow agents to adapt their bidding policies to those of other agents. The sequential model can be applied in settings where combinatorial and simultaneous models are infeasible (e.g., when agents enter or leave markets over time, or when agents require resources from multiple sellers). Preliminary results are encouraging and suggest that desirable behavior often emerges.

We have suggested several possible extensions of the model, some of which we are currently exploring. These include developing continuous bidding models, models with reselling/return, incorporating correlated bid distributions and exploring the interactions between decision theoretic planning and bidding for the resources needed to implement plans and policies.

There are several more immediate directions we hope to pursue. One is the investigation of models where prices are estimated with greater weight placed on more recent prices. Along with correlated price distributions, the use of limited "opponent" models may be helpful: by identifying which agents tend to need which resources, a bidder can make more informed decisions. Additional revealed information about specific auctions (such as who bid what amount) could also lead to more informed decisions. This information may be appropriate in team situations, where distributed decision makers are not directly in competition.

Apart from such myopic mechanisms, we would also like to develop a Bayes-Nash equilibrium formulation of the sequential model, and study the extent to which myopic

---

[15] This is reminiscent of the mechanism suggested in [9].

models like our simple learning scheme approximate it. The conditions under which our model converges to interesting allocations (socially optimal allocations, equilibria, etc.) is also worthy of exploration. Other avenues to be considered are the development of different auction ordering heuristics to maximize social welfare, seller's revenue or other objective criteria; and the development of generalization methods to speed up dynamic programming. We are also integrating the sequential auction model for resource allocation into the general planning context described in Section 1.

Acknowledgments

The authors acknowledge partial support from the DARPA Co-ABS program (through Stanford University contract F30602-98-C-0214). Bikash Sabata was funded in part by DARPA through the SPAWARSYSCEN under Contract Number N66001-97-C-8525. Craig Boutilier was partially supported by NSERC Research Grant OGP0121843. Thanks to Bill Walsh, Piero La Mura, Tuomas Sandholm, Yoav Shoham and Mike Wellman for their helpful comments, suggestions and pointers to relevant literature.

References

1. Sushil Bikhchandani and John W. Mamer. Competitive equilibria in and exchange economy with indivisibilities. *Journal of Economic Theory*, 74:385–413, 1997.
2. Craig Boutilier, Thomas Dean, and Steve Hanks. Decision theoretic planning: Structural assumptions and computational leverage. *Journal of Artificial Intelligence Research*, 11:1–94, 1998.
3. Craig Boutilier, Moisés Goldszmidt, and Bikash Sabata. Continuous value function approximation for sequential bidding policies. In *Proceedings of the Fifteenth Conference on Uncertainty in Artificial Intelligence*, pages 81–89, Stockholm, 1999.
4. George W. Brown. Iterative solution of games by fictitious play. In T. C. Koopmans, editor, *Activity Analysis of Production and Allocation*. Wiley, New York, 1951.
5. Scott Clearwater, editor. *Market-based Control: A Paradigm for Distributed Resource Allocation*. World Scientific, San Mateo, 1995.
6. Morris H. Degroot. *Probability and Statistics*. Addison-Wesley, New York, 1986.
7. A. P. Dempster, N. M. Laird, and D. B. Rubin. Maximum likelihood from incomplete data via the EM algorithm. *Journal of the Royal Statistical Society*, B 39:1–39, 1977.
8. Richard Engelbrecht-Wiggans and Robert J. Weber. A sequential auction involving assymetrically informed bidders. *International Journal of Game Theory*, 12:123–127, 1983.
9. Yuzo Fujisima, Kevin Leyton-Brown, and Yoav Shoham. Taming the computational complexity of combinatorial auctions. In *Proceedings of the Sixteenth International Joint Conference on Artificial Intelligence*, Stockholm, pages 548–553, 1999.
10. Donald B. Hausch. Multi-object auctions: Sequential vs. simultaneous sales. *Management Science*, 32(12):1599–1610, 1986.
11. Shlomit Hon-Snir, Dov Monderer, and Aner Sela. A learning approach to auctions. *Journal of Economic Theory*, 82(1):65–88, 1998.
12. Junling Hu and Michael P. Wellman. Online learning about other agents in a dynamic multi-agent system. In *Proceedings of the Second International Conference on Autonomous Agents*, Minneapolis, 1998.

13. R. Preston McAfee and John McMillan. Auctions and bidding. *Journal of Economic Literature*, 25:699–738, 1987.
14. Roger B. Myerson. *Game Theory: Analysis of Conflict*. Harvard University Press, Cambridge, 1991.
15. Martin L. Puterman. *Markov Decision Processes: Discrete Stochastic Dynamic Programming*. Wiley, New York, 1994.
16. S. J. Rassenti, V. L. Smith, and R. L. Bulfin. A combinatorial auction mechanism for airport time slot allocation. *Bell Journal of Economics*, 13:402–417, 1982.
17. Michael H. Rothkopf. Bidding in simultaneous auctions with a constraint on exposure. *Operations Research*, 25:620–629, 1977.
18. Michael H. Rothkopf, Aleksander Pekeč, and Ronald M. Harstad. Computationally manageable combinatorial auctions. *Management Science*, 1998. To appear.
19. Tuomas Sandholm. An algorithm for optimal winner determination in combinatorial auctions. In *Proceedings of the Sixteenth International Joint Conference on Artificial Intelligence*, Stockholm, pages 542–547, 1999.
20. William Vickrey. Counterspeculation, auctions, and competitive sealed tenders. *Journal of Finance*, 16(1):8–37, 1961.
21. Michael P. Wellman, William E. Walsh, Peter R. Wurman, and Jeffrey K. MacKie-Mason. Auction protocols for decentralized scheduling. (manuscript), 1998.

Profit-Driven Matching in E-Marketplaces: Trading Composable Commodities

Apostolos Dailianas, Jakka Sairamesh, Vibby Gottemukkala, and Anant Jhingran[1]

IBM T. J. Watson Research
Hawthorne
New York, NY, 10532
{jramesh,vibby}@watson.ibm.com

Abstract. We are witnessing the dawn and emergence of a new breed of businesses over the Internet, such as electronic intermediaries, which are not only reducing search costs, but also aiming to create efficient markets for businesses and consumers to conduct commerce over the Internet. Among these intermediaries, Electronic Marketplaces are emerging to provide value by streamlining commerce among diverse buyers and sellers and creating fair trading environments.

We envision that these E-Marketplaces will play a very significant role in matching buyers and sellers and increasing market efficiency by satisfying a variety of objectives ranging from pure profit maximization to guaranteeing a target market liquidity. In this paper, we consider a specific E-Marketplace for trading soft composable commodities such as bandwidth and application quality of service, where buyers and sellers submit bids and offers to the marketplace to trade bandwidth products. We develop and analyze the performance of novel computationally efficient matching heuristics. The experimental results demonstrate that these heuristics perform as well as the exact computationally intensive matching algorithms.

Keywords: Electronic Marketplaces, Electronic Trading Systems, Trading Models, Trading Objectives, Trading Algorithms, Electronic Commerce Intermediaries, Bandwidth Markets

1 Introduction

The rapid proliferation of the Internet and the low costs of computing and communication are driving businesses to move some or all their commercial transactions over the Internet. Businesses can now reach new markets and increase efficiency in commerce transactions and day-to-day business. In the coming years, we envision that these and other factors will cause many types of electronic intermediaries to emerge and provide value added services to businesses conducting commerce by streamlining the process of searching, purchasing, ordering and delivery. Among these intermediaries, E-Marketplaces are envisioned to become

A.Moukas, C.Sierra, F.Ygge (Eds.): AMEC'99, LNAI 1788, pp.153-179, 2000.
© Springer-Verlag Berlin Heidelberg 2000

the main focal trading places, where complex products/services will be traded[2, 4, 9].

In the recent years, several E-Marketplaces have already started emerging in various consumer retail and industrial sectors, providing some or all of the commerce functions such as seller product catalogs, searching, matchmaking, negotiation and finally settlement and fulfillment. In addition, they are providing mechanisms for third party intermediaries to participate in the fulfillment of commerce transactions, enforcing the regulatory policies, and auditing the transactions[1, 2, 4, 9]. There is already strong evidence of E-Marketplaces evolving in various industries such as telecommunications (bandwidth markets) [11, 12], steel, energy[15], computer and electronic components[13, 14], bio-chemicals, pharmaceuticals[16], supply chain management, financial products, insurance, automobile, and consumer retail.

There are various ways to define and characterize physical and electronic marketplaces. These definitions will evolve with the roles the marketplaces will play in the electronic world. The business models of the entities controlling them will have an impact on the kind of value they provide to their participants, and the kinds of role they play in facilitating commerce transactions. We define E-Marketplaces as electronic intermediaries that bring buyers, sellers and other intermediaries together, and perform the following: (i) organize the seller product information; (ii) organize the buyer needs and preferences; (iii) facilitate commerce transactions between the buyers and sellers (search, matchmaking, negotiation, etc.); and (iv) provide a flexible environment for multiple intermediaries to participate in the fulfillment of the commerce transactions.

We conjecture that unlike traditional non-profit physical Marketplaces, a large number of profit oriented E-Marketplaces will emerge, where profit will be made from value added services offered to the participants of the E-Marketplaces. We envision that E-Marketplaces will become viable businesses, and the revenue for these marketplaces could come from a combination of registration fees, advertising fees, transaction commission fees and usage, and revenue from bid-ask spreads in high volume markets. We envision that E-Marketplaces will be networked for business reasons and for reasons of efficiency in trading products and services. These networks of E-Marketplaces will provide a combined value and one-stop shopping to a wide variety of buyers. With increasing number of products and services sold over the Internet, E-Marketplaces will act as brokers/dealers on behalf of buyers and sellers and they will aggregate products and services to maximize profit.

In this paper, we focus on marketplaces for bandwidth in a network services economy that consists primarily of three types of players: Backbone ISPs or NSPs who offer backbone services to local ISPs and consumers (businesses); local ISPs who offer Internet access services to buyers (homes and small businesses)[1]; consumers who select ISPs (local or backbone) based on services offerings, reputation, quality and price. With the emerging differentiated services over the

---

[1] Large business have enough resources to connect directly to backbone ISPs for business reasons and critical performance needs.

Internet, a whole range of network qualities of service will be offered to support a variety of applications, and this will create a need for a marketplace to match the buyers with the right set of suppliers.

The current Internet houses about 5000 ISPs, about 40 of which are backbone ISPs offering access services to various consumer types. In the past the backbone ISPs were connected via public access points (public NAPs), which provided trusted cross-over points for network traffic. Recently, Marketplaces have emerged by establishing connectivity and peer-to-peer networking among the backbone ISPs. In such a marketplace each ISP would advertise its services across the Internet to attract potential customers (whether they are homes, businesses or other ISPs). With multiple providers offering a multitude of qualities of services, it is natural for intermediaries to find a niche in matching the buyer application QoS requirements to the offerings of the sellers[6].

Bandwidth Marketplaces such as Band-X[12] and Rate-X[11] offer both a software exchange and a facilities exchange. Through the software exchange the trading entities (buyers and sellers) place bids and offers. Once the match is done by the marketplace, the contracts are transfered to the hardware exchange so that buyer packet traffic is routed along the seller links through the facilities exchange. With the emergence of enabling technologies for setting up virtual paths and private networks in real-time (dynamic VPNs and SVCs[2]), we envision more of these bandwidth marketplaces to emerge, offering services to trade and switch bandwidth. Bandwidth marketplaces will find a niche in providing various kinds of bandwidth services such as futures contracts (e.g., reserving bandwidth in the future) on network services and other value added services.

In this paper, we examine a few of the potential roles E-Marketplaces can play, and demonstrate their computational feasibility and their usefulness. Section 2 presents an architecture of a distributed E-Marketplace for trading soft and physical goods and services, and describes the economic model assumptions for the operation of the marketplace. Section 3 presents the trading model in detail. In this section, we also present the various objectives that the marketplace is attempting to satisfy. Section 4 presents the heuristics developed to satisfy the objectives outlined in Section 3. Section 5 presents some numerical results comparing the heuristics based on the profit made by the E-Marketplace, and their ability to satisfy the given objectives.

Our main contributions in this paper are the following: (a) a prototype and architecture of an E-Marketplace to support trading of soft and physical products and services; (b) economic model of a specific profit-oriented marketplace, where complex range of objectives can be satisfied based on the business requirements of the owner of the marketplace; (c) novel heuristics to match buyer demand and seller offers, and a comparison of the performance of these heuristics.

---

[2] VPN stands for Virtual Private Networks, and SVC stands for Shared Virtual Circuits

2   E-Marketplace Architecture and Economic Model

2.1   Architecture

In Figure 1, we illustrate a simple architecture of an E-Marketplace, where several buyers and sellers gather to trade goods and services[7]. The E-Marketplace provides software tools for buyers to express their bids and for the sellers to advertise their products. The marketplace keeps a catalog of seller products and product attributes. Buyers submit bids by placing constraints on the attributes of the products. The marketplace matches buyers demand and seller offers, sets prices and allocates resources efficiently based on the objectives and constraints/preferences placed by the buyers and sellers.

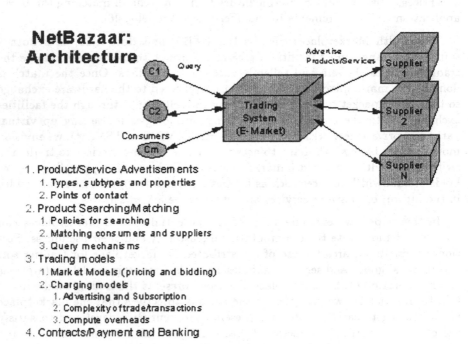

NetBazaar: Architecture

1. Product/Service Advertisements
   1. Types, subtypes and properties
   2. Points of contact
2. Product Searching/Matching
   1. Policies for searching
   2. Matching consumers and suppliers
   3. Query mechanisms
3. Trading models
   1. Market Models (pricing and bidding)
   2. Charging models
      1. Advertising and Subscription
      2. Complexity of trade/transactions
      3. Compute overheads
4. Contracts/Payment and Banking

Fig. 1. E-Marketplace: Architecture

A prototype of this architecture has been built and is currently operational. The prototype is being used to test and explore novel algorithms for matchmaking and price discovery. The main functionality for sellers and buyers include the following:

- A list of product/service types and subtypes.
- A list of attribute-value pairs for each product advertised. Attributes include the following: Price, Quantity, Quality, availability, delivery time, and other product specific attributes.

- Terms and conditions for each product advertised.
- A contact address or a reference to reach the seller.

2.2 Economic Model

In this paper we focus on a marketplace where bandwidth products and services are traded. The economy consists of the following three players: buyers who submit bids for bandwidth (capacity); sellers who offer bandwidth products and services over one or more links; and the E-Marketplace that matches buyers and sellers, and provides settlement and fulfillment services.

Bandwidth products are generally characterized by their quantity, quality, the source-destination of the link, price per unit bandwidth, the cost for reserving the bandwidth for a certain period of time and other terms and conditions on usage and quality of service. For products such as virtual private networks, the product description is more complex.

3 Trading Model

In this section we describe the various trading models and objectives an E-Marketplace can support and exploit in order to profit. Using these models, an E-Marketplace can derive revenue from aggregation and brokering of products; the marketplace aggregates demands from customers and satisfies them by acquiring the appropriate quantity of bandwidth from service providers. The marketplace may also derive revenues through dealership and risk-taking, i.e., by buying products in advance and re-selling them to the buyers in order to derive profit from the spread.

The E-Marketplace collects the bids and offers and runs matching algorithms (auctions) periodically to match buyer demand and seller offers. The mechanism for collecting the bids and disseminating the market information is via a single-round sealed bid auction model, where buyers submit either single bids (bid-points) or multiple bids (bid-curves), and sellers submit multiple bids (offer-curves). The marketplace clears the trades at multiple clearing prices; different participants may see different prices for the same good. Each participant gets to know only if their bids/offers were satisfied/taken and the respective price.

3.1 Scenario of a Trade

Consider the following scenario of a trade: two buying organizations (businesses) place a bid each for 10 T1 lines from New York to Los Angeles from March 1st, 2000, to October 1st, 2000. A selling organization will place an offer of 100 T1 lines between New York and Los Angeles starting from February 1st, 2000, to November 1st, 2000. In addition, the seller specifies a price per unit (T1) for the duration of the offer, and the buyer specifies its willingness to pay per unit demand. The E-Marketplace captures these bids and offers and performs a match taking into account the rest of the bids and offers in the system.

Given that the E-Marketplace has information about the market (bids and offers), it can intelligently aggregate demand and supply, and reduce the costs for the buyers by buying a larger quantity of bandwidth for a lower per unit price from the selected sellers. We assume that the price per unit of good traded (bandwidth in this example) drops as the quantity increases. Under this assumption, by aggregating the demand, the marketplace can buy the goods at lower prices than the individual buyers. The marketplace allocates resources efficiently among the buyers and reduces the overall costs of searching and transacting.

Depending on the objective of the marketplace, the profits derived from aggregation can be used in any of the following ways: (1) as a profit for the marketplace, (2) to offer lower prices to buyers, (3) to indirectly subsidize customers that would not be able to buy goods on an individual basis, since the price they can afford is lower than the price asked for by the providers, or (4) any combination of (1)-(3).

3.2   The trading parameters

The above examples and trading scenario illustrate the multitude of parameters to consider for trading bandwidth or other products in general. In the following we capture these parameters.

The buyer bid consists of the following parameters: resource type, willingness to pay, quantity, time of delivery, duration of resource and other quality of service parameters. More formally the bid can represented by the following:

$$Bid : \{W, Z, T, D, Src, Dest, QoS1, QoS2, ..\} \tag{1}$$

Here, W is the willingness to pay for the quantity Z demanded. The parameter T is the time at which the bandwidth must be delivered, and D is the duration of the possession of the bandwidth resource. The bandwidth capacity requested is for a link represented by a source-destination pair$(Src, Dest)$. The rest of the parameters are the quality of service parameters describing the link, such as the average packet loss, the average packet delay, and others.

The seller offer consists of the following parameters: resource type, price per unit, quantity available, time of availability, duration of resource availability and other quality of service parameters.

Formally the offer can be represented by the following:

$$\{P, X, T, D, Src, Dest, QoS1, QoS2, ..\} \tag{2}$$

Here, P is the price per unit quantity. X is the quantity available. The parameter T is the time at which the bandwidth is available for use, and D is the duration of the availability of the Bandwidth resource. The bandwidth capacity available is for a link represented by a source-destination pair$(Src, Dest)$. The rest of the parameters are the quality of service parameters describing the link, such as the average packet loss, the average packet delay, and others.

3.3   Matching Models

There are many ways in which an E-Marketplace can match buyers and sellers based on its objectives and criteria of the participants. Figure 2 depicts four possible ways in which an E-Marketplace can match buyers and sellers.

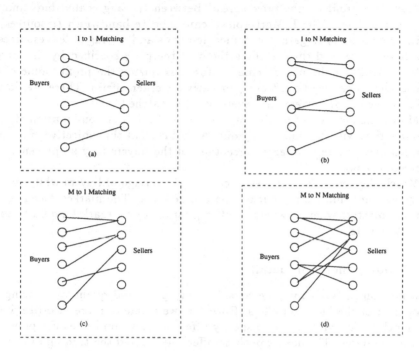

Fig. 2. Matching Models

In the current literature and practice, most of the models of matching and trading are focussed on one-to-one, one-to-many and many-to-one matching models as shown in figure 2 (a), (b), and (c). Many businesses that have emerged in the recent years - such as Netbuy[13]- have based their business models on the one-to-many and many-to-one matching models.

However, not much research work and practice exists in matching many buyers to many sellers, though there are new businesses emerging in the recent years to explore these models as potential business opportunities. In this paper, we focus on the many-to-many matching model, and explore a variety of business objectives driven by profit motives detailed in the following subsection.

3.4   Objectives of the E-Marketplace

The E-Marketplace can exploit its knowledge of the seller offers and buyer bids to derive profit by aggregating demand. In addition, it can take risk by buying bandwidth resources in anticipation of the future demand. Buyers submit bids to the marketplace in the form of price and quantity points or curves. Similarly, sellers submit offers, where the offers are either points or curves in the price-quantity space. Given this model, the following are some of the objectives for the E-Marketplace.

- Maximize profit on the price spread between the aggregated bids and aggregated offers. The E-Marketplace can allocate bandwidth (resources) to the buyers by aggregating customer demands and buying seller resources at a lower price, and then reselling them at the price specified by the buyers. In aggregating the buyer demands for maximizing the profit, some of the user demands may be left out (similarly for seller offers). Therefore, in this objective not all buyers and sellers will be matched.
- Match the demand of *all* the buyers and find the best combination of seller offers that will maximize the profit. A variation of this objective is to maximize the welfare of a large percentage of the buyers (say 95 percent), and maximize profit.
- Match the demands of at least a certain percentage of buyers while guaranteeing some minimum profit for the marketplace. The marketplace may use this objective when it wants to offer guarantees on market liquidity to its participants.

3.5 Trading model in detail

From now on in this paper, we consider only price and quantity as being the parameters of the bids and offers. However, we promote more **complexity** in the model, by allowing sellers to specify offer-curves or multiple offer points for the same resource. The details of these offer models and the trading models are described in the following.

From now on in this paper, we consider only price and quantity as being the parameters of the bids and offers. However, we promote more **complexity** in the model, by allowing sellers to specify offer-curves or multiple offer points for the same resource. The details of these offer models and the trading models are described in the following.

Each **buyer** c_i submits bids to the E-Marketplace. The bid is either a simple tuple ($< w_i, z_i >$) specifying the price w_i per unit quantity the buyer is willing to pay for a given quantity z_i , or a bid curve expressed either as a collection of such tuples, or as a function $w_i(z_i)$. The buyer bids are generated based on their utility function, which depends on the current average price per unit bandwidth advertised by the E-Marketplace.

Each **seller** s_j submits one or more offer curves to the E-Marketplace. An offer curve is expressed either as a collection of tuples ($< p_j, x_j >$) or as a function $p_i(x_j)$ where $p_i(x_j)$ is the price per unit quantity offered by seller s_i for an allocation of bandwidth x_j. For now, we assume that each seller s_j requires a minimum purchase quantity of bandwidth B_j^0, therefore the range of $x_j = [B_j^0, B_j]$, where B_j is the bandwidth supply of seller s_j. The offer curves of two sellers, with limitations on the bandwidth capacity, is shown in figure 3.

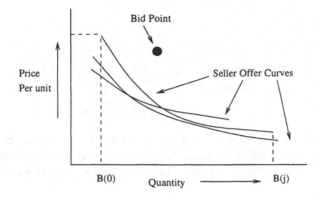

Fig. 3. Buyer Bid points and Seller Offer Curves.

More complex offer curves could incorporate the time of possession of the bandwidth, the time in the future the bandwidth refers to, and others. The sellers can update their offer curves and available bandwidth whenever needed. For now, we will focus on the simplest case of price versus bandwidth allocation offer curve of the seller, along with other attribute values which are static.

The utility function of the buyers (which is internal to the buyer) captures the following:

- If the bids are single points (single-bid model), then the utility is zero if the final allocation is less that what was demanded.
- If the buyer bids are curves (multi-bid model), then the utility function increases with increasing allocation of resources as long as the minimum requirement is met.

The utility function of the sellers captures the following values given a certain offer model:

- If the offers are single points (single-bid model), then the seller utility is zero if the allocation is more that what was demanded.
- If the offers are curves (multi-bid model), then the utility function increases with increasing allocation of resource as long as the minimum allocation requirement is met.

3.6   E-Marketplace Objectives

Objective 1: Profit Maximization The goal of this objective is the find an optimal matching strategy that maximizes the profit of the marketplace. The solution identifies a set of buyers C^* and an allocation z^* of bandwidth to them, that match with a set of sellers S^* and an allocation of bandwidth x^* bought from them. More formally, the objective can be described by the following:

$$find: \quad \{C^*, z^*, S^*, x^*\} \tag{3}$$
$$that\ maximizes: \sum_{i \in C^*} z_i w_i - \sum_{j \in S^*} x_j p_j$$
$$constraints: \quad \sum x_j \geq \sum_i z_i$$
$$x_j \in [B_j^0, B_j]$$

It is possible that a only a few buyers and a few sellers will be matched in order to obtain the maximum profit. This may or may not be beneficial for the E-Marketplace if it wants to attract a large number of buyers and sellers.

Objective 2: Buyer Satisfaction The goal of this objective for the marketplace is to find the best match of sellers such that all the buyers' demand is satisfied. The EM will try to achieve this objective as long as it does not incur a loss. The E-Marketplace can ensure this by simply checking that the aggregate buyer willingness to pay is higher than the cost of acquiring the demanded bandwidth from the suppliers. The formal definition of the problem is as follows:

$$find: \quad \{z^*, S^*, x_j^*\} \tag{4}$$
$$that\ maximizes: \sum_i z_i^* w_i - \sum_{j \in S^*} x_j^* p_j$$
$$constraints: \quad \sum_i z_i^* \leq \sum_{j \in S^*} x_i$$
$$x_j \in [B_j^0, B_j]$$

The problem, therefore, is to find the optimal allocation of resources from the various sellers which will satisfy the demands of all the buyers.

Objective 3: Minimum Liquidity The goal of this objective for the marketplace is to find a set of buyers C^* that satisfies at least a percentage y of buyers and an allocation z^* of bandwidth to them, and match it with a set of sellers S^* and an allocation of bandwidth x^* purchased from them, while guaranteeing a minimum profit Pr for the marketplace. The formal definition of the problem is as follows:

$$find: \quad \{C^*, z^*, S^*, x^*\} \tag{5}$$
$$that\ maximizes: \quad \|C\|$$
$$and\ \left(\sum_{i \in C^*} z_i * w_i - \sum_{j \in S^*} x_j * p_j\right)$$
$$constraints: \quad \|C\|/100 \geq y$$
$$\sum_{i \in C^*} z_i * w_i - \sum_{j \in S} x_j * p_j \geq Pr$$
$$\tag{6}$$

4 Matchmaking Algorithms

We now describe algorithms that compute the optimal solution for the different marketplace objectives presented earlier. We consider both exact and heuristic-based algorithms.

4.1 Exact Algorithm for Objective 1

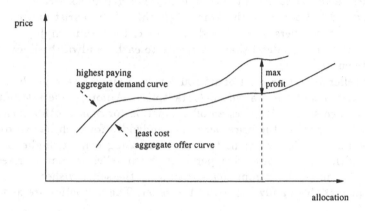

Fig. 4. Algorithm for Objective 1

Exact Algorithm The following algorithm finds the exact solution to Objective 1 outlined earlier. Refer to Figure 4 for a graphical representation of the algorithm.

- Construct the highest-paying aggregate demand curve. The aggregate demand curve is computed as follows: for each allocation of bandwidth find all combinations of buyers' demand that sum up to the particular allocation. Among these combinations, pick the one with the highest total willingness to pay. This highest willingness is chosen as a point on the highest-paying demand curve for this particular bandwidth allocation.
- Compute the least cost aggregate offer curve. This is constructed in a similar fashion as the highest-paying aggregate demand curve, by picking the combination of sellers with the lowest total ask price for each bandwidth allocation.
- Compute the maximum distance between the least cost aggregate seller curve and the highest paying aggregate buyer curve. The distance is the vertical distance between the two curves. The maximum profit allocation is the one that corresponds to the maximum distance. At this allocation, some or all buyers are matched to one or more sellers.

The straightforward algorithm presented above exhibits a very high computational complexity. The complexity here is caused by the need to compute all possible combination of bids (offers) that would add up to a particular allocation of bandwidth, in order to find the highest paying (lowest asking) set of buyers (sellers) for the particular allocation. This makes it computationally prohibitive if large numbers of buyers and sellers participate in the E-Marketplace.

Heuristics-based Algorithms for Objective 1 We now propose some heuristics to compute an approximate solution for Objective 1. All the heuristics presented here attempt to avoid the complexity incurred in constructing the aggregate offer and bid curves in the exact algorithm. The heuristics presented here simply order the buyers/sellers based on some criteria and simplify the selection of the set of buyers (sellers) that contribute to each bandwidth allocation in the aggregate curves.

Each seller advertises a set of attribute-value pairs for each product type and product that it advertises at the E-Marketplace. Among these attributes is the price, and each seller advertises an offer function for bandwidth allocation. The offer function specifies the price per unit bandwidth for each bandwidth allocation. We assume offer functions that are decreasing convex; higher allocations of bandwidth incur a lower cost per unit. Each seller is characterized by the shape of the curve, the minimum allocation B_j^0 the seller wishes to sell, and the maximum available bandwidth B_j of the seller. The heuristics are as follows:

- Least per unit cost (LPUC)
  - Order the sellers in increasing order of their price per unit at $\min[B_j]$.
  - Start from the lowest cost curve.
  - Allocate upto B_j^{max} from the curve to the buyer.
  - Go to the next lowest seller.
  - Continue this till the buyer demand is met. The fractional bandwidth left over can be chosen from a least cost seller for that allocation[3]
- Highest available bandwidth (MaxAvail)
  - Order the sellers according to their largest available capacity (B_j).
  - The sellers are selected one by one till the demand can be satisfied.
  - This continues until the allocation satisfies the aggregate buyer demand. If it doesn't, then only some of the buyers are satisfied. In this case, we order the buyers based on their willingness to pay.
- Minimum cost (MinCost)
  - Order the sellers according to their area which is computed by multiplying the p_j at B_j and B_j.
  - The seller who has the least cost capacity is selected first
  - The next seller in the list is selected next, and so on till the aggregate buyer demand is exhausted.

---

[3] Note that this is still an approximation of the heuristic.

4.2   Algorithms for Objective 2 (Buyer satisfaction)

Since the marketplace wants to satisfy *all* buyers we will assume that the available supply is greater than the demand. The exact algorithm for this problem involves finding the least cost supplier combination at the aggregate demand point (similar to the construction of the least cost offer curve in the exact algorithms for Objective 1). Furthermore, we have to ensure that the aggregate willingness to pay at this point is greater than the cost of acquiring the bandwidth from the suppliers at this point.

It is easy to see that it is fairly straightforward to apply the heuristics-based algorithms for Objective 1 to achieving Objective 2 while obeying the constraints for Objective 2.

4.3   Heuristic-based Algorithm for Objective 3 (Minimum liquidity)

In this section we present a solution for Objective 3 outlined above. The complexity of an exact solution for satisfying this objective is similar to that for satisfying Objective 1. In the case of Objective 1, the fact that we do not care what percentage of buyers contributes to the highest-paying aggregate curve, allows for some computational optimizations that make the algorithm feasible for small number of participants in the EM. Unlike Objective 1, we cannot apply similar optimizations to the exact algorithm for Objective 3. This necessitates the development of approximations. The approximate solution presented in this section is based on intuitive arguments and its performance depends on the characteristics of the customer bids. Yet, it dramatically reduces the computational complexity of the problem and its operation can be tuned to focus either on satisfying the time constraints for providing a solution or on optimizing the produced solution.

The algorithm operates as follows:

- Construct the least cost aggregate offer curve in the same fashion as in the exact algorithm for Objective 1. The outcome of this process is a curve $A(x)$, where $A(x)$ is the price per unit of the aggregate offer curve for x units of bandwidth. The value of x in the aggregate curve is between B_{min} (the minimum bandwidth offered among all providers) and B_{tot} (the sum of the maximum bandwidth offered by all participating providers).
- Define a uniform *profit per unit* $Pr_u = Pr/B_{tot}$ be the profit per unit if we were to sell B_{tot} units of bandwidth. The implicit assumption here is that we will try to sell all the bandwidth we can buy. This is not a restriction of the algorithm; instead of B_{tot} we could pick any other bandwidth allocation.
- For each allocation x advertise two prices:
  - High: $A(x) + Pr_u + delta$ (high curve)
  - Low: $A(x) + Pr_u$ (low curve)
- For each allocation allow a customer to bid either on the low or the high price for the allocation. Figure 5 shows an example where only two customers are submitting their bids. Notice that a customer may chose not to bid for

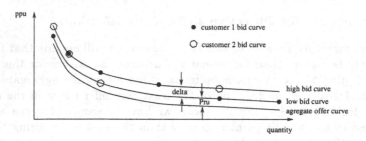

Fig. 5. Heuristic for Objective 3

a particular allocation. Later in this section the algorithm is generalized to allow for non-constrained bids.

- Transform the percentage y of bids to be satisfied, to the number of offers c to be satisfied.
- Define the *average allocation per satisfied bid* as $m = B_{tot}/c$. This is the amount we would give to each of the c customers if we were to give each of them the same amount of bw.
- Among the available bids pick the following to satisfy (*as many as possible* in what follows means that the sum of all selected bid allocations does not exceed B_{tot}):
  - Pick as many bids as possible from the high curve at $x = m$
  - Pick as many pairs of bids $< b_1, b_2 >$ as possible, both from the high curve at $x_1 = m + j$ and $x_2 = m - j$, for all $j = 1, ..., m - B_{min}$
  - Pick as many pairs of bids $< b_1, b_2 >$ as possible, one from the high curve at $x_1 = m + j$ and one from the low curve at $x_2 = m - j$, for all $j = 1, ..., m - B_{min}$
  - Pick as many pairs of bids $< b_1, b_2 >$ as possible, one from the low curve at $x_1 = m + j$ and one from the low high at $x_2 = m - j$, for all $j = 1, ..., m - B_{min}$
  - Pick any bid that will make the sum equal to B_{tot} (notice that due to the way we pick the bids to satisfy, this may not be possible). Start with allocation around the value of m. For every allocation, first select bids lying in the high curve

Notice a few things about the above algorithm. First, the constrained allocation and the uniform per unit gain of the trading system encoded in these constraints has two consequences: (a) in the allocation of bw to users we can substitute any bid from the upper curve with any other combination of bids from the upper curve that adds up to the same demand, without affecting the gain of the trading system. The same holds for bids lying in the lower curve. (b) as long as we pick bids that add up to Btot we guarantee the minimum gain the trading system wants to make. Second, the algorithm performs a deterministic ordering of the bids to be satisfied. This ordering is not unique. The ordering presented above aims at maximizing the gain of the trading system (while guaranteeing a minimum profit). Third, the reason for picking bids to satisfy in pairs is that in order to satisfy $y\%$ of customers, whenever we satisfy a bid for more than m units, we have to also satisfy another bid for less than m units. Finally, the algorithm is not guaranteed to generate the optimal solution. It is a greedy algorithm that does not posses the optimal sub-structure property. This is apparent in the last step, where due to earlier bids we may have satisfied, we may not find bids that would make the total allocation equal to B_{tot}.

Generalization of the algorithm for Objective 3 The above approach can be generalized by removing the above strict bidding constraints and instead allowing for *bidding bands*; buyer bids must lie within these bands. The algorithm then becomes the following:

- The low limit of the band at x has to be the same as in the previous case to guarantee the minimum profit Pr produced by the solution. There is no limitation on the high limit of the band at x.
- Users are allowed to bid for each allocation anywhere within the band
- The band is divided in n discrete, equally-spaced values. Each bid within a band is mapped to the closest of these discrete values. The value of n determines the computational complexity of the algorithm (and the quality of the achieved solution) and can be adjusted to meet the running time constraints of the algorithm.
- The bids to be satisfied are picked by a simple generalization of the above ordering sequence:
  - Pick as many bids as possible from the highest curve at $x = m$
  - Pick as many pairs of bids $< b_1, b_2 >$ as possible, both from the highest curve at $x_1 = m + j$ and $x_2 = m - j$, for all $j = 1, ..., m - B_{min}$
  - Pick as many pairs of bids $< b_1, b_2 >$ as possible, one from the highest curve at $x_1 = m + j$ and one from the second highest curve at $x_2 = m - j$, for all $j = 1, ..., m - B_{min}$
  - Pick as many pairs of bids $< b_1, b_2 >$ as possible, one from the highest curve at $x_1 = m + j$ and one from the third highest curve at $x_2 = m - j$, for all $j = 1, ..., m - B_{min}$
  - ...
  - Pick as many pairs of bids $< b_1, b_2 >$ as possible, one from the second highest curve at $x_1 = m + j$ and one from the highest curve at $x_2 = m - j$, for all $j = 1, ..., m - B_{min}$
  - Pick as many pairs of bids $< b_1, b_2 >$ as possible, one from the third highest curve at $x_1 = m + j$ and one from the highest curve at $x_2 = m - j$, for all $j = 1, ..., m - B_{min}$
  - ...

5   Experimental Results

The algorithms described in Section 3 were implemented to evaluate their performance. The evaluation for Objectives 1 (profit maximization) and 2 (buyer satisfaction) compares how well the heuristics perform with respect to the computationally very intensive exact solution. The LPUC heuristic was found to outperform the rest; LPUC results are typically in the range of 1% from the exact solution. The evaluation for Objective 3 (minimum liquidity) examines how well the proposed heuristic performs with respect to the set goals. We varied the number of sellers and buyers and their offer and bidding parameters and found that the heuristic performs satisfactorily in all cases.

5.1   Seller and Buyer Characteristics

We assume that each seller j commits to selling any quantity x between a minimum quantity (B_j^0), and a maximum quantity (B_j), at a price expressed by the following equation:

$$Price\,per\,unit_j(x) = (P_{o,j}(1 - e^{-b_j x}) + a_j)/x \qquad (7)$$

The seller has full control over all of the parameters $(P_0, a, b, B^0$ and $B)$ characterizing the offer. Notice that the algorithms presented in this paper are not in any way limited to the price per unit equation in (7). Equation (7) is chosen only because it is adequate for capturing a wide and realistic range of seller behaviors.

Figures 6 through 8 depict the effect of the parameters P_0, a and b in the price per unit each seller advertises. b controls how fast the price per unit changes with respect to the quantity x (Figure 8). P_0 (Figure 6) and a (Figure 7) collectively control the placement of the curves along the y axis. The effects of P_0 and a differ. Their qualitative difference can best be appreciated through figures 9 through 11 showing the actual price a perspective buyer would pay to purchase a given quantity x.

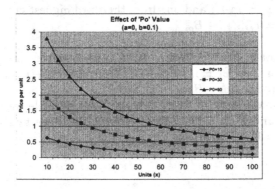

Fig. 6. Price per unit for varying P_0 values - $(a = 0, b = 0.1)$

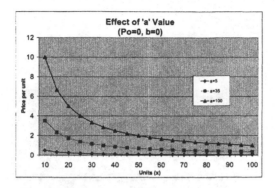

Fig. 7. Price per unit for varying a values - ($P_0 = 0$, $b = 0.1$)

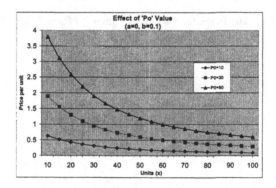

Fig. 8. Price per unit for varying b values - ($P_0 = 50$, $a = 0$)

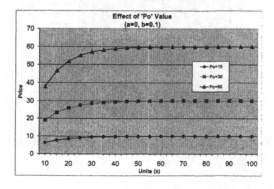

Fig. 9. Price for varying P_0 values - ($a = 0$, $b = 0.1$)

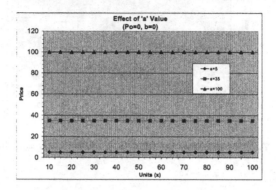

Fig. 10. Price for varying a values - $(P_0 = 0, b = 0.1)$

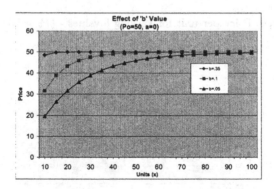

Fig. 11. Price for varying b values - $(P_0 = 50, a = 0)$

We assume that each buyer i submits a bid point characterized by two parameters:

$$Z_i : \ quantity\,demanded \tag{8}$$

$$W_i : \ willingness\,to\,pay\,for\,Z_i \tag{9}$$

5.2   Sets of Parameters used in Evaluation

The performance of the algorithms was evaluated against four sets of parameters specifying the marketplace. The sets are presented in Table 1. In this table, r signifies a random variable whose value is uniformly distributed in the interval $[0, 1]$.

Set 1 in Table 1 corresponds to a small marketplace of 20 sellers whose offers have quite different characteristics. Similarly the bids placed by perspective buyers are quite different from one another. The second set corresponds to another small marketplace of 20 sellers, whose offers are very similar to each other; competition among sellers tends to create such marketplaces. All the values specifying the offers differ by no more than 10% from one another. Similarly, buyers have similar needs and valuations; their bids differ by no more than 20% from each other. Set 3 consists of sellers and buyers with the same characteristics as those in the marketplace of Set 1; Set 3 describes a larger marketplace consisting of 100 sellers. Similarly, Set 4 consists of sellers and buyers with the same characteristics as those in the marketplace of Set 2; Set 4 simulates a larger marketplace consisting of 100 sellers. The number of buyers in all sets is varied between 10 and 190.

	Set 1	Set 2	Set 3	Set 4
P_0	10+60r	35+3.5r	10+60r	35+3.5r
a	70r	10+r	70r	10+r
b	.5r	.3+.03r	.5r	.3+.03r
$B_j{}^0$	1	1	1	1
B_j	10+190r	130+13r	10+190r	130+13r
# sellers	20	20	100	100
# buyers	10-190	10-190	10-190	10-190
W_i	35+15r	40+8r	35+15r	40+8r
Z_i	10+20r	20+4r	10+20r	20+4r

Table 1. Sets of parameters for experimenting with Objectives 1 and 2

5.3   Objective 1: Profit Maximization

Figures 12 through 15 present the comparison of the heuristics and the exact algorithm in computing the profit from the spread between the buyers bids and the sellers offers (offer curves). Figure 12 corresponds to the marketplace of Set 1 in Table 1, Figure 13 to Set 2, Figure 14 to Set 3 and Figure 15 to Set 4.

The results presented in these figures show that the LPUC heuristic performed as well as the exact algorithm to compute the best match which maximizes the profit of the E-Marketplace. The results produced by LPUC are typically on the order of 1% poorer than the exact solution. The other heuristics also performed reasonably well, but in most cases, they produced results which were inferior to those of the LPUC heuristic.

It is worth noticing that when sellers have similar offer characteristics and buyers similar biding characteristics (Figures 13 and 15) all of the algorithms perform almost indistinguishably.

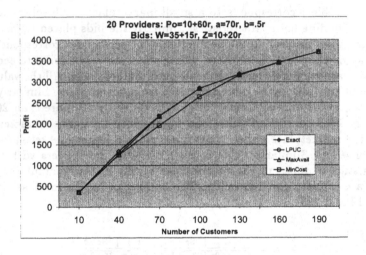

Fig. 12. Profit maximization – Set 1 (20 sellers, differentiated offers/bids)

5.4   Objective 2: Buyer Satisfaction

The second objective function attempts to maximize the profit of the E-Marketplace, while satisfying all of the buyers demands. Figures 16 through 19 present the comparison of the heuristics and the exact algorithm in computing the profit from the spread between the buyer bids and seller offers when satisfying all of the buyer bids. Figure 16 corresponds to the marketplace of Set 1 in Table 1, Figure 17 to Set 2, Figure 18 to Set 3 and Figure 19 to Set 4.

Similar to the results in Figures 12-15 for objective 1, the results in Figures 16-19 show that the LPUC heuristic performs better than the other heuristics and very close to the exact algorithm in all the trading configurations. Once again the differences are accentuated in the case of differentiated characteristics

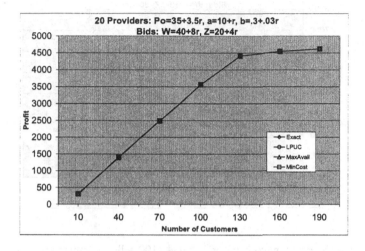

Fig. 13. Profit maximization – Set 2 (20 sellers, similar offers/bids)

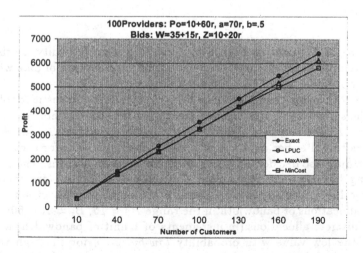

Fig. 14. Profit maximization – Set 3 (100 sellers; differentiated offers/bids)

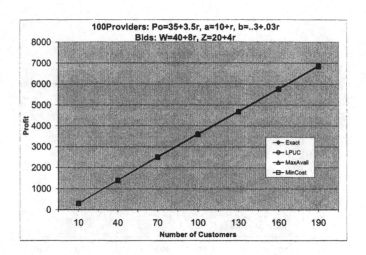

Fig. 15. Profit maximization – Set 4 (100 sellers; similar offers/bids)

(Figures 16 and 18). They are almost indistinguishable in marketplaces where participants have similar characteristics (Figures 17 and 19).

Notice that in Figures 16 and 17 the number of buyers goes only up to 100 and not up to 190 as in the rest of the graphs. This occurs because for the given bid and offer characteristics, there is not enough supply to satisfy all of the demand.

Objective 3: Minimum Liquidity The Minimum Liquidity heuristic algorithm attempts to satisfy more than a minimum percentage of bids while guaranteeing a minimum profit for the marketplace.

Tables 2 through 4 summarize the performance of the heuristic for objective 3 versus the set goals. The parameters describing the sellers offers are those of Set 1 in Table 1. The heuristic algorithm for this objective (see Section 4.3) allows customers to bid either on a low or a high advertised price for each allocation. The user may also decide not to bid at all for some allocations. The parameters describing bidding behavior in Sets 1 through 4 in Table 1 are therefore not applicable here. Instead, each customer's bid curve consists of set of discrete bids for allocations of bandwidth in the range $B_j^0 = 10$, $B_j = 10 + 60r$. For each of these discrete allocations (in increments of 1 unit of bandwidth) a customer bids for the low value with probability *low-bid prob*, for the high value with probability *high-bid prob*, and does not bid at all with probability *1-(low-bid prob + high-bid prob)*.

As the number of participants in the marketplace increases, the heuristic for objective 3 has a simpler task to perform in terms of achieving the set goals.

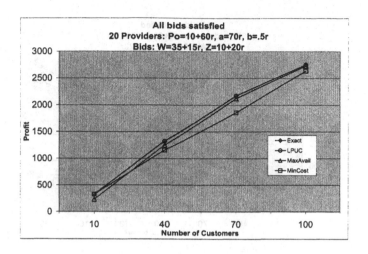

Fig. 16. Buyer Satisfaction – Set 1(20 sellers; differentiated offers/bids)

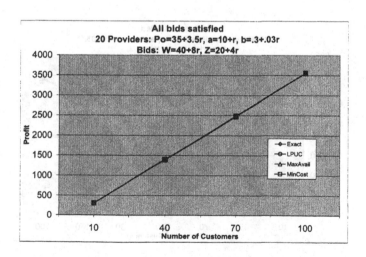

Fig. 17. Buyer Satisfaction – Set 2 (20 sellers; similar offers/bids)

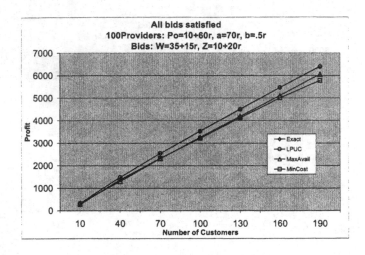

Fig. 18. Buyer Satisfaction – Set 3(100 sellers; differentiated offers/bids)

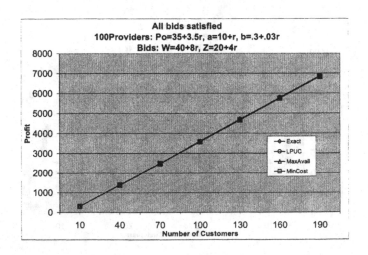

Fig. 19. Buyer Satisfaction – Set 4 (100 sellers; similar offers/bids)

Tables 2 through 4 present the results for two relatively small marketplaces. Table 2 summarizes the performance for the case where the difference *delta* (see Figure 5) between the high and the low bidding prices is very small (*delta* = $Pr_u/100$). The percentage of customers to be satisfied is varied between 50% and 95%. The bidding behavior of the customers is also varied. These variations are captured by their decision to bid for the low value (with probability *low-bid prob*) or the high value (with probability *high-bid prob*) or not bid at all for a specific allocation of bandwidth.

# customers	# providers	low-bid prob	high-bid prob	% goal	% sat.	Profit goal	Actual profit
200	30	.1	.1	50	50.5	500	499.4
200	30	.1	.1	80	82.5	500	501
200	30	.1	.1	90	91.5	500	493.9
200	30	.1	.1	95	98.5	500	488.5
200	30	.2	.2	50	51	500	505
200	30	.2	.2	80	80	500	484.8
200	30	.2	.2	90	87.5	500	471.6
200	30	.2	.2	95	97.5	500	499.2

Table 2. Results for Objective 3 (Minimum liquidity) – Low difference between low and high bids (*delta* = $1\%Pr_u$)

Table 3 is similar to table 2, but for a greater difference *delta* between the high and the low bidding prices (*delta* = $Pr_u/10$). Comparing Tables 2 and 3 one can see that in the later case (higher value of *delta*) the profit is met in all cases, whereas this is not the case in Table 2.

# customers	# providers	low-bid prob	high-bid prob	% goal	% sat.	Profit goal	Actual profit
200	30	.1	.1	50	50.5	500	543.9
200	30	.1	.1	80	82.5	500	545.4
200	30	.1	.1	90	91.5	500	536
200	30	.1	.1	95	98.5	500	527.5
200	30	.2	.2	50	51	500	550
200	30	.2	.2	80	80	500	527.7
200	30	.2	.2	90	87.5	500	513.4
200	30	.2	.2	95	97.5	500	543.2

Table 3. Results for Objective 3 (Minimum liquidity) – High difference between low and high bids (*delta* = $10\%Pr_u$)

Table 4 is the same as Table 3 for a much smaller number of customers and providers. Comparing Table 4 to Table 3, one can observe that the algorithm performs better for a larger number of participants, but still performs reasonably well even for a small number of participants.

# customers	# providers	low-bid prob	high-bid prob	% goal	% sat.	Profit goal	Actual profit
50	10	.1	.1	50	50	500	516.4
50	10	.1	.1	80	78	500	509
50	10	.1	.1	90	86	500	510.4
50	10	.1	.1	95	98	500	525.4
50	10	.2	.2	50	54	500	545
50	10	.2	.2	80	76	500	518
50	10	.2	.2	90	86	500	508.2
50	10	.2	.2	95	96	500	502.5

Table 4. Results for Objective 3 (Minimum liquidity) – Small number of participants ($delta = 10\%Pr_u$)

6   Conclusions

E-Marketplaces are already emerging in various sectors of the human economy, and businesses are beginning to realize that a majority of commerce in the 21st century will be done over the Internet. E-Marketplaces will play a major role in creating an efficient and competitive commerce environment. In this paper we presented a model for a specific type of profit oriented E-Marketplace, where the objective of the marketplace is to exploit the benefit of aggregating demand for bandwidth and thus acquiring supply at a much lower cost than otherwise possible. We show that the exact solution to the problem of maximizing the profit in a bid/offer marketplace is computationally complex, given that the offers are functions instead of just price-capacity points.

We designed and implemented a collection of heuristics and compared their performance in terms of profit as a function of the number of buyers in the marketplace. The model was static; we fixed the number of buyers and sellers and we computed the profit made by the marketplace for each of the heuristics we proposed. We found that a simple heuristic, LPUC, performed as well as the exact algorithm for the best possible match for maximizing profit under both the objectives. We attribute this behavior to the convexity of the offer functions. If the offer functions are non-convex and non-continuous, then we might see substantial differences between the heuristics and exact analysis. Furthermore, we presented a heuristic-based solution for a marketplace that is interested in offering certain minimal liquidity under a profit constraint. We evaluated the performance of the solution against the specified objectives and found that the algorithm achieves the objectives under a variety of conditions.

As mentioned earlier, the algorithms in this paper operate under static (or snapshot) market conditions. Furthermore, the match-making considers all the supply in the market to homogeneous. We intend to study the dynamics of market under various matching algorithms for profit-oriented intermediaries for dynamic markets and also where multi-attribute match-making may be required. We implemented a version of the E-Marketplace using IBM's middleware and commerce technology[7]. A newer version is currently being implemented with support for various heuristics for searching, matchmaking and price discovery in a complex product space, defined by many attributes.

References

1. J. P. Bailey and Y. Bakos, "An Exploratory Study of the Emerging Role of Electronic Intermediaries," *International Journal of Electronic Commerce*, Vol. 1, No. 3, Spring 1997.
2. Y. Bakos, "the Emerging Role of Electronic Marketplaces on the Internet," *Journal of CACM*, August 1998.
3. W. Elmaghraby, "Capturing Non-Convexities in a Multi-Unit Auction: An Application to Electricity Markets," *Submitted to Management Science*, September 1998.
4. R. Guttman, A. Moukas and P. Maes, "Agent Mediated Electronic Commerce: A Survey," *Knowledge Engineering Review*, June, 1998.
5. M. D. Ilic, "Price Dynamics in the Deregulated California Energy Market," *Energy Laboratory Consortium Workshop*, Cambridge, MA, Feb. 4, 1999.
6. J. Sairamesh and J. Kephart, "Dynamics of Price and Quality Differentiation in Information and Computation Markets," *Proceedings of the ICE-98*, October 25-28, 1998.
7. J. Sairamesh and C. Codella, "NetBazaar: Networked Electronic Markets,", *proceedings of the 7th Delos Workshop on Electronic Commerce*, Springer Verlag, September, 1998.
8. J. Tirole, "The Theory of Industrial Organization," The MIT Press, Cambridge, Massachusetts, 1995.
9. S. M. H. Wallman, "Technology takes to Securities Trading," *IEEE Spectrum*, February 1997.
10. P. Visudhiphan and M. D. Ilic, "Dynamic Games-based Modeling of Electricity Markets," *Proceedings of the IEEE PES Winter Meeting*, New York, NY, January 1999.
11. Rate Exchange URL: http:/www.ratexchange.com.
12. Band-X: The bandwidth exchange: URL: http://www.band-x.com.
13. NetBuy: Electronic Marketplace for Electronic Components: URL: http://www.netbuy.com
14. NECX: Electronic Marketplace for Electronic Components: URL: http://www.necx.com
15. ALTRANET: Energy Exchange: URL: http://www.altranet.com
16. Chemdex: Electronic Marketplace for Chemical Products: URL: http://www.chemdex.com

Two-Sided Learning in an Agent Economy for Information Bundles

Jeffrey O. Kephart[1], Rajarshi Das[1], and Jeffrey K. MacKie-Mason[2]

[1] Institute for Advanced Commerce, IBM Research
PO Box 704, Yorktown Heights, NY 10598
{kephart,rajarshi}@watson.ibm.com
[2] School of Information and Department of Economics
University of Michigan, Ann Arbor, MI 48109
jmm@umich.edu

Abstract. Commerce in information goods is one of the earliest emerging applications for intelligent agents in commerce. However, the fundamental characteristics of information goods mean that they can and likely will be offered in widely varying configurations. Participating agents will need to deal with uncertainty about both prices and location in multi-dimensional product space. Thus, studying the behavior of learning agents is central to understanding and designing for agent-based information economies. Since uncertainty will exist on both sides of transactions, and interactions between learning agents that are negotiating and transacting with other learning agents may lead to unexpected dynamics, it is important to study two-sided learning.

We present a simple but powerful model of an information bundling economy with a single producer and multiple consumer agents. We explore the pricing and purchasing behavior of these agents when articles can be bundled. In this initial exploration, we study the dynamics of this economy when consumer agents are uninformed about the distribution of article values. We discover that a reasonable albeit naïve consumer learning strategy can lead to disastrous market behavior. We find a simple explanation for this market failure, and develop a simple improvement to the producer agent's strategy that largely ameliorates the problem. But in the process we learn an important lesson: dynamic market interactions when there is substantial uncertainty can lead to pathological outcomes if agents are designed with "reasonable" but not sufficiently adaptive strategies. Thus, in programmed agent environments it may be essential to dramatically increase our understanding of adaptivity and learning if we want to obtain good aggregate outcomes.

Keywords: Information economy, information bundling, two-sided learning, economic agents.

A. Moukas, C. Sierra, and F. Ygge (Eds.): AMEC'99, LNAI 1788, pp. 180–205, 2000.
© Springer-Verlag Berlin Heidelberg 2000

1 Introduction

Within a few years, we anticipate that software agents will participate in a wide variety of commercial transactions, and may even become economic players in their own right [8]. One important domain for agent economies is the production and distribution of information goods and services, such as news articles, entertainment and other service reviews, and instructional materials. As is the case with physical goods, producers can reduce costs or increase the surplus extracted from consumers by *bundling* information goods together [1].

We expect negotiations over the composition and prices for bundles to become a natural application for software agents. Agents representing producers could use up-to-date information about market conditions and consumer demand to explore not just prices, but also locations in a multi-dimensional bundled product space. Agents representing consumers could gather relevant information by purchasing bundles from multiple producers, always keeping an eye out for new opportunities that arise as the producers change their offerings in an effort to gain a competitive advantage. While they will have their limitations, software agents will have important advantages over humans: they are likely to respond more quickly to changing market conditions and deal more easily with pricing structures that are more complex than might be feasible in an all-human economy. On the other hand, economic software agents are endowed with less common sense than their human counterparts, and interactions among them may lead to strange and undesirable market dynamics [2]. To avoid adverse and possibly disastrous individual, firm and market consequences, humans must design their economic software agents carefully, taking into account their likely interactions with their environment and with other agents.

Although there is a growing literature on commodity bundling in the context of information goods [1,4], much remains to be learned before we can design competent software agents that buy and sell bundled information goods. Very little is understood about strategic search over the joint information good price and product space (that is, search for which products to offer, in which combinations, at what prices)[3]. Agents competing in this space must learn about the distribution of preferences across a heterogeneous and changing customer population, must learn about the strategies being followed by their competitors, and then must optimize their strategies to take into account the new understanding of customers and competitors. Consumers, on the other hand, attempt to optimize their purchases by learning about the quantity, quality and price of bundled items offered by the various producers, all of which may change over time. Learning and optimization are both difficult search problems, and in the market context they are closely related.

---

[1] For example, articles are bundled together into a single journal or newspaper issue, and a monthly or daily series of these are bundled together in subscriptions [4, 11].

[2] See references [6, 8, 9] for an example of the instabilities that can result when competing broker agents search a restricted price and product space.

[3] For some recent work on multi-agent search, see, e.g., [23, 24].

Our recent work on strategic pricing for bundles [5] represents the first study of bundling in a market with multiple producers. In that work, we assumed that all of the relevant parameters were known by the producers. We distinguished between conditions in which firms prefer to offer comprehensive bundles at a single price, those in which they prefer to sell items individually, and those in which they prefer to offer consumers a choice between a bundle or individual components.

In this paper we examine a considerably more general problem, although for this initial foray we maintain some simplifying restrictions. We envision an agent economy with one information broker agent and many consumer agents. The consumer agents are heterogeneous: they value each item differently, and these values are drawn from a different distribution for each agent. To set profit-maximizing prices, the broker agent desires, but may not know, the parameters of the consumers' valuation distributions. The consumers also may not know their valuation parameters until they gain experience with the broker's offered information goods. Therefore, both sides wish to learn. The broker can set prices strategically, learning about consumer valuations from their purchasing behavior at different prices. The consumers can purchase strategically, learning about the distribution of information good values by sampling.

This environment is very rich and will permit us to explore many interesting questions. In this paper we focus on one surprising result: that when consumer agents follow a plausible but overly naïve learning strategy, even if the producer is fully informed (but also somewhat naïve), the economy can continuously degenerate with disastrous overall performance. We find a simple explanation for the initial failure, and develop a simple improvement to the producer agent's strategy that largely ameliorates the problem. But in the process we learn an important lesson: dynamic market interactions when there is substantial uncertainty can lead to pathological outcomes if agents are designed with "reasonable" but not sufficiently adaptive strategies. Thus, in programmed agent environments it may be essential to dramatically increase our understanding of adaptivity and learning if we want to obtain good aggregate outcomes.

This paper is the first in a series of studies directed towards understanding and developing robust adaptive learning techniques that are effective for individual agents and lead to acceptable collective (market) behavior. We are also extending the model to study the much more common setting in which there is competition among multiple producers of information goods. Of course, this setting exacerbates the learning problem, since the producers need to learn about each other's strategies in addition to learning about consumer valuations.

In the next section we discuss the model. We introduce two relevant distributions: first, a parameterized distribution g from which a given consumer's valuations are drawn, and second, a distribution h describing the population of consumers — the distribution from which an individual consumer's valuation distribution parameters are drawn. For tractability, we assume that the broker is restricted to two-part tariff pricing schemes [16]: it can charge consumer agents a subscription price to examine the current items, and a per item price for each item the consumer subsequently purchases.

In a general analysis section, we derive the optimal strategies for fully informed broker and consumer agents as functions of the article value and consumer type distributions g and h. Then in Section 4 we explore specific cases of exploration and exploitation through analysis and simulation. When agents are underinformed and engage in learning, we consider plausible (but not necessarily fully optimal) agent strategies, and examine the resulting system outcomes. We close with a summary of our current results and plans for future work.

2   Model

A single producer periodically (at discrete times $t = 0, 1, 2, \ldots$) generates sets of N articles. It sets a subscription fee F and a price schedule $\boldsymbol{P} = \{P(1), \ldots, P(N)\}$ where $P(k)$ represents the price it charges for a subset of $k \in \{1, \ldots, N\}$ of the N articles.

At a given time t, each of M consumers are informed about $(F, \boldsymbol{P})$, and they decide whether to subscribe. Then, each subscribing consumer receives abstracts of all N articles, and uses them to assess its value w_j from reading each article, for $j \in \{1, \ldots, N\}$. We assume that these values are generated randomly according to a distribution $g(\boldsymbol{q_i}; w)$, where $\boldsymbol{q_i}$ is the set of parameters that define the distribution for consumer i. The parameters $\boldsymbol{q_i}$ that represent consumer i's valuation distribution are themselves generated randomly prior to time 0 from a distribution $h(\boldsymbol{r}, \boldsymbol{q})$. Once the $\boldsymbol{q_i}$ parameters are generated for consumer i, they remain fixed for the rest of time (though the agents may not know their true values for a while, if ever).

After assessing the value of each article, a subscriber decides which articles to purchase. It does this by choosing a set of articles K to maximize surplus $s = (\sum_{j \in K} w_j) - P(|K|)$. Henceforth we assume that the articles have been sorted by consumer j so that the w_j are ordered highest to lowest, and thus the set K consists of the first $k = |K|$ articles.

The subscription decision depends on consumer *expectations*. If a consumer believes correctly that its valuations are drawn from a distribution with parameters $\boldsymbol{q_i}$, then its expected surplus from purchasing k articles would be

$$\langle s_k \rangle = \left\langle \sum_{j=1}^{k} w_j \right\rangle - P(k). \tag{1}$$

The consumer can then derive the vector of values p_k, the probabilities that any k is the expected surplus maximizing number of articles. Then the consumer's optimized expected surplus is

$$\langle s \rangle = \sum_{k=1}^{N} p_k \langle s_k \rangle. \tag{2}$$

The consumer should subscribe [4]if and only if the expectation $\langle s \rangle$ exceeds the subscription fee F.

If consumer i does not know its own q_i for the articles offered by this broker, then values $\hat{w}_j$ are the consumer's *beliefs* drawn from a distribution $g(\hat{q}_i; w)$ after reviewing the abstracts, where the $\hat{q}_i$ are the agent's current best estimate of the valuation parameters q_i. When the agent purchases and reads articles, it learns their true values w_j and can then use this sample information to update its beliefs $\hat{q}_i$ about the distribution of article values. Therefore, a good consumer strategy should take into account the value of learning. For example, when uncertainty about q_i is high, the consumer might deliberately subscribe even when its estimated surplus is less than F, simply to experience more articles to improve its valuation estimates. Or, having subscribed the consumer might purchase more articles than would maximize expected surplus from current reading.

Turning to the producer's problem, it can choose a subscription fee F and a price schedule P in each period. These should be chosen to maximize some function of expected current and future profits, where current profit can be expressed as:

$$\pi = \sum_{i=1}^{M} \theta_i \left(F + P(k_i) - C(k_i) \right). \tag{3}$$

with $\theta_i = 1$ if consumer i chooses to subscribe, and 0 otherwise. The cost of delivering k_i articles to consumer i is denoted as $C(k_i)$.

In performing its maximization, the producer must take into account the effect of P and F on the consumer's subscription decisions, and the effect of P on the distribution of k_i across the set of subscribers. Higher prices will decrease the number of subscribers and the expected number of articles purchased, of course. To compute the optimal subscription fee and price schedule the broker wants to know the distribution $h(r, q)$ from which the consumers' parameters were generated, and the consumer strategies for subscribing and purchasing. Based on its current beliefs about r and consumer strategies, the broker can simulate a consumer population and its responses to various (F, P) schedules, and then pick (F, P) to maximize a value function. In practice, the broker may not know the consumer type parameters r, nor the consumer strategies. Thus, the broker may choose (F, P) to balance current expected profit according to equation (3), against the increase in expected future profit from learning about consumer preferences by observing their behavior when confronted with varying (F, P) combinations.

---

[4] We assume consumers are *risk neutral*. A *risk averse* agent would want to optimize the expectation of a concave function of surplus, and optimal behavior would depend on second and possibly higher moments of the induced distribution of surplus, not just the expected surplus. See, e.g., [12].

3   General Analysis

In this section, we first analyze the expected surplus and number of articles purchased per subscription period for a rational, fully-informed consumer with a given valuation distribution g. Then, we derive an expression for a monopolistic producer's expected profit as a function of its price schedule and the distribution h of valuation parameters q across the consumer population, assuming that all consumers are rational and fully-informed about their valuation distribution. A rational, fully-informed producer would choose its price schedule so as to maximize its expected profit.

Suppose that a given consumer has its valuations w drawn from a probability density function $g(q; w)$. (The distribution parameters q may vary from one consumer to another.) For the sake of simplicity, we assume that the producer constrains itself to a linear price schedule: $P(k) = k\Delta$. Then a rational consumer will purchase k articles, where k is the number of articles with valuations exceeding the threshold $P(k) - P(k-1) = \Delta$. The probability p_k for exactly k articles to have valuations $w > \Delta$ is

$$p_k = \binom{N}{k} G(q; \Delta)^{N-k} (1 - G(q; \Delta))^k \qquad (4)$$

where $G(q; w)$ represents the cumulative distribution function that corresponds to $g(q; w)$, i.e. it is the probability for an article to be valued at less than w. From this we can compute the expected number of articles purchased:

$$\langle k(q, \Delta) \rangle = \sum_{k=1}^{N} k\, p_k = N\,[1 - G(q; \Delta)] \qquad (5)$$

where the last equality follows from simple manipulations of binomial coefficients.

The expected surplus $\langle s \rangle$ can be obtained from Eq. 2, provided that we first compute $\langle s_k \rangle$, the expected surplus given that exactly k articles prove to have valuations $w > \Delta$. The conditional probability distribution for a single draw from $g(q; w)$ *given* that $w > \Delta$ is

$$\tilde{g}(q; w) = \frac{g(q; w)}{1 - G(q; \Delta)} \Theta(w - \Delta) \qquad (6)$$

where $\Theta(x)$ represents the step function, equal to 1 if $x > 0$ and 0 otherwise. The expected valuation for this distribution is

$$\bar{w}(q; \Delta) = \int_{\Delta}^{\infty} dw\, w\, \tilde{g}(q; w) \qquad (7)$$

The expected sum of k draws from this conditional distribution is $k\bar{w}(q; \Delta)$. Subtracting the price $P(k) = k\Delta$, we obtain:

$$\langle s_k \rangle = k(\bar{w}(\Delta) - \Delta) \qquad (8)$$

Inserting this result into Eq. 2, we obtain:

$$\langle s(\boldsymbol{q}, \Delta) \rangle = \sum_{k=1}^{N} p_k k \left[\bar{w}(\boldsymbol{q}; \Delta) - \Delta \right] = \left[\bar{w}(\boldsymbol{q}; \Delta) - \Delta \right] \langle k(\boldsymbol{q}, \Delta) \rangle \qquad (9)$$
$$= N \left[\bar{w}(\boldsymbol{q}; \Delta) - \Delta \right] \left[1 - G(\boldsymbol{q}; \Delta) \right]$$

Note that the consumer will subscribe if and only if $\langle s(\boldsymbol{q}, \Delta) \rangle$ is greater than the subscription fee F.

Now we take the producer's perspective. If we assume (for simplicity) that the cost of producing and delivering k items is $C(k) = k\gamma$, then the expected profit is

$$\langle \Pi(F, \Delta) \rangle = \sum_{i=1}^{M} \Theta(\langle s(\boldsymbol{q}_i, \Delta) \rangle - F)(F + (\Delta - \gamma) \langle k(\boldsymbol{q}_i, \Delta) \rangle) \qquad (10)$$

$$\approx \int_{\boldsymbol{q}} d\boldsymbol{q} \, h(\boldsymbol{r}, \boldsymbol{q}) \, \Theta(\langle s(\boldsymbol{q}, \Delta) \rangle - F) \, (F + (\Delta - \gamma) \langle k(\boldsymbol{q}, \Delta) \rangle)$$

where $h(\boldsymbol{r}, \boldsymbol{q})$ is the probability distribution for the consumers' $\boldsymbol{q}$ parameters, as defined previously. In effect, the last approximation replaces the actual realized set of consumer distribution parameters $\{\boldsymbol{q}_i\}$ with an ensemble average over all possible realizations of a set of M consumers generated from the distribution h, and this approximation grows increasingly accurate in the limit of large M. Note that a producer that knows h can compute this profit landscape. A fully knowledgeable and rational producer would set Δ and F so as to maximize $\langle \Pi(F, \Delta) \rangle$.

4   Rational and Bounded-Rational Players

In the remainder of the paper, we shall assume simple functional forms for g and h, and explore what happens when the consumers and/or the producer must learn these distributions. In particular, we suppose that g is a one-parameter exponential distribution given by $g(\mu; w) = \mu e^{-\mu w}$, and that $h(\mu)$ is a uniform distribution in the interval from $\mu_{\min}$ to $\mu_{\max}$.

4.1   Fully-Informed Producer and Consumers

As a reference point, we analyze the case where the consumers are fully informed about their individual values of μ, the producer knows the distribution $h(\mu)$, and the producer and the consumers act so as to maximize their expected gain.

Integrating g, we obtain the cumulative distribution $G(\mu; w) = 1 - e^{-\mu w}$. From Eq. 6 we can compute the conditional distribution

$$\tilde{g}(\mu; w) = \frac{g(\mu; w)}{1 - G(\Delta)} \Theta(w - \Delta) \qquad (11)$$

$$= \mu e^{-\mu(w-\Delta)} \Theta(w - \Delta).$$

The average valuation for this conditional distribution is $\bar{w}(\mu, \Delta) = \Delta + \mu^{-1}$. Using Eqs. 5 and 9, we obtain the expected number of purchased articles and the expected surplus (assuming the consumer subscribes):

$$\langle k(\mu) \rangle = Ne^{-\mu\Delta} \tag{12}$$

$$\langle s(\mu) \rangle = \frac{N}{\mu}e^{-\mu\Delta}.$$

To compute the producer's expected profit as a function of Δ and F, we can substitute Eqs. 12 into Eq.10, which yields:

$$\langle \Pi(F, \Delta) \rangle = \frac{1}{(\mu_{max} - \mu_{min})} \int_{\mu_{min}}^{\mu'} d\mu \left(F + N(\Delta - \gamma)e^{-\mu\Delta} \right) \tag{13}$$

$$= \frac{(\mu' - \mu_{min})F + N(1 - \frac{\gamma}{\Delta})\left(e^{-\Delta\mu_{min}} - e^{-\Delta\mu'} \right)}{(\mu_{max} - \mu_{min})},$$

where μ' is defined as $\mu' = \min(\mu_{max}, \tilde{\mu})$ and $\tilde{\mu}$ is defined as the unique solution to $Ne^{-\tilde{\mu}\Delta} = F\tilde{\mu}$.

Eq. 13 can be visualized as a profit landscape in which the expected profit is plotted as a function of F and Δ. It is convenient to define a normalized expected profit $\pi = \Pi/N$ and a normalized fee $f = F/N$. Fig. 1 illustrates the landscape for two different production costs: $\gamma = 0.1$ and $\gamma = 0.5$.

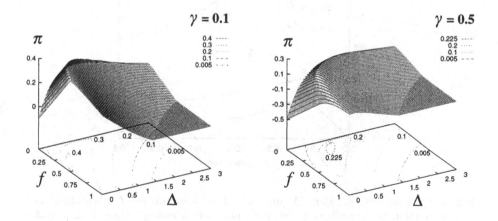

Fig. 1. Profit landscape $\pi(f, \Delta)$. h is a uniform distribution with $\mu_{min} = 0.5$, $\mu_{min} = 2.0$. a) Production cost $\gamma = 0.1$. b) Production cost $\gamma = 0.5$.

In each such landscape, there are two ridges. The lower ridge, which demarcates the boundary beyond which the producer attracts no consumers and thus makes no profit, is defined by $e^{-\mu_{min}\Delta} = f\mu_{min}$. The upper ridge is described by a piecewise joining of two nonlinear curves, the simpler one being described by the relation $e^{-\mu_{max}\Delta} = f\mu_{max}$. This portion of the ridge has the following characteristics:

- it is formed by a discontinuous derivative with respect to f and Δ (it changes abruptly from positive to negative)
- for price settings along this ridge, all consumers subscribe
- if the production cost $\gamma < \gamma_{crit}$, the optimal setting of (f, Δ) occurs along this part of the ridge. For the examples of Fig. 1, the critical production cost γ_{crit} is found [5] to be approximately 0.28, so that Fig. 1a ($\gamma = 0.1$) is in this regime, while Fig. 1b ($\gamma = 0.5$) is not.

The other portion of the ridge is defined by a more complex nonlinear relation between f and Δ. It is less sharp, resulting from derivatives with respect to f and Δ being zero rather than jumping discontinuously from positive to negative [6].

Figure 2 shows the dependence of the optimal f and Δ upon the production cost γ. There is a discontinuous derivative at $\gamma = \gamma_{crit}$, due to the switchover between the two nonlinear curves that define the upper ridge in the landscape. As one might guess, the profit π decreases monotonically with the production cost. The proportion m of consumers that subscribe is 1 for all $\gamma \leq \gamma_{crit}$; for γ exceeding this threshold the proportion of subscribers is strictly less than one, and is given by $(\tilde{\mu} - \mu_{min})/(\mu_{max} - \mu_{min})$.

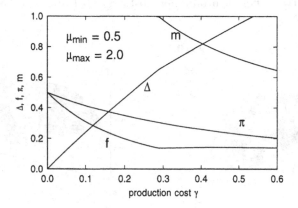

Fig. 2. Optimal price-per-item Δ, normalized subscription fee f, normalized profit π, and fraction of subscribers m vs. item production cost γ, where h is a uniform distribution with $\mu_{min} = 0.5$, $\mu_{min} = 2.0$.

---

[5] It can be shown that, for exponential g and uniform h, $\gamma_{crit} = \frac{\Delta(\gamma_{crit})\mu_{min}\mu_{max}+\mu_{min}}{\mu_{max}^2} \geq \frac{\mu_{min}}{\mu_{max}^2}$, which is positive when $\mu_{min} > 0$.

[6] These characteristics only pertain to the case where g is exponential and h is uniform; we have explored other combinations of functional forms for g and h that yield profit landscapes that are topographically different. For example, if g is exponential and h consists of a number of well-separated mass points, the landscape can contain multiple ridges and peaks.

4.2 Uninformed Consumers

For a variety of reasons, a consumer agent may have to rely on adaptive estimates of its valuation distribution, g. Suppose for example that consumer i knows that g is an exponential distribution, but does not know its individual parameter μ_i. Depending on the consumer's beliefs about the dynamics of the environment, it might wish to place more or less weight on recent observations. Since the mean of the distribution $g(\mu; w) = \mu \exp^{-\mu w}$ is $1/\mu$, one reasonable and flexible approach to estimating μ is to start with an assumed prior μ_0 and after each period of subscription to update the estimate $\hat{\mu}$ according to

$$\hat{\mu}_{t+1} = (\phi * \sigma_t + (1 - \phi)(\hat{\mu}_t)^{-1})^{-1}, \tag{14}$$

where σ_t is the mean of the N valuations received during the subscription period t, and ϕ is the consumer's "flightiness" factor. This factor could be set to a constant, or be time-varying; in fact, if $\phi = 1/t$, all observations are weighted equally, yielding the standard maximum likelihood estimator of μ for exponential distributions [7].

Fig. 3 presents one view of what happens when the consumers all start with exactly the right estimates of their μ parameters, but update their estimates in accordance with Eq. 14 with $\phi = 0.5$. The profit landscape of Fig. 3 was generated as follows: for each pair of f and Δ in a large grid, a simulation was run for 200 subscription periods, and the average profit during that period was recorded on the vertical axis. Compared to Fig 1a, the landscape peaks at a lower value of f and a higher value of Δ, and the overall profit at that peak is lower. More precisely, the peak of the landscape of Fig. 3 occurs at $(f, \Delta, \pi) = (0.0, 1.1, 0.291)$, as compared to the "ideal" peak of Fig. 1a, which occurs at $(f, \Delta, \pi) = (0.30878, 0.24098, 0.41367)$. In other words, if the producer is constrained to a fixed price schedule, then over the course of 200 subscription periods it is most profitable to eliminate subscription fees entirely, compensating only partly by raising the price-per-item by a large factor. The optimal Δ and π in Fig. 3 obtained from simulation are consistent with Eq. 13: with F fixed at 0, optimization with respect to Δ yields an optimal $\Delta = 1.04141$ and a corresponding $\pi = 0.28296$.

Figure 4 provides a different perspective on how consumer learning affects the producer's price-setting strategy and profits. Suppose that the producer were to fix its price parameters f and Δ to their ideal values as given by Fig. 2. Again, we suppose that the production cost is $\gamma = 0.1$, so the ideal values are $(f, \Delta) = (0.30878, 0.24098)$, the corresponding "ideal" profit $\pi = 0.41367$, and the fraction of subscribers $m = 1$. As before, we suppose that the consumers all start with correct estimates of their μ parameters and then update their estimates in accordance with Eq. 14 with $\phi = 0.5$ as they continue to purchase items. Fig. 4a illustrates the resultant profit (normalized by dividing by the "ideal" value of 0.41367) and consumer subscription rate as a function of time. Both continue to diminish over time. Interestingly, they do so at almost exactly the same rate, suggesting that the loss of profit is almost entirely attributable to the continual loss of consumers.

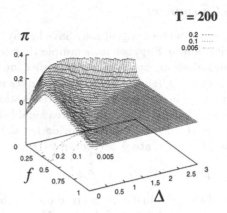

Fig. 3. Profit landscape $\pi(f, \Delta)$ when consumers estimate their μ values, and the flightiness parameter is $\phi = 0.5$. The graph shows the expected average profit after 200 subscription periods when f and Δ are held fixed. The market consists of $M = 1000$ consumers and one seller offering $N = 10$ articles per subscription period. As in Fig 1a, h is a uniform distribution with $\mu_{min} = 0.5$, $\mu_{min} = 2.0$, and the production cost $\gamma = 0.1$.

Fig. 4b offers some insight into the phenomenon of consumer leakage. It shows the distribution of estimated $\hat{\mu}$ in the consumer population at iteration 0 (the dashed line, representing the original distribution $h(\mu)$) and at iteration 40. Although the distribution of $\hat{\mu}$ is uniform at iteration 0, it evolves to a bimodal distribution by iteration 40. As consumer i continually updates its estimate $\hat{\mu}_i$, this estimate exhibits a random walk about its correct value μ_i. If $\hat{\mu}_i$ drifts above a certain critical threshold μ_{crit}, the expected value of subscribing falls below the subscription fee, and consumer i opts out of the market. Once this occurs, consumer i has no further source of information that might demonstrate that its estimated valuation is overly pessimistic, so it remains permanently disenfranchised from the market. The threshold value μ_{crit} therefore acts as an absorbing boundary; its value can be computed implicitly from Eq. 12: $e^{-\hat{\mu}_{crit}\Delta}/\hat{\mu}_{crit} = f$. In the scenario presented in Fig. 4b, $\hat{\mu}_{crit} = 2.0$. Consumers with $\hat{\mu}$ below this value are still subscribing; a consumer i with $\hat{\mu}_i$ above this value will never subscribe again unless the producer entices it back into the market by lowering f or Δ sufficiently to raise the threshold μ_{crit} above $\hat{\mu}_i$.

Fig. 4b shows that there is a large portion of consumers with $\hat{\mu}$ only slightly more than $\hat{\mu}_{crit}$. Even a slight lowering of f and/or Δ by the producer would encourage these consumers to re-enter the market. To help illustrate this point, Fig. 5 shows a profit landscape as a function of f and Δ conditioned on the distribution of $\hat{\mu}$ at iterations a) 0, b) 40, and c) 200. In other words, the simulation is run with the ideal settings of f and Δ for t iterations, and then f and Δ are changed suddenly to different values at iteration $t + 1$. The landscapes show

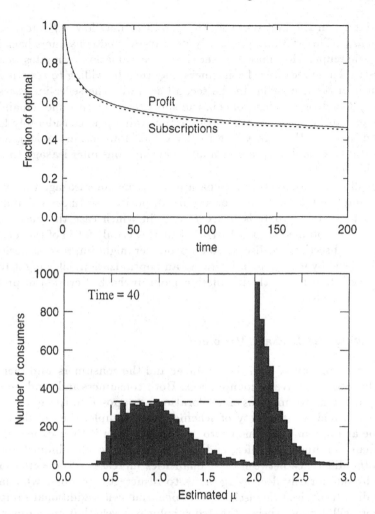

Fig. 4. (a)Profit π (normalized to its ideal value) and proportion of subscribed consumers m vs. time (in subscription periods) when consumers estimate their μ values; flightiness parameter $\phi = 0.5$. Both π and m diminish indefinitely and nearly identically, although the rate of reduction slows with time. The market consists of $M = 10000$ consumers and one seller offering $N = 10$ articles per subscription period. (b) Histogram of $\hat{\mu}$ in the consumer population at iteration 40. The dashed line indicates the initial distribution of $\hat{\mu}$.

the expected profit for iteration $t + 1$. According to Fig. 4b, the profit landscape initially peaks at the ideal values $(f, \Delta) = (0.30878, 0.24098)$, but as time passes the peak quickly develops into an ever-deepening trough that is bordered by two ridges, each of which contains a peak. The producer could do better by switching to either of the two peaks — either by lowering or raising its price parameters appropriately. In the first scenario, the producer may lower f and/or Δ so as to lower $\hat{\mu}_{\mathrm{crit}}$. This will lure previously disenfranchised consumers back into the market, whereupon they may discover that their valuation estimates were overly pessimistic. These recaptured consumers may then be willing to stay in the market even if prices rise again. In the second scenario, the seller increases profits by *raising* f and/or Δ. This works in the short term because the remaining consumers tend to be those for whom the actual value μ is considerably less than $\hat{\mu}_{\mathrm{crit}}$, and therefore they are willing to pay more. However, in the long term, this reduces the threshold $\hat{\mu}_{\mathrm{crit}}$ substantially, causing consumer leakage to occur at a much higher rate.

Regardless of γ, ϕ, or other such parameters, consumer leakage will eventually lead to complete market failure for any fixed, positive settings of f and Δ. The only way to sustain profits is to fix $f = 0$, in which case the maximal profit $\pi = 0.28296$ is obtained at $\Delta = 1.04141$. But this is only 0.684 of the ideal profit. In the next subsection, we discuss how a producer might improve its performance above this level by using *dynamic* pricing and optimization, allowing it to charge finite subscription fees without suffering from unchecked erosion of profits and subscription levels.

4.3 Solving the Leakage Problem

Consumer leakage hurts both the producer and the consumers, and therefore all players have an incentive to counteract it. Both consumers and producers can do this by putting more emphasis on exploration as opposed to (pure) exploitation. Consumers could use a variety of schemes; for example, they could choose to subscribe at random with a non-zero probability even if their expected surplus is less than the subscription fee, and this probability could diminish monotonically as the difference between these quantities increases. Producers could fight leakage by temporarily decreasing prices to resurrect consumers who have mistakenly disenfranchised themselves, in hopes that, with additional samples, the consumers will increase their estimated surplus to levels that can support higher prices. One might expect that consumers could be enticed back into the market even with small discounts, since, once their $\hat{\mu}$ ventures into a realm where subscription appears to be unprofitable, it is frozen at this just-barely-unprofitable value [7].

Here we focus on the producer's strategy for enticing overly pessimistic consumers back into the market. (This is not to deny that consumers' exploration strategies merit serious study.) From our study of consumer leakage, it is apparent that the producer's strategy must involve dynamic pricing, and that it must cope with a profit landscape that changes dynamically due to shifts caused by

---

[7] Economists have studied behavior of this sort in order to explain temporal price dispersion, such as "sales", temporary discounts, and introductory pricing. A mixture of reasons have been modeled, including attempts to price discriminate between better and worse informed customers, and inducing potential customers to bear some search costs to find a better price or product. See [18], [19], and [22].

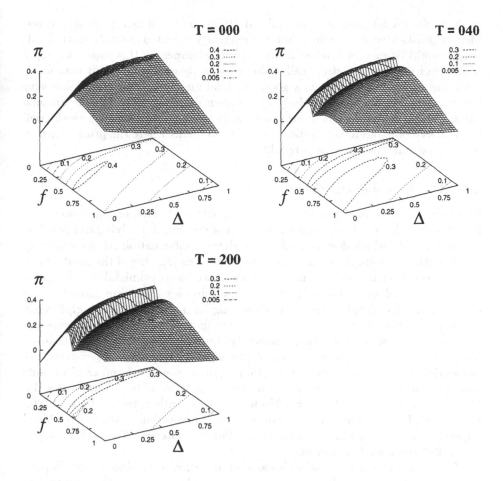

Fig. 5. Profit landscape showing the mean profit per article per consumer as a function of f and Δ conditioned on the distribution of $\hat{\mu}$ a) at iteration 0, b) at iteration 40, and c) at iteration 200. Consumers are assumed to estimate their μ values with flightiness parameter $\phi = 0.5$. (Note that, compared to Fig 1a and Fig 3, this figure uses a smaller range along the axis representing Δ.)

consumers' ongoing attempts to learn an estimate of g. It also seems most likely that the pricing strategy would involve stochastic search on this dynamically changing landscape, rather than following some pre-planned schedule.

The dynamically changing nature of the profit landscape in our problem limits the applicability of standard stochastic optimization techniques. For example, approaches such as simulated annealing implicitly assume that the search is being conducted on a static landscape as the value of its temperature parameter is lowered. On the other hand, standard gradient-based optimization approaches are of limited use because it is often too hard to determine the gradient of the profit landscape for general g and h distributions or for different price structures. More sophisticated approaches that are currently oriented towards static landscapes might be modified to handle dynamic landscapes. In this paper, we apply a simple direct search method called the *amoeba* algorithm for profit maximization. The amoeba algorithm is a good candidate optimizer since it makes very few assumptions about the underlying problem domain. Although the amoeba can get stuck at local optima, our preliminary work indicates that it works well for a variety of g and h distributions, even in problems where the price structure involves as many as ten parameters [3].

4.4   The Amoeba Algorithm

Consider the unconstrained optimization problem of maximizing a nonlinear function $\mathcal{F}(x)$ for $x \in \Re^n$. A well-known class of methods for solving this problem is direct search, which does not rely on derivative information (either explicitly or implicitly), but employs only function evaluations [2]. One of the most widely used direct search methods for nonlinear unconstrained optimization problems is the Nelder-Mead *simplex* algorithm [15]. (This simplex algorithm should not be confused with the simplex algorithm of Dantzig for linear programming.) Nelder-Mead's algorithm is parsimonious in the number of function evaluations per iteration, and is often able to find reasonably good solutions quickly. On the other hand, the theoretical underpinnings of the algorithm, such as its convergence properties, are less than satisfactory [10, 13]. In response, a number of variants have been proposed in the literature which attempt to address such issues [14, 20, 21]. For a detailed survey of the Nelder-Mead algorithm, the reader may refer to [25, 26]. In this paper, we focus on one implementation of the Nelder-Mead algorithm as described in the popular handbook *Numerical Recipes* [17], where it is called the *amoeba* algorithm.

The amoeba algorithm maintains at each iteration a nondegenerate simplex, a geometric figure in n dimensions of nonzero volume that is the convex hull of $n + 1$ vertices, $x_0, x_1, \ldots, x_n$, and their respective function values. In each iteration, new points are computed, along with their function values, to form a new simplex. The algorithm terminates when the function values at the vertices of the simplex satisfy a predetermined condition.

One iteration of the amoeba algorithm consists of the following steps:

1. **Order:** Order and re-label the $n + 1$ vertices as $x_0, x_1, \ldots, x_n$, such that $\mathcal{F}(x_0) \geq \mathcal{F}(x_1) \geq \ldots \geq \mathcal{F}(x_n)$. Since we want to maximize, we refer to x_0 as the *best* vertex or point, to x_n as the *worst* point, and to x_{n-1} as the *next-worst* point. Let $\bar{x}$ refer to the centroid of the n best points in the vertex (i.e., all vertices except for x_n) : $\bar{x} = (\sum_{i=0}^{n-1} x_i)/n$.

2. **Reflect.** Compute the *reflection* point x_r,

$$x_r = \bar{x} + \alpha(\bar{x} - x_n). \tag{15}$$

Evaluate $\mathcal{F}(x_r)$. If $\mathcal{F}(x_0) \geq \mathcal{F}(x_r) > \mathcal{F}(x_n)$, accept the reflected point x_r and terminate the iteration.

3. **Expand.** If $\mathcal{F}(x_r) > \mathcal{F}(x_0)$, compute the *expansion* point x_e,

$$x_e = x_r + \beta(x_r - \bar{x}). \tag{16}$$

If $\mathcal{F}(x_e) > \mathcal{F}(x_r)$ accept x_e and terminate the iteration; otherwise (i.e., if $\mathcal{F}(x_r) \geq \mathcal{F}(x_e)$) accept x_r and terminate the iteration.

4. **Contract.** If $\mathcal{F}(x_r) < \mathcal{F}(x_{n-1})$, perform a contraction between $\bar{x}$ and x_n

$$x_c = \bar{x} + \zeta(\bar{x} - x_n). \tag{17}$$

If $\mathcal{F}(x_c) \geq \mathcal{F}(x_n)$ accept x_c and terminate the iteration.

5. **Shrink Simplex.** Evaluate $\mathcal{F}$ at the n new vertices for $i = 1, \ldots, n$.

$$x_i = x_0 + \eta(x_i - x_0). \tag{18}$$

For the four coefficients, the standard values reported in the literature are: $\alpha = 1, \beta = 1, \zeta = 0.5, \eta = 0.5$.

4.5 Applying Amoeba to Increase Profit

In the model delineated in this paper, the producer faces a profit maximization problem with two independent variables: the normalized subscription fee f and the price-per-item Δ. For this problem, the amoeba employs a two dimensional simplex (*i.e.*, a triangle) to search in the profit landscape. In the scenario in which the consumers know their valuations and the producer knows both g and h, the producer can compute the profit landscape and use amoeba offline to compute the optimal f and Δ to several digits of accuracy within a few dozen iterations. This takes little more than a second on a modest processor. It then sets f and Δ to their computed values. If the consumers know their valuations, but the producer does *not* know g and h, the producer can still use amoeba, but it must do so in an online configuration. In this case, each iteration of the amoeba samples the profit landscape by experimentation. Thus each step is slow and costly, and the producer has to expect non-optimal profit during the exploration phase of the algorithm. Nonetheless, after a few dozen iterations, the producer will have found near-optimal settings of f and Δ, and will enjoy the same steady-state profits as a producer that was fully informed from the beginning.

The situation becomes more interesting when the producer uses amoeba in a market in which the consumers learn their own valuations by sampling items and updating their estimates via Eq. 14. The producer's knowledge of g and h is now immaterial: its profit landscape is determined by the consumers' *beliefs* about their valuations. As has been seen, the distribution of estimated $\hat{\mu}$ can diverge substantially from $h(\mu)$, resulting in a profit landscape that shifts dramatically over time. Can the amoeba algorithm cope with a dynamic landscape?

Fig. 6a illustrates what happens when the amoeba algorithm is started with very small, low-profit values of f and Δ. Quickly, it finds profitable values for these parameters. Having reached a high-profit region, the amoeba begins to contract its simplex. However, once the price parameters stabilize, consumer leakage begins to set in, and the amoeba is unable to escape from an ever-deepening trough similar in nature to that of Fig. 5c. Amoeba falls into this trap because it never bothers to resample vertices that it has already evaluated. In particularly, it fails to consider that the profit obtained at the best vertex in its simplex may change over time — it (falsely) believes that the best vertex is an ever-sharper needle sitting in a ever-deepening trough in the profit landscape. Once the amoeba finds a high-profit region, it is compelled to shrink its simplex, and it is completely blind to the ever-diminishing profits that occur throughout that simplex.

The amoeba algorithm can be improved considerably for this application by having it occasionally resample previously sampled points and by conditionally expanding its simplex from time to time. Specifically, we propose a modified amoeba that is more suitable for dynamic landscapes by replacing Step 5 (**Shrink Simplex**) in the amoeba algorithm as follows:

5. **Resample Best Vertex.** Evaluate $\mathcal{F}$ at x_0. Denote the new evaluate as $\mathcal{F}_{new}(x_0)$.
   If $\mathcal{F}_{new}(x_0) < \mathcal{F}(x_0)$ then *expand simplex*, by computing the n new vertices for $i = 1, \ldots, n$:

$$x_i = x_0 + \eta(x_i + x_0). \tag{19}$$

   Else, (i.e., $\mathcal{F}_{new}(x_0), \geq \mathcal{F}(x_0)$) *shrink simplex*, and compute the n new vertices for $i = 1, \ldots, n$:

$$x_i = x_0 + \eta(x_i - x_0). \tag{20}$$

Fig. 7 illustrates that the modified amoeba algorithm avoids long-term profit and consumer leakage. Leakage is thwarted because the modified amoeba briefly lowers its prices to recapture disenfranchised consumers, and then raises them again to enjoy increased profits from consumers who have learned again to appreciate the value of the producer's wares. In steady state, the average profit (computed between iterations 50 and 200 to avoid transient effects) is 0.31683, or 0.766 of the ideal profit. This is approximately a 12% improvement over the highest profit that can be sustained with fixed prices, which was $(f, \Delta, \pi) = (0, 1.04141, 0.28296)$.

Fig. 8 illustrates how the distribution of $\hat{\mu}$ responds to lowering of prices by the modified amoeba. In iteration 40, the producer makes a profit $\pi = 0.34327$ by setting $(f, \Delta) = (0.34103, 0.37486)$. In Fig. 8a, less than 65% of the consumer population subscribes — the ones whose estimates $\hat{\mu}$ are below the critical threshold for those price parameters, $\hat{\mu}_{crit} = 1.5$.

The situation changes dramatically in iteration 41 when the producer sets $(f, \Delta) = (0.04457, 0.38722)$. While the profit decreases temporarily ($\pi = 0.22429$), *all* consumers are now encouraged to subscribe because the critical threshold has risen to $\hat{\mu}_{crit} = 4.1$. The consumers re-estimate their μ values, and the overall distribution now shifts to that illustrated in Fig. 8b. This sets the stage for the producer to obtain profit $\pi > 0.34$ in the next four time steps by increasing f (but reducing Δ).

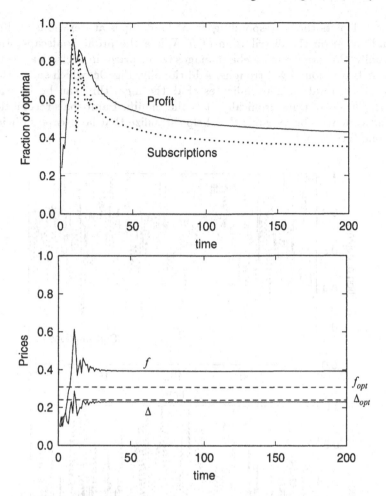

Fig. 6. (a) Profit π (solid line; normalized to "ideal" value of 0.41367) and proportion of subscribed consumers m (dashed line) vs. time (in subscription periods) and (b) f (solid) and Δ (dashed) vs. time when the producer uses amoeba for online learning and the consumers estimate their μ values with flightiness parameter $\phi = 0.5$. The horizontal dashed lines indicate the optimal f and Δ values for fully informed consumers. As before, the market consists of $M = 10000$ consumers and one seller offering $N = 10$ articles per subscription period. For a simplex in two dimensions (a triangle), we have used the standard coefficients $\alpha = 1, \beta = 1, \zeta = 0.5, \eta = 0.5$ for the amoeba algorithm. In this and all subsequent experiments involving the amoeba algorithm, the initial simplex consists of the following (f, Δ) values: $(0.10, 0.10)$, $(0.10, 0.15)$, and $(0.15, 0.10)$.

Fig. 9 depicts the corresponding profit landscapes at iterations a) 40 and b) 41 conditioned on the distribution of $\hat{\mu}$. While the profit landscape still shifts continually, the modified amoeba manages to set prices in such a way as to avoid the formation of long-lived troughs. Additionally, Fig. 9c, which shows the profit landscape at iteration 200, indicates that the algorithm can be be successful for long periods of time. Ironically, it is the modified amoeba's recognition that the landscape may be dynamic that helps stabilize that landscape sufficiently to yield long-term profits.

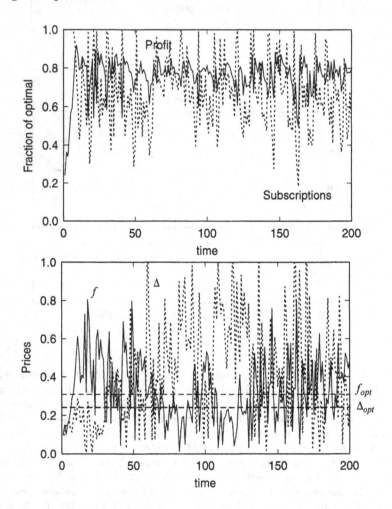

Fig. 7. (a)Profit π (solid line; normalized to "ideal" value of 0.41367) and proportion of subscribed consumers m (dashed line) vs. time (in subscription periods) and (b) f (solid) and Δ (dashed) vs. time when the producer uses the modified amoeba algorithm for online learning. The parameter settings remain unchanged from Fig. 6.

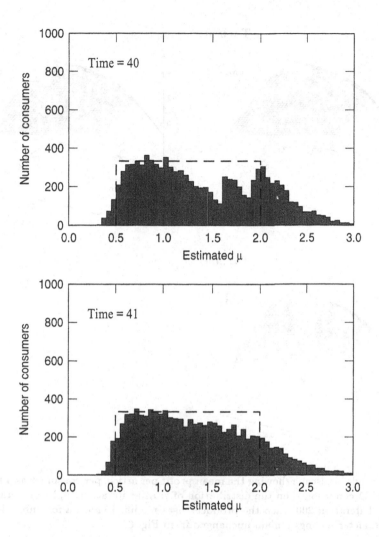

Fig. 8. Estimated μ distributions at (a) time 40 and (b) time 41 (in subscription periods) when the producer uses modified amoeba for online learning. The dashed line represents the initial distribution of $\hat{\mu}$.

5 Conclusions

Commerce in information goods is one of the earliest emerging applications for intelligent agents in commerce. However, the fundamental characteristics of information goods mean that they can and likely will be offered in widely varying configurations. Participating agents will need to deal with uncertainty about both prices and location in multi-dimensional product space. Thus, studying the behavior of learning agents is central to understanding and designing for

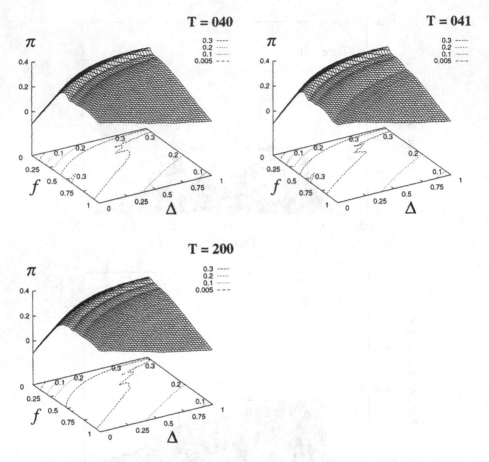

Fig. 9. Profit landscape showing the mean profit per article per consumer as a function of f and Δ conditioned on the distribution of $\hat{\mu}$ a) at iteration 40, b) at iteration 41, and c) at iteration 200 when the producer uses modified amoeba for online learning. The parameter settings remain unchanged from Fig. 6.

agent-based information economies. Since uncertainty will exist on both sides of transactions, and interactions between learning agents that are negotiating and transacting with other learning agents may lead to unexpected dynamics, it is important to study two-sided learning.

We presented a simple but powerful model of an information bundling economy with a single producer and multiple consumer agents. We then explored the pricing and purchasing behavior of these agents when articles can be bundled. In this initial exploration, we studied the dynamics of this economy when consumer agents are uninformed about the distribution of article values. We discovered that a reasonable albeit naïve consumer learning strategy can have a profound influence on market behavior — in this case, a strikingly bad influence.

Our consumer and producer agents were rather naïve in our first learning experiments. This could be viewed as a criticism of our modeling. However, especially early in the development of adaptive agent intelligence, it may well be that agent-based markets are quite vulnerable to odd behavior and dysfunctional dynamics of the sort we observed. Our consumer agents did not recognize the option value of new information, and thus suffered by not undertaking sufficient exploration relative to exploitation. Our producer agent did not initially adapt to the pathological dynamics induced by the consumer agent naïveté, and thus suffered by relying too confidently on its "perfect" but static knowledge. Although it was fairly easy for us to see what was going wrong, and to modify the producer agent in a simple way that ameliorated much of the problem, our environment is artificially simple and static. In more realistic settings it may be quite difficult for even relatively intelligent agents to adapt to emergent pathologies. Human markets may not be as susceptible because human behavior is less rote and more reflective. The lesson for agent design is to search for strategies that are dynamically robust and adaptive in the face of substantial uncertainty.

We have started to explore how to make our simple mechanism more robust in realistic settings. For example, the search technique employed by the amoeba algorithm is likely to get stuck at local optima. For the uniform h there is a single peak in the profit landscape, but that is not at all general. Several powerful optimization techniques exist for static landscapes with multiple optima. Extensions to these that handle changing, noisy landscapes may lead to robustly adaptive agent learning strategies.

We have an active agenda of continuing work on this topic. For example, we have begun to consider less naive consumer strategies that balance exploration against exploitation. We are considering producer strategies that adapt based on the number of recent subscribers relative to the producer's model of the optimal number of subscribers. Perhaps most challenging — but essential to a more general understanding of the problem — is the extension of our work into an economy with multiple producers who are underinformed about each other's competitive strategies as well as about consumer valuations.

In this and earlier work we have found that initial plausible but simple designs of economically-intelligent agents lead to dynamic market interactions that can be surprising and unsuccessful. The value of intelligent agents in electronic commerce will depend on the ability to understand the problems of learning and adaptivity, and to design agents that interact robustly in the presence of substantial uncertainty about both parameters and the strategies of other underinformed agents.

Commerce in information goods is one of the earliest emerging applications for intelligent agents in commerce. However, the fundamental characteristics of information goods mean that they can and likely will be offered in widely varying configurations. Participating agents will need to deal with uncertainty about both prices and location in multi-dimensional product space. Thus, studying the behavior of learning agents is central to understanding and designing for agent-based information economies. Since uncertainty will exist on both sides of transactions, and interactions between learning agents that are negotiating and transacting with other learning agents may lead to unexpected dynamics, it is important to study two-sided learning.

We presented a simple but powerful model of an information bundling economy with a single producer and multiple consumer agents. We then explored the pricing and purchasing behavior of these agents when articles can be bundled. In this initial exploration, we studied the dynamics of this economy when consumer agents are uninformed about the distribution of article values. We discovered that a reasonable albeit naïve consumer learning strategy can have a profound influence on market behavior — in this case, a strikingly bad influence.

Our consumer and producer agents were rather naïve in our first learning experiments. This could be viewed as a criticism of our modeling. However, especially early in the development of adaptive agent intelligence, it may well be that agent-based markets are quite vulnerable to odd behavior and dysfunctional dynamics of the sort we observed. Our consumer agents did not recognize the option value of new information, and thus suffered by not undertaking sufficient exploration relative to exploitation. Our producer agent did not initially adapt to the pathological dynamics induced by the consumer agent naïveté, and thus suffered by relying too confidently on its "perfect" but static knowledge. Although it was fairly easy for us to see what was going wrong, and to modify the producer agent in a simple way that ameliorated much of the problem, our environment is artificially simple and static. In more realistic settings it may be quite difficult for even relatively intelligent agents to adapt to emergent pathologies. Human markets may not be as susceptible because human behavior is less rote and more reflective. The lesson for agent design is to search for strategies that are dynamically robust and adaptive in the face of substantial uncertainty.

We have started to explore how to make our simple mechanism more robust in realistic settings. For example, the search technique employed by the amoeba algorithm is likely to get stuck at local optima. For the uniform h there is a single peak in the profit landscape, but that is not at all general. Several powerful optimization techniques exist for static landscapes with multiple optima. Extensions to these that handle changing, noisy landscapes may lead to robustly adaptive agent learning strategies.

We have an active agenda of continuing work on this topic. For example, we have begun to consider less naive consumer strategies that balance exploration against exploitation. We are considering producer strategies that adapt based on the number of recent subscribers relative to the producer's model of the optimal number of subscribers. Perhaps most challenging — but essential to a more general understanding of the problem — is the extension of our work into an economy with multiple producers who are underinformed about each other's competitive strategies as well as about consumer valuations.

In this and earlier work we have found that initial plausible but simple designs of economically-intelligent agents lead to dynamic market interactions that can be surprising and unsuccessful. The value of intelligent agents in electronic commerce will depend on the ability to understand the problems of learning and adaptivity, and to design agents that interact robustly in the presence of substantial uncertainty about both parameters and the strategies of other underinformed agents.

Acknowledgments

MacKie-Mason gratefully acknowledges support from an IBM University Partnership grant and from DARPA/ITO grant F30602-97-1-0228.

References

1. Y. Bakos and E. Brynjolfsson. Bundling information goods: Pricing, profits and efficiency. In B. Kahin and H. Varian, editors, *Internet Publishing and Beyond: The Economics of Digital Information and Intellectual Property*. MIT Press, Cambridge, Massachusetts, 2000.
2. D. P. Bertsekas. *Nonlinear Programming*. Athena Scientific, Belmont, 1995.
3. C. H. Brooks, S. Fay, R. Das, J. K. Mackie-Mason, J. O. Kephart, and E. H. Durfee. Automated search strategies in an electronic goods market: Learning and complex price scheduling. In *Proceedings of the ACM Conference on Electronic Commerce*, 1999.
4. J. C. Chuang and M. A. Sirbu. Network delivery of information goods: Optimal pricing of articles and subscriptions. In B. Kahin and H. Varian, editors, *Internet Publishing and Beyond: The Economics of Digital Information and Intellectual Property*. MIT Press, Cambridge, Massachusetts, 2000.
5. S. Fay and J. K. MacKie-Mason. Competition between firms that bundle. Manuscript, Dept. of Economics, University of Michigan, 1998.
6. J. E. Hanson and J. O. Kephart. Spontaneous specialization in a free-market economy of agents. In *Proceedings of Workshop on Artificial Societies and Computational Markets at the Second International Conference on Autonomous Agents*, May 1998.
7. N. L. Johnson, S. Kotz, and N. Balakrishnan. *Continuous Univariate Distributions*, volume 1. John Wiley & Sons, Inc., New York, 1995.
8. J. O. Kephart, J. E. Hanson, D. W. Levine, B. N. Grosof, J. Sairamesh, R. B. Segal, and S. R. White. Dynamics of an information-filtering economy. In *Proceedings of Second International Workshop on Cooperative Information Agents (CIA-98)*, Paris, July 1998.
9. J. O. Kephart, J. E. Hanson, and J. Sairamesh. Price-war dynamics in a free-market economy of software agents. In *Proceedings of Alife VI*, June 1998.
10. J. C. Lagarias, J. A. Reeds, M. H. Wright, and P. E. Wright. Convergence properties of the Nelder–Mead simplex method in low dimensions. *SIAM Journal on Optimization*, 9(1):112–147, 1998.
11. J. K. MacKie-Mason and J. Riveros. Economics and electronic access to scholarly information. In B. Kahin and H. Varian, editors, *Internet Publishing and Beyond: The Economics of Digital Information and Intellectual Property*. MIT Press, Cambridge, Massachusetts, 2000.
12. A. Mas-Colell, M. Whinston, and J. Green. *Microeconomic Theory*. Oxford University Press, 1995.

13. K. I. M. McKinnon. Convergence of the Nelder-Mead simplex method to a non-stationary point. *SIAM Journal on Optimization*, 9(1):148–158, 1998.
14. L. Nazareth and P. Tseng. Gilding the lily: a variant of the Nelder-Mead algorithm. Department of Mathematics, University of Washington, Seattle, 1998.
15. J. A. Nelder and R. Mead. A simplex method for function minimization. *Computer Journal*, 7:308–313, 1965.
16. W. Oi. A Disneyland dilemma: Two-part tariffs for a Mickey Mouse monopoly. *The Quarterly Journal of Economics*, 85(1):77–96, February 1971.
17. W. H. Press, B. P. Flannery, S. A. Teukolsky, and W. T. Vetterling. *Numerical Recipes in C: The Art of Scientific Computing*. Cambridge University Press, Cambridge, 1988.
18. S. Salop and J. Stiglitz. Bargains and ripoffs: A model of monopolistically competitive price dispersion. *Review of Economic Studies*, 44:493–510, October 1977.
19. Y. Shilony. Mixed pricing in oligopoly. *Journal of Economic Theory*, 14:373–388, April 1977.
20. V. Torczon. On the convergence of pattern search algorithms. *SIAM Journal on Optimization*, 7(1):1–25, 1997.
21. P. Tseng. Fortified-descent simplical search method: a general approach. Department of Mathematics, University of Washington, Seattle, 1998.
22. H. R. Varian. A model of sales. *American Economic Review*, 70:651–659, September 1980.
23. J. M. Vidal and E. H. Durfee. The moving target problem in multi-agent learning. In *Proceedings of the Third International Conference on Multi-agent Systems (ICMAS98)*, 1998.
24. J. M. Vidal and E. H. Durfee. Learning nested agent models in an information economy. *Journal of Experimental and Theoretical Artificial Intelligence (special issue on learning in distributed artificial intelligence systems)*, 1999. to appear.
25. F. H. Walters, L. R. Parker, S. L. Morgan, and S. N. Deming. *Sequential Simplex Optimization*. CRC Press, Boca Raton, Florida, 1991.
26. M. H. Wright. Direct search methods: once scorned, now respectable. In D. F. Griffiths and G. A. Watson, editors, *Numerical Analysis: Proceedings of the 1995 Dundee Biennial Conference in Numerical Analysis*, pages 191–208, Harlow, United Kingdom, 1996. Addison-Wesley Longman.

Appendix: List of Symbols

$C(k_i)$: The cost of delivering k_i articles to consumer i.

F: Subscription fee.

f: Normalized subscription fee $= F/N$.

$\mathcal{F}$: Any nonlinear function $\mathcal{F}(x)$ for $x \in \Re^n$.

$G(q; w)$: Cumulative distribution function of $g(q; w)$.

$g(q; w)$: The probability density function from which the consumer valuations w are drawn. q is the distribution parameter which may vary from one consumer to another.

$h(r; q)$: The probability distribution for the consumers' q parameter. r is the distribution parameter.

i: Index of consumers as in consumer i.

j: Index of valuations as in w_j.

K: Set of articles.

k: Index of articles; $k \in \{1, \ldots, N\}$.

M: Total number of consumers in the system.

m: Proportion of subscribing consumers.

N: Number of articles generated by the producer in each subscription period.

n: Dimension of problem space as in $\Re^n$.

P: The price schedule $= \{P(1), \ldots, P(N)\}$.

$P(k)$: The price charged for a subset of $k \in \{1, \ldots, N\}$ of the N articles.

p_k: The vector of probabilities that any k is the expected surplus maximizing number of articles.

q: The distribution parameter in $g(q; w)$.

r: The distribution parameter in $h(r; q)$.

s: Consumer surplus.

t: Index of the subscription period.

w_j: Consumer valuation of article j.

x: $x \in \Re^n$.

α: Reflection coefficient in the amoeba algorithm.

β: Expansion coefficient in the amoeba algorithm.

γ: Normalized production cost assuming linear production cost; $C(k) = k\gamma$.

Δ: Normalized price-per-item assuming linear price schedule; $P(k) = k\Delta$.

ζ: Contraction coefficient in the amoeba algorithm.

η: Simplex shrink/expand coefficient in the amoeba algorithm.

θ_i: Hard threshold function. Equals 1 if consumer i subscribes, else it is 0.

μ: Parameter for the exponential distribution of consumer valuations; $g(\mu; w) = \mu e^{-\mu w}$.

π: Normalized expected profit; Π/N.

Π: Expected profit.

σ_t: The mean of the N valuations received during the subscription period t.

ϕ: The consumer's "flightiness" factor.

Optimal Auction Design for Agents with Hard Valuation Problems

David C. Parkes*

Computer and Information Science Department
University of Pennsylvania, Philadelphia PA 19104
dparkes@unagi.cis.upenn.edu

Abstract. As traditional commerce moves on-line more business transactions will be mediated by software agents, and the ability of agent-
mediated electronic marketplaces to efficiently allocate resources will be
highly dependent on the complexity of the decision problems that agents
face; determined in part by the structure of the marketplace, resource
characteristics, and the nature of agents' local problems. We compare
auction performance for agents that have hard local problems, and uncertain values for goods. Perhaps an agent must solve a hard optimization
problem to value a good, or interact with a busy and expensive human
expert. Although auction design cannot simplify the valuation problem
itself, we show that good auction design can simplify *meta*-deliberation
– providing incentives for the "right" agents to deliberate for the "right"
amount of time. Empirical results for a particular cost-benefit model
of deliberation show that an ascending-price auction will often support
higher revenue and efficiency than other auction designs. The price provides agents with useful information about the value that other agents
hold for the good.
Keywords: Agent-mediated electronic commerce, valuation problem,
metadeliberation, auction theory.

1 Introduction

As traditional commerce moves on-line more business transactions will be mediated by software agents, and dynamically negotiated between multiple and
fluidly changing partners. The ability of agent-mediated electronic marketplaces
to efficiently allocate resources will be highly dependent on the complexity of the
decision problems that agents face; determined in part by the structure of the
marketplace, resource characteristics, and the nature of agents' local problems.

While many of the costs that are associated with traditional auctions, such as
the cost of participation (making bids and watching the progress of an auction),
are unimportant in agent-mediated electronic auctions, the cost of valuation remains important [17]. The value of a good is often uncertain, and an accurate

---

* This research was funded in part by the National Science Foundation under Grant
SBR 97-08965.

A. Moukas, C. Sierra, and F. Ygge (Eds.): AMEC'99, LNAI 1788, pp. 206–219, 2000.
© Springer-Verlag Berlin Heidelberg 2000

valuation can require that an agent solves a hard optimization problem, or interacts with a busy and expensive human expert. In fact, electronic markets may
make the valuation problem more difficult, because of mitigating factors such as
decreased aggregation, increased product differentiation, and increased dynamics [1, 4, 5]. In this paper we compare auction performance for agents that have
hard local problems, and uncertain values for goods.

Just as careful market design can reduce the complexity of the bidding problem, for example by providing incentives for agents to reveal their true value for
a good [28], careful market design can also reduce the loss in efficiency that is
associated with agents that have hard valuation problems. Unlike the bidding
problem, market design can not simplify the valuation problem itself. However
market design can improve the quality of an agent's decisions about when to
reason about the value of a good. A well structured marketplace can provide
information to enable the "right" agents to deliberate for the "right" amount of
time. Roughly, agents with high values should deliberate more than agents with
low values.

For example, consider a bidding agent that participates in an on-line auction
for a flight to Stockholm, initialized by a user with a *lower bound* $\underline{v}$ on value.
The user does not know her exact value for the flight, but finds it relatively
easy to bound her value. Although the agent can absorb the costs of monitoring
the auction and placing bids, the agent cannot easily refine the user's value for
the flight. The value of non-standard and short-supply goods is often subjective,
and can depend on many factors that an agent cannot know. However, in an
ascending-price auction the agent can bid up to $\underline{v}$, and then prompt the user
for a more accurate value. Compare this to a sealed-bid auction where the user
needs *a priori* information about the distribution of bids from other agents to
make a good decision about how much time to spend deliberating about her
value for the flight. The ascending-price auction provides dynamic information
on the value of other participants, and can enable the user to avoid deliberation
altogether – for example if the price increases above an *upper bound* on value.

We compare the performance of three market designs with agents that have
hard valuation problems: a posted-price sequential auction; a second-price sealed-
bid auction; and a first-price ascending-price auction [12]. In the posted-price
auction the seller offers the good at a fixed price to each agent in turn, and
does not sell the good if no agent accepts the price. The price is set dynamically
in the ascending- and sealed-bid auctions, and we allow the seller to optimize
the ask price for distributional information about the values of agents in the
posted-price auction.

In Section 2 we introduce a simple model for agents with hard valuation problems that allows the derivation of optimal expected-case metadeliberation and
bidding strategies for risk-neutral agents in each auction; we describe the optimal strategies in Section 3. Section 4 presents empirical results from simulation,
comparing the efficiency and revenue in each auction for different numbers of
agents and different levels of local problem complexity. Finally we discuss related

work in auction theory, artificial intelligence, and economics, before presenting our conclusions.

2 The Valuation Problem

In standard auction theory agents either know their value for a good (private values) or the value is common across all agents but unknown because of missing information (common-values) [12]. We model an auction with agents that have private independent values for a good, but uncertainty about the value. We believe that this model is especially relevant in on-line auctions, where agents can have hard local problems (e.g. a manufacturing agent that bids for components), or goods are non-standard and difficult to value (e.g. collectibles at www.ebay.com). We assume that agents have an option to refine their value for a cost. The cost is considered to represent the actual cost of consulting an expensive expert, or the cost that results from suboptimal or missed bids because of lost deliberation about the value of goods in other marketplaces.

Conceptually, one can partition the decision problem of a bidding agent into three sub-problems: *metadeliberation*, *valuation*, and *bidding*. The optimal bidding strategy depends on the auction and an agent's (possibly approximate) solution to its valuation problem. The optimal metadeliberation strategy follows from an analysis of an agent's valuation problem and bidding strategy. An agent bids only when it has decided to perform no more deliberation about the value of the good.[1] Previous models of agent-mediated markets have addressed the complexity of the *bidding problem*, that is deciding on an optimal bid given the value of a good, but largely ignored the valuation and metadeliberation problems (although see [24, 25]).

2.1 A Simple Theoretical Model

We propose a simple model for the valuation problem of an agent, that enables the derivation of optimal metadeliberation and bidding strategies for agents in each auction. The model matches some of the properties of standard algorithmic techniques for solving hard optimization problems, such as Lagrangian relaxation, depth-first search, and branch-and-bound. Furthermore, the model supports a mode of interaction between people and software bidding agents that is provided in some current on-line auctions [17]. We do not expect the valuation

---

[1] In an alternative model agents do not explicitly solve the valuation problem, but select a bidding strategy directly, based on the payoff from past bids [2]. It is often useful to separate the valuation and bidding phases because: (a) there might be a separation of skills/information – for example when a software agent *bids* for a person that *values* the good; (b) in a business context, separation can enable a bidding agent to leverage existing decision analysis tools and models for the valuation problem; (c) in some markets (for example incentive compatible markets) the bidding problem is trivial.

problems and decision procedures of real agents (or real experts) to have characteristics that match the precise assumptions (e.g. distributional assumptions) of our model. However, we believe that the general results from our analysis will hold in many real problem domains for agents with hard valuation problems.

Every agent i has an unknown true value v_i for a good, and maintains a lower bound $\underline{v}$ and upper bound $\overline{v}$ on its value, see Fig 1 (a). Agent i believes that its true value is uniformly distributed between its bounds, $v \sim U(\underline{v}, \overline{v})$. Given this belief the expected value for the good is $\hat{v} = (\underline{v} + \overline{v})/2$. As an agent deliberates its bounds are refined and its belief about the value of the good changes, with expected value $\hat{v}$ converging to v over time.

Let $\Delta = \overline{v} - \underline{v}$ denote an agent's current uncertainty about the value of the good. Agents have a deliberation procedure that adjusts the bounds on value, reducing uncertainty by a multiplicative factor α, where $0 < \alpha < 1$. The new bounds are $\alpha\Delta$ apart, and consistent with the current bounds (but not necessarily adjusted symmetrically), see $\underline{v}'$ and $\overline{v}'$ in Fig 1 (a). For a small α the uncertainty is reduced by a large amount, and we refer to $(1 - \alpha)$ as the "computational effectiveness" of an agent's deliberation procedure. Furthermore, we model the new expected value $\hat{v}'$ for the good after deliberation as uniformly distributed $\hat{v}' \sim U(\underline{v} + \alpha\Delta/2, \overline{v} - \alpha\Delta/2)$, such that the new bounds are consistent with the current bounds. After deliberation an agent believes the value of the good is uniformly distributed between its new bounds. Agents incur a cost C for each deliberation step, that we assume is constant for all steps, and independent of the final outcome of the auction.

3   The Metadeliberation Problem

The *metadeliberation problem* is to determine how much deliberation to perform before placing a bid. The decision is a tradeoff between reducing uncertainty about the value of the good so that the bid is accurate, and avoiding the cost of deliberation. An agent's optimal metadeliberation strategy *does* depend on the bids that other agents will make, even in incentive compatible auctions (unlike an agent's optimal bidding strategy).

Given our model of an agent's valuation problem and decision procedure we derive optimal metadeliberation strategies for agents within the general framework of Russell and Wefald [22]. The key observation is that the value of deliberation is derived from the effect of deliberation on an agent's bid. Deliberation can only be worthwhile when: (1) it changes an agent's bid; (2) the new bid has greater expected utility than the old bid. For example, an agent should never deliberate about its value for a good if its current upper bound on value is less than the ask price, because further deliberation can never cause the agent to accept the price. Metadeliberation is hard because of uncertainty, about: the effect of placing a bid b in an auction (this can depend on the bids of other agents); the outcome of further deliberation (otherwise deliberation is unnecessary!), and the value of goods. We describe normative metadeliberation strategies for agents in each auction below, but see [19] for derivations. We assume risk-neutral agents, who receive utility $v_i - p$ for purchasing a good at price p.[2]

3.1   Second-Price Sealed-Bid

In a second-price sealed-bid (Vickrey) auction agents need distributional information about the bids from other agents to make good metadeliberation decisions. For example, if an agent does not have any information about the bids from other agents it cannot know the probability of winning the auction with a bid b, or its expected surplus if it wins (this depends on the second-highest bid received). Uninformed agents are left to either follow a worst-case metadeliberation strategy (don't deliberate), a best-case strategy (that recommends too much deliberation), or an ad-hoc strategy that makes implicit assumptions about the bids from other agents. We do not consider the mechanism (for example Bayesian learning) with which agents become informed, but provide agents with approximately correct distributional information about the bids from other agents.

Informed agents can follow expected-utility maximizing metadeliberation strategies; agents compare the expected utility of placing an optimal bid after deliberation with the expected utility of placing an optimal bid before deliberation, given their beliefs about deliberation, the value of the good, and the bids of other agents. The mapping from expected value $\hat{v}$ to expected utility for an agent's optimal bid ($b^* = \hat{v}$) is non-linear, because an agent is more likely to win the auction with a higher bid. Although an agent's mean expected value $\hat{v}'$ after deliberation is equal to an agent's expected value $\hat{v}$ before deliberation, deliberation can have positive utility because of this non-linear mapping. The number of deliberation steps that an agent performs depends on the number of agents in the auction, an agent's current beliefs $[\underline{v}, \overline{v}]$, and the computational effectiveness and cost of its deliberation procedure. Agents with large uncertainty and high expected values tend to deliberate more than other agents.

3.2   Posted-Price Sequential

In a posted-price sequential auction an agent that receives an ask-price p for the good holds an exclusive offer until it accepts or rejects the price. The only uncertainty in an agent's metadeliberation problem is due to the agent's own uncertainty about the value of the good. There is no uncertainty from the actions of other agents in the auction. Although agents that receive the offer can make good metadeliberation decisions, the revenue and efficiency is often less than for auctions that set the price dynamically.

---

[2] The optimal bidding strategy for a risk-neutral agent with an uncertain value for the good is "expected-value equivalent" to the optimal bidding strategy for an agent that knows its value for the good. For example, when offered a good at a fixed price p, an agent with beliefs $[\underline{v}, \overline{v}]$ should buy the good for a price $p < \hat{v}$. Similarly, in a second-price sealed-bid auction an agent should bid $\hat{v}$.

The optimal expected-value metadeliberation and bidding strategy for an agent that faces a fixed price p and has beliefs $[\underline{v}, \overline{v}]$ is to deliberate while its expected value $\hat{v}$ is close to the ask price, and then accept a price $p < \hat{v}$, and reject the price otherwise, see Fig 1 (b). An agent deliberates while its expected value $\hat{v}$ is within $\gamma^* \Delta / 2$ of the price, for a threshold $\gamma^*(\alpha, C, \Delta)$ that depends on the computational effectiveness $(1 - \alpha)$ of its deliberation procedure, its cost C for deliberation, and its current uncertainty Δ in value. The threshold decreases as an agent deliberates, and eventually an agent will not deliberate for any ask price (when $\gamma^* = 0$).

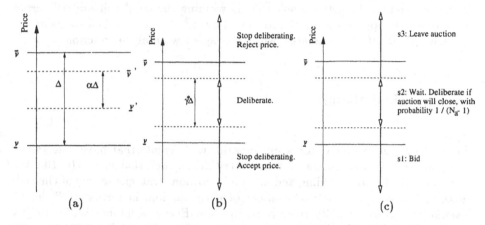

Fig. 1. (a) Valuation problem. Upper and lower bounds $\overline{v}$ and $\underline{v}$ on value before deliberation, with uncertainty $\Delta = \overline{v} - \underline{v}$; new bounds after deliberation $\overline{v}'$ and $\underline{v}'$ are $\alpha \Delta$ apart and consistent with the initial bounds. Optimal Metadeliberation and Bidding Strategies: (b) Posted-price auction; (c) Ascending-price auction.

3.3 Ascending-Price

The auctioneer in an ascending-price auction announces an initial ask price, p, and increases the price a minimum bid increment ϵ whenever a bid is received. The auction closes when no bids are received, with the good sold to the highest bidder for the price that it bid. The optimal metadeliberation and bidding strategy in the ascending-price auction is different than in the posted-price auction because: (1) the price of the good can increase over time; (2) an agent that bids for the good at price p cannot be sure that it will win the good. In addition to choosing to deliberate or bid, it can also be useful for agents to wait because the price can increase as the result of bids from other agents. Every agent hopes that another agent will deliberate and place a new bid that increases the price. Agents are locked into a deliberation "waiting game". If the price increases above an agent's upper bound $\overline{v}$ on value the agent can avoid deliberation completely.

Agents can be in one of three states, depending on the relative position of the ask price with respect to their beliefs $[\underline{v}, \overline{v}]$ about the value of the good, see Fig

1 (c). Agents in state *s1* always bid, and therefore the ask price in the auction is always ϵ (the minimum bid increment) above the second-highest lower threshold on deliberation for all agents (after a bidding war between all agents in state *s1*). Agents in state *s3* leave the auction because the ask price is greater than their upper thresholds on deliberation, and can only increase. Agents in state *s2* remain *active*, and are locked into a waiting game. Every active agent will deliberate to prevent the auction closing, but prefers to wait for another agent to deliberate. The unique symmetrical Nash equilibrium of the waiting game has all active agents that are not currently winning the auction play a mixed strategy: deliberate with probability $1/(N_a - 1)$ when the auction is about to close, for N_a active agents (the active agent that is winning the good will not deliberate because it is happy for the auction to terminate).[3] When there is a single active agent left the auction terminates, with that agent winning the auction.

4   Empirical Results

We model a simple market for a single good, with agents that have true values v_i for the good drawn from a uniform distribution, such that $v_i \sim U(0, 10)$. We implement the optimal bidding and metadeliberation strategies for agents in each auction, and compare the performance of each auction, in terms of efficiency, revenue and average utility from participation. Every agent has initial beliefs $\underline{v} = 0$ and $\overline{v} = 10$, and a deliberation procedure with computational effectiveness $(1 - \alpha)$ and cost C. We simulate deliberation to match the agents' simple model. After assigning a true value for the good to each agent we use a stochastic procedure to generate new bounds after deliberation such that: (1) the true value remains between the bounds; (2) the true value is uniformly distributed between the bounds over all possible stochastic sequences of deliberations.[4]

Efficiency is computed as the (true) value for the good of the agent that wins the auction, as a fraction of the maximum value over all agents. Revenue is computed as the price paid for the good, as a fraction of the maximum value over all agents. Finally, the average utility to an agent for participation in the auction is computed as the surplus $(v_i - p)$ to agent i that wins the auction for price p, minus the total cost of deliberation for all agents, and divided by the number of agents in the auction. Agents can lose utility from participation because of assumptions made in deriving metadeliberation strategies, for example about

---

[3] The agents need to know how many agents remain active to implement the Nash equilibrium. We could ask the agents to pay a small "participation fee" in each round of the auction to remain active, so that the auctioneer can report this information in each round.

[4] Actually, this requires that the new expected value for the good in simulation is not uniformly distributed with respect to the current bounds, but favors more central values.

the bids of other agents and an agent's own deliberation procedure.[5] We check that the utility for participation is positive to validate agent strategies.

We compare the performance of each auction as we vary the number of agents, N, and the computational effectiveness $(1-\alpha)$ and cost C of agents' deliberation procedures. All results are averaged over at least 1000 trials. Efficiency is often the primary performance measure of mechanism design, but if the auctioneer is also the seller then revenue can be important. We write $M_1 \succ M_2$ if mechanism M_1 dominates M_2 in terms of efficiency and revenue, or $M_1 \approx M_2$ if the mechanisms have conflicting ordering for revenue and efficiency, or very similar performance; A denotes the ascending-price auction, S the sealed-bid auction, and P the posted-price auction.

4.1   Adjusting the Number of Agents

Fig 2 (a) compares the performance of each auction mechanism as the number of agents is varied between 5 and 100 (log scale). All agents have deliberation procedures with $\alpha = 0.7, C = 0.1$. We plot efficiency (i), revenue (ii), average computational-cost (iii), and average utility (iv). The bid-increment in the ascending-price auction is set to enable agents to achieve positive expected utility from participation in the auction, while maximizing performance.

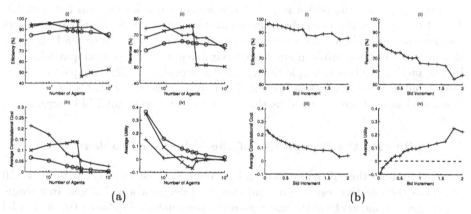

Fig. 2. (a) Auction performance: 'x' sealed-bid; 'o' posted-price sequential; '+' ascending-price. Agents with $\alpha = 0.7, C = 0.1$. Bid increment in the ascending-price auction is adjusted to provide agents with positive expected utility from participation. Averaged over 1000 trials. (b) Performance of ascending-price auction. $N = 10$ agents, $\alpha = 0.7, C = 0.1$.

For $N < 10$ we have $A \succ S \succ P$, with agents achieving positive expected utility for participation in all auctions. For $10 < N < 35$ it at first appears

---
[5] Agents that deliberate in the ascending-price auction assume that they will win the good for current ask price p if they bid. The auction actually remains open and other agents can bid.

that $S \succ A$, however the agents in the sealed-bid auction now have negative utility for participation (iv).[6] So, discounting the performance of the sealed-bid auction, for $10 < N < 70$ agents we have $A \succ P \succ S$. Finally, for large numbers of agents, $N > 70$ we have $P \succ A \succ S$. Therefore, the ascending-price auction performs best for small to medium numbers of agents ($N < 70$), and the posted-price auction performs better than the sealed-bid auction for medium to large numbers of agents ($N > 10$), and better than the ascending-price auction for large numbers of agents ($N > 70$).

Although the surplus to the winning agent remains approximately constant in all auctions as the number of agents increases (unlike in regular auctions, where it falls), the average utility for participation can only remain positive if the total computational cost also remains approximately constant (or increases to no more than the surplus). The only auction that can sustain a fixed but positive amount of deliberation as the number of agents increases is the posted-price mechanism, because it isolates agents from the effect of more agents by offering the good sequentially to each agent. Efficiency and revenue tend to decrease as the number of agents increases, again contrary to the performance markets with agents that have easy valuation problems. Performance decreases because the surplus from participation is less able to support the amount of deliberation that is necessary for high efficiency and revenue with large numbers of agents.

Fig 2 (b) plots the performance of the ascending-price auction for $\alpha = 0.7$, $C = 0.1$ and $N = 10$, as the bid-increment ϵ is increased. Small bid increments support more efficient allocations and higher revenue, but also lead to more deliberation and can result in agents receiving negative utility from participation in the auction. In this example the agents have positive utility for participation with a bid increment $\epsilon > 0.25$, see Fig 2 (b) iv, and the seller is able to achieve a revenue that is almost as good as that possible with very small bid increments.

4.2   Adjusting the Complexity of the Valuation Problem

Fig 3 compares the efficiency (a), and revenue (b), for markets with $N = 10$ agents as the effectiveness $(1 - \alpha)$ and cost C of deliberation changes. In a single experiment all agents have the same α and C parameters. Equivalently, we model agents with the same bounded resources, but easy local problems for large $(1-\alpha)$ and relaxed time-constraints for small costs C.

In this market, with $N = 10$ agents, when agents have small deliberation costs ($C = 0.05$) then $A \succ S \succ P$, and $A \approx S \succ P$ for $C = 0.1$. Auctions with dynamic prices, such as the ascending-price or sealed-bid auctions, perform better than the posted-price auction for small C. For medium deliberation costs ($C = 0.5$), the sealed-bid auction fails and $A \approx P \succ S$. For large deliberation costs (e.g.

---

[6] This is because there are no homogeneous beliefs that agents can hold about the distribution of bids from agents that are consistent with the actual distribution of bids that occurs when agents hold the beliefs. The inaccuracy in agents' models leads to a loss in utility.

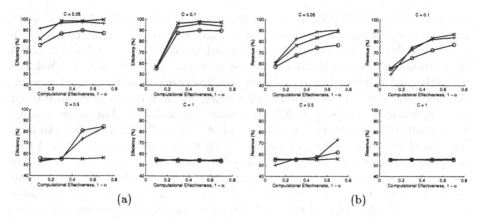

Fig. 3. Auction performance for $N = 10$ agents with different levels of deliberation effectiveness and cost. '+' ascending-price; 'x' sealed-bid; 'o' posted-price sequential auctions. Bid increment $\epsilon = 0.4$, 1000 trials. (a) Efficiency; (b) Revenue.

$C = 1$) there is no deliberation in any auction, and auction design does not matter. Efficiency and revenue increase as deliberation effectiveness increases, and decrease as deliberation cost increases. The ascending-price and sealed-bid auctions become approximately *revenue equivalent* for small deliberation costs and high computational effectiveness (c.f. easy local problems), see Fig 3 (b) i, $C = 0.05, 1 - \alpha = 0.7$.

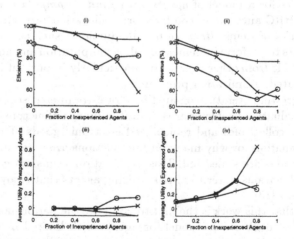

Fig. 4. Performance of the sealed-bid 'x', ascending-price '+', and posted-price 'o' auctions as the fraction of inexperienced agents in the system increases. $N = 10, \alpha = 0.3, C = 0.5$. The results are computed over 2000 trials. Bid increment $\epsilon = 0.2$.

Finally, consider a market with a *mixture* of agents; some with hard valuation problems ("inexperienced agents"), and some with easy valuation problems ("experienced agents"). We assume a fraction f of inexperienced agents; and a fraction $1 - f$ of experienced agents that know their value v_i for the good. Fig 4 plots results for $N = 10$, and inexperienced agents with $\alpha = 0.3$ and $C = 0.5$. The ascending-price auction has the best performance, but the sealed-bid auction often outperforms the posted-price auction, even though the efficiency and revenue comes only from experienced agents. For a small to medium fraction of inexperienced agents, $f < 0.4$, the sealed-bid and ascending-price auctions are approximately *revenue equivalent*, and $A \approx S \succ P$. For a medium to large fraction of inexperienced agents, $0.4 < f < 0.8$, we have $A \succ S \succ P$, and with many inexperienced agents the sealed-bid auction fails and $A \succ P \succ S$. The posted-price auction performs badly for heterogeneous markets, e.g. $f = 0.6$, because the seller must choose an ask price to target one type of agent. The other auctions are better able to involve both agent types. Also, we see that when there are only a few experienced agents they are able to use their informational advantage, and achieve high average utility from participation in the auction, see Fig 4 (iv).

5   Related Work

In Parkes and Ungar [15] we introduce a formal definition for *bounded-rational compatible* (BRC) auctions, to describe auctions in which agents can bid optimally with approximate values. Iterative auctions are a special class of BRC auctions which can compute optimal allocations with enough agent computation. Empirical results for a model of agents with *limited computation* highlight the importance of BRC auctions in combinatorial allocation problems, with agents that need *bundles* of items. *Iterative* bundle auctions, such as *i*Bundle [16, 18], that allow agents to perform incremental value computation and adjust their bids in response to bids from other agents, are particularly important in applications to hard distributed optimization problems.

There is a growing literature on auctions for e-commerce, see [7] for an introduction. Hard valuation problems are relevant in many online consumer auctions, for example for collectibles and refurbished electronic goods. This provides an appealing explanation for why many on-line auctions are ascending-price, while few on-line auctions are sealed-bid. This explanation seems more probable than alternative explanations in terms of risk-seeking agents that enjoy risk-taking in iterative auctions [13].

We believe that this work is the first to compare the performance of auctions with a normative deliberation model for agents with limited or costly computation. Early work in market-oriented programming [29] assumed that agents were provided with closed-form solutions to their local valuation problems, so minimizing agent valuation work was not important. Problems associated with limited or costly computation in the *auctioneer* have received recent attention, in particular with respect to the generalized Vickrey auction [27]. Interesting recent work explores methods to introduce approximate solutions but retain the incentive-compatibility property (such that truth-telling remains optimal for self-interested agents) [8, 9, 14]. However, these methods still require that agents compute their values for all possible outcomes, which is often impossible. Shoham and Tennenholtz [26] consider the communication complexity of auction mechanisms.

Sandholm [25] proposed TRACONET, a decentralized system for dynamic task reallocation via negotiation between agents, with an application to a transport scheduling problem in which agents have hard local valuation problems. Safe and opportunistic strategies are proposed for contracting strategies with approximate valuations. Sandholm and Lesser [23] introduce decommitment to allow agents that make early mistakes because of approximate values and uncertainty to backtrack, and increase allocative efficiency. The technique allows agents to integrate local deliberation with negotiation between many other agents. The focus is on a *decentralized* system, while our work considers techniques for auction systems— with a centralized auctioneer.

Parunak *et al.* [20] describe a market-based constraint system for interactive decision support between cooperative agents. The MARCON system aims to reduce agents' work; agents can express broad initial preferences and must only refine preferences as necessary to compute a good system-wide solution.

Models of economic search with one-time participation costs have demonstrated that *posted-price* sequential auctions can reduce agent uncertainty and improve performance when agents are uninformed about the bids of other agents [3, 10]. Rothkopf and Harstad [21] argue that auction design should be considered in the context of a marketplace, with agents that take active participation decisions. Although some auction models consider agents with *one-time* participation costs [6, 11], the models cannot distinguish between sealed-bid and iterative auctions.

6   Conclusions

We have presented the results of an empirical comparison of the performance of first-price ascending, second-price sealed and posted-price sequential auctions, for a simple model of agents with hard valuation problems. The empirical results show clear support for the bounded-rational compatible [15] properties of ascending-price and other iterative auctions, first identified by Parkes *et al.* [17] as important for on-line auctions. It is interesting that the *revenue-equivalence theorem* [12] fails when agents have hard valuation problems and limited or costly computation.

The ascending-price auction dominates the sealed-bid auction, in terms of allocative efficiency and revenue, when there are more than a few agents in the market (e.g. $N > 5$). This holds even when agents are uninformed about the values of other agents in the ascending-price auction but informed in the sealed-bid auction. Iterative auctions do more than provide agents with useful information about the values of other agents, they can also reduce an agent's *uncertainty* about the outcome, i.e. about the final prices and allocation.

Posted-price auctions are often necessary with many agents (e.g. $N > 50$) because they eliminate a bidder's uncertainty about the outcome of the auction. An agent knows that if it accepts the price of an item it will definitely receive the item, and at that price. This simplifies an agent's metadeliberation problem. However, with small numbers of agents posted-price auctions are typically less efficient than auctions with dynamic pricing unless the seller is very well informed about agents' values.

Agents with information about the likely outcome of an auction can deliberate more efficiently about the values of different outcomes, for example quickly eliminating from their possibility set all bundles of items that are very expensive. Iterative auctions provide agents with this information dynamically during the auction as bids are received. The "right" agents can deliberate for the "right" amount of time, shifting deliberation away from agents with low values and towards agents with high values, and towards values for bundles that fit into good global solutions.

Another approach to improve deliberation efficiency could provide agents with historical information about clearing prices from previous problem instances, to allow agents to predict likely outcomes even before an auction begins. This is a useful role for *middleware* in agent-mediated auctions.

References

1. Bakos, Y. 1997. Reducing buyer search costs: Implications for electronic marketplaces. *Management Science* 43(12).
2. Boutilier, C.; Goldszmidt, M.; and Sabata, B. 1999. Sequential auctions for the allocation of resources with complementarities. In *Proc. 16th International Joint Conference on Artificial Intelligence (IJCAI-99)*, 527–534.
3. Ehrman, C., and Peters, M. 1994. Sequential selling mechanisms. *Economic Theory* 4:237–253.
4. Greenwald, A., and Kephart, J. O. 1999. Shopbots and pricebots. In *Proc. 16th International Joint Conference on Artificial Intelligence (IJCAI-99)*, 506–511.
5. Guttman, R. H., and Maes, P. 1998. Cooperative vs. competitive multi-agent negotiations in retail electronic commerce. In *Proc. 2nd International Workshop on Cooperative Information Agents (CIA'98)*.
6. Hausch, D. B., and Li, L. 1993. A common value auction model with endogeneous entry and information acquisition. *Economic Theory* 3:315–334.
7. Huhns, M. H., and Vidal, J. M. 1999. Online auctions. *IEEE Internet Computing* 3(3):103–105.
8. Kfir-Dahav, N. E.; Monderer, D.; and Tennenholtz, M. 1998. Mechanism design for resource bounded agents. Technical report, Technion.
9. Lehmann, D.; O'Callaghan, L.; and Shoham, Y. 1999. Truth revelation in rapid, approximately efficient combinatorial auctions. In *Proc. ACM Conference on Electronic Commerce (EC-99)*.
10. Lippman, S. A., and McCall, J. J. 1976. The economics of job search: A survey. *Economic Inquiry* 14:155–189.
11. McAfee, R. P., and McMillan, J. 1987a. Auctions with entry. *Economic Letters* 23:343–347.

12. McAfee, R. P., and McMillan, J. 1987b. Auctions and bidding. *Journal of Economic Literature* 25:699–738.
13. Monderer, D., and Tennenholtz, M. 1998. Internet auctions - are they gamblers' attraction? Technical report, Technion.
14. Nisan, N., and Ronen, A. 1999. Algorithmic mechanism design (extended abstract). In *Proc. 31st Annual Symposium on Theory of Computing (STOC99)*.
15. Parkes, D. C., and Ungar, L. H. 2000a. Bounded rational compatible auctions. Submitted for publication.
16. Parkes, D. C., and Ungar, L. H. 2000b. Iterative combinatorial auctions: Theory and practice. To appear, *Proc. 18th National Conference on Artificial Intelligence (AAAI-00)*.
17. Parkes, D. C.; Ungar, L. H.; and Foster, D. P. 1999. Accounting for cognitive costs in on-line auction design. In Noriega, P., and Sierra, C., eds., *Agent Mediated Electronic Commerce (LNAI 1571)*. Springer-Verlag. 25–40. Earlier version appeared at the Agents'98 Workshop on Agent Mediated Electronic Trading, 1998.
18. Parkes, D. C. 1999a. *i*Bundle: An efficient ascending price bundle auction. In *Proc. ACM Conference on Electronic Commerce (EC-99)*, 148–157.
19. Parkes, D. C. 1999b. On agent metadeliberation strategies in auctions. Technical report, University of Pennsylvania.
20. Parunak, V.; Ward, A.; and Sauter, J. 1998. A systematic market approach to distributed constraint problems. Poster session, *Proc. 3rd International Conference on Multi-Agent Systems (ICMAS-98)*, 455–456.
21. Rothhopf, M. H., and Harstad, R. M. 1994. Modeling competitive bidding: A critical essay. *Management Science* 40(3):364–384.
22. Russell, S., and Wefald, E. 1991. Principles of metareasoning. *Artificial Intelligence* 49:361–395.
23. Sandholm, T. W., and Lesser, V. R. 1996. Advantages of a leveled commitment contracting protocol. In *Proc. 14th National Conference on Artificial Intelligence (AAAI-96)*, 126–133.
24. Sandholm, T. W., and Lesser, V. R. 1997. Coalitions among computationally bounded agents. *Artificial Intelligence* 94(1–2):99–137.
25. Sandholm, T. 1993. An implementation of the Contract Net Protocol based on marginal-cost calculations. In *Proc. 11th National Conference on Artificial Intelligence (AAAI-93)*, 256–262.
26. Shoham, Y., and Tennenholtz, M. 1999. What can a market compute, and at what expense? Technical report, Technion.
27. Varian, H., and MacKie-Mason, J. K. 1995. Generalized Vickrey auctions. Technical report, University of Michigan.
28. Varian, H. R. 1995. Economic mechanism design for computerized agents. In *Proc. USENIX Workshop on Electronic Commerce*. Minor update, 2000.
29. Wellman, M. P. 1993. A market-oriented programming environment and its application to distributed multicommodity flow problems. *Journal of Artificial Intelligence Research* 1:1–23.

Auctions without Auctioneers: Distributed Auction Protocols

Marc Esteva * and Julian Padget **

[1] Artificial Intelligence Research Institute, IIIA
Spanish Council for Scientific Research, CSIC
08193 Bellaterra, Barcelona, Spain.
marc@iiia.csic.es
[2] Department of Mathematical Sciences
University of Bath, BATH BA2 7AY, UK
jap@maths.bath.ac.uk

Abstract. It is quite natural for electronic institutions to follow the structure of their physical counterparts. However, this is not always appropriate or desirable in a virtual setting. We report on the prototyping of an alternative architecture for electronic auctions based around the concept of an *interagent* and building on the considerable body of work in the distributed algorithms literature to plot a path toward *resilient* trading frameworks. In particular, we have adapted the classical Leader Election algorithm for resolving bids in a generic auction scheme as well as identifying the factors which differentiate the physical auction protocols in such a way that new auction protocols can be plugged into the scheme by the specification of the relevant (sub-)processes. We have used the process algebra called the π-calculus to specify both the generic scheme and the specific protocols of first-price, second-price, Dutch and English. The bid resolution process has been prototyped in Pict and is now going to be integrated into the FishMarket electronic auction house.

Keywords: Electronic commerce, auctions, distributed programming, process calculi.

1 Introduction

Electronic commerce has become more and more important with the growth of the Internet. In particular, auctioning has become one of most popular mechanisms of electronic trading, as we can see from the proliferation of on-line auctions on the Internet. Multi-agent systems appear to offer a convenient mechanism for automated trading, due mainly to the simplicity of their conventions for interaction when multi-party negotiations are involved. AI researchers have been interested in two areas: auction

* This work has been partially supported by ESPRIT LTR 25500-COMRIS Co-Habited Mixed-Reality Information Spaces project and Marc Esteva enjoys the CIRIT doctoral scholarship FI/99-00012

** Julian Padget's work has been partially supported by EPSRC grant GR/K27957 (http://www.maths.bath.ac.uk/~jap/Denton) and the CEC/HCM VIM project, contract CHRX-CT93-0401 (http://www.maths.bath.ac.uk/~jap/VIM)

A. Moukas, C. Sierra, and F. Ygge (Eds.): AMEC'99, LNAI 1788, pp. 220–238, 2000.
© Springer-Verlag Berlin Heidelberg 2000

marketplaces and the trading agents' strategies and heuristics [5, 18, 20]. Apart from web-based trading, auctions are the most prevalent coordination mechanism for agent-mediated resource allocation problems such as energy management [20, 19], climate control[6], flow problems[6], computing resources [4], public monopolies [1] and many others [2].

From the point of view of multi-agent interactions in auction-based trading, the situation is deceptively simple. Trading within an auction house demands that buyers merely decide an appropriate price to bid, and that sellers essentially only have to choose the time to submit their goods.

The work related here is a continuation of the FishMarket (FM) project[17, 16]. The goal of FM is to develop means for the specification and design of electronic institutions, where by *electronic institution* we mean an organization [12] where the agents can interact following some protocols. Commonly, the institution is formed from a set of connected scenes and the agents can move from one to another when they satisfy some institution-defined conditions. The scenes are the basic elements of the institutions and it is there where the interactions between agents take place. Each scene has its own protocol that defines the interaction between the agents and the agents within a scene have to observe this protocol.

As an example of an electronic institution a group at IIIA have implemented the FishMarket[21]. The FM is an electronic auction house used as a test-bed for trading agents. The FM has six scenes, two for admissions (buyers and sellers), one for the staff, two for settlements and the auction room itself.

In this paper we focus on the auction room, and especially the process used for the resolution of bids. In all the versions of the FM to date, this process has been carried in a centralized manner. While that corresponds to the physical reality of auctions, it is not necessarily an appropriate model in a computing context due to two problems that are not common in physical situations (*pace* telephone bidders!): breakdown of processes or communications — so-called stopping failures — and intermittently faulty processes or communications, leading to unreliable messages — so-called Byzantine failures [7]. As a first step to addressing these problems we here present a distributed solution to which other techniques may later be added to handle resilience issues, which effectively does away with the auctioneer, thus removing a central single point of failure. In some sense the interagents — the market interfaces for the buyers —, as we shall see later, are really replications of the auctioneer, in common with the architecture proposed in [3].

In the current FM all the bids are submitted to an agent called the auctioneer who controls the whole auctioning process and determines the result of the round. From this point of view, the resolution of the bidding protocol is centralized. What we do in this new version is distribute this process among the buyers' market interface agents (called interagents) — see Figure 1. Thus, the auctioneer sends the buyers (via the interagents) the information about the lot and then waits until one buyer interagent sends it the result of the round. During the intervening period the buyer interagents resolve the bids using a distributed protocol. Thus, the work of the auctioneer is reduced to:

- controlling which buyers participate in the auction,
- starting the rounds by sending the information on the lots
- waiting for the result of the round

We have two motivations: to have another way of applying auction protocols and to have a way to avoid the auctioneer becoming a bottleneck. With this new mechanism, the load of messages is distributed between all the buyers. The idea is that this algorithm can be applied to an existing auction house, providing an alternative way to deliver different auction protocols.

The basis of the distributed approach is the Leader Election algorithm [8]. It can be understood simply as an algorithm for choosing one processor in a network of many and the version we have adapted here derives from that used in token ring networks, where it is used to regenerate the token.

In the next section (2) we explain the new organization in the auction room in order to apply the algorithm. In section 3 we give a brief summary of π-calculus. In section 4 we outline how to apply the Leader Election algorithm in auction protocols. Finally (sections 5-9) we explain how to use this algorithm for a range of auction protocols and give their specification in π-calculus too.

2   Organization of the Auction Room

On first looking at the auction room we can see that we have two kind of agents, the auctioneer and the buyers. The auctioneer is an institutional agent who controls the correct running of the auctions. It controls when buyers enter and leave, starts the round and receives the result of it. Finally, it declares the end of the auctions when it has no further lots to auction.

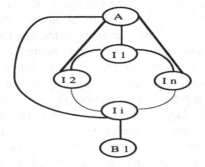

Fig. 1. Organization of the agents in the auction room

We have added another kind of institutional agent, the so-called *interagent*, [9] an autonomous software agent which mediates interactions between a buyer and the agent society wherein it is situated. An interagent is connected to a buyer and abstracts it from communication problems. Thus, each buyer only has to communicate with its interagent so it can focus on its strategies for bidding. The use of an interagent also has advantages for the institutions, because the interagent also forces the buyer to follow the auction room protocol. For example, the interagent will prevent the buyer from making a bid between rounds. The interagents also implement the resolution of the bidding protocol.

Previously, this task was done by the auctioneer, whereas now it is distributed among the interagents, which are linked in a ring in order to apply the particular version of Leader Election we have chosen [8].

An important point here, is that the change in the process of bidding resolution does not affect the buyers. It is an internal change of the system. This process is opaque to the buyers which cannot see the information passed between interagents in order to resolve the bidding protocols. In other words, from the point of view of the buyers there is no difference between centralized bid resolution and the new scheme.

The buyers are the participants in the auctions. As we have said, each one is connected to one interagent in order to communicate with the other agents. Of course, we cannot specify the buyers here because each one is potentially unique. All we can define are the channels with which the buyer will be supplied in order to communicate with its interagent, the messages that it will receive and when it is allowed to submit a bid or leave the system. Therefore, in the auction room there is one auctioneer, a set of buyers and one interagent for each buyer (see Figure 1).

We will focus on the specification of the distributed resolution of the bidding protocol. We omit the specification of the auctioneer but note that its principal work now is to send the information about the lots at the start of each round.

3   The π-Calculus in Brief

The main features of the π-calculus—and those necessary to read the remainder of this paper—are the means to read and write information over channels, the creation of channels, and parallel, alternative and sequential composition. Terms in the π-calculus are described as prefixes followed by terms, which is intentionally a recursive definition. Syntactic details are outlined below[1].

3.1   Summary of π-Calculus Syntax and Semantics

In order to keep this paper to a reasonable length, we cannot provide a full introduction to the π-calculus, limiting ourselves instead to this summary. For more information, the interested reader is referred to Pierce's excellent article [14] and subsequently to Milner [10] and the wider literature [11].

$x(y)$: Reads an object from channel x and associates it with the name y. This operation blocks until the writer is ready to transmit. The scope of y is limited to the process definition in which y occurs. Channel names, on the other hand may be local (see ν below), parameters to process definitions (see below), or global.

$\overline{x}\langle y\rangle$: Writes the object named by y to the channel x. This operation blocks until the reader is ready to receive.

---

[1] A word of warning: this description should not be taken as definitive, since there are numerous interpretations which vary slightly in details of syntax, and sometimes of semantics. It does however represent π-calculus adequately for the purposes of the discussion in this paper.

$\nu x \ldots$: Creates a new channel named x. The scope of x is limited to the ν expression, but the channel may be passed over another channel for use by another process. For example, a common idiom is to create a channel using ν, transmit it to another process and then wait for a reply on that channel:

$$\nu (x) \, \overline{y} \, \langle x, question \rangle \, . \, x(answer)$$

$P \, | \, Q$: The terms P and Q behave as if they are running in parallel. For example, $\overline{x} \langle 1 \rangle \, | \, \overline{y} \langle 2 \rangle$ outputs 1 on channel x and 2 on channel y simultaneously.

$P + Q$: Either one or the other (non-deterministic choice) of P and Q proceeds. Normally, the prefixes of P and Q are operations which could block, such as channel transactions, and this operation allows us to express the idea of waiting on several events and then proceeding to act upon one of them when it occurs. For example, $x(a) + y(a)$ waits for input on channels x and y, associating the information in both cases with a. As soon as one branch of such an alternative succeeds, the others can be considered to have aborted (see discussion in section 3.2).

$P \, . \, Q$: The actions of term P precede those of term Q. For example $x(y) \, . \, \overline{z} \, \langle y \rangle$ reads y from x then writes y on z.

In addition, we include an ability to associate a term with a name — that is a definition — and furthermore, that in so doing a global channel is declared with that name, as in: $P(x1, x2, x3) = \ldots$, which defines a process P taking a three-tuple. In practice this also means we have declared a channel P such that we may invoke the process P by writing a three-tuple to the channel named P. We will use this convention to obtain a form of parameterization, allowing us to pass processes as arguments (high-order processes) by passing the channel by which they are invoked. This syntactic convenience can be described primitively in the π-calculus but we omit these details here.

3.2   Events and Choice

Of the many variants of the π-calculus, we chose as a starting point, the basic synchronous form as found in [10]. One of the essential properties of the kinds of markets we want to model is liveliness, which in practical terms means an event-based model. The non-deterministic choice (sum) operator has therefore been invaluable—although it also raises some interesting questions. To quote [10]:

> The summation form $\sum \pi_i . P_i$ represents a process able to take part in one—but only one—of several alternatives for communication. The choice is not made by the process; it can never commit to one alternative until it occurs, and this occurrence precludes the other alternatives.

When viewed as a mathematical description, for example, for the purpose of determining bisimilarity, there is no problem. However, when viewed as a program to run, there is an element of time and therefore sequence involved. Consider the process $\overline{c_1}.P_1 + \overline{c_2}.P_2$. If a message arrives on c_1 just before one arrives on c_2, do we expect to become P_1, or do we expect a non-deterministic choice of P_1 or P_2? Certainly, we *can* become P_1, but most people (and the quote above can be interpreted to support this), would say we *should* become P_1. If not then the π-calculus would be a difficult tool indeed, requiring many synchronizations to enforce this natural behaviour, and these synchronizations would generally have no counterpart in a "real" program. In the following descriptions we have assumed that the natural interpretation is the case, this is, choices are determined as and when messages arrive on channels.

A further issue, of wanting to give priority to one channel over another, is addressed by the definition of the test/0 process, which is much used later on. This process is used to check if there is information waiting to be read on a channel but without blocking the process attempting to read.

test/0(*event, then, else*) =
$\quad \nu\ (c1, c2, c3)$
$\quad\quad \overline{c3} \langle\rangle$
$\quad\quad | \ event() . c2() . \overline{c1} \langle then\rangle \ + \ c2() . \overline{c1} \langle else\rangle$
$\quad\quad | \ c3() . \overline{c2} \langle\rangle . c1(x) . \overline{x} \langle\rangle$

The function tries to read from the channel *event* and if it succeeds writes on channel *then*, otherwise writes on channel *else*. The version presented here does not read any data from the channel *event* but we assume that we have other versions that do and writes it to *then*. We will differentiate the number of arguments passed by adding arity to the name of the process (following a Prolog convention). Then the function test/0 is the one that does not pass information, the process test/1 is the one that passes one item and so on.

4 Leader Election

Leader election is a distributed algorithm used in some kinds of networks to elect a leader. For example, it is used in a token ring network when the token is lost and it is necessary to generate a new one. The algorithm assumes that all the nodes are identical, except in each having an unique identifier and they have to select one node to generate the token, but only one because there can only be one token in the ring.

There are different versions for solving the Leader Election problem and we have based our work on the LCR version [8]. This algorithm uses only unidirectional communication and does not rely on knowledge of the size of the ring. Other algorithms use more knowledge (equals more constraints) to reduce the complexity of the algorithm, but do not change it in essence.

It is presumed that the unique identifiers support an ordering so that the leader will be the process with the largest identifier. First of all, each node sends a message with its identifier around the ring. When a process receives a message there are three possible actions:

1. If the identifier in the message is greater than its own, it passes the message on.
2. If the identifier in the message is less than its own, it discards the message.
3. If the identifier in the message is equal to its own, it declares itself the leader.

Thus, only the process with the greatest identifier will receive again its message and it will declare itself as a leader. We can see that all the other messages will be eliminated because at some point they will arrive at a process with a greater identifier.

The important point of the algorithm that we have to bear in mind is that it only uses local information in each process and all of them are identical except in their identifiers. The processes do not have global information.

The next step is to see how we can apply this strategy to the auction protocols. The first and obvious point is that we have to compare the bids submitted for the buyers. The winner will be the buyer with the greatest bid. When a process receives a message, it will have to compare the bid in the message with its bid. There is one aspect that makes processing bids trickier than straight leader election: all the identifiers were different, but it is quite possible there will be equal (highest) bids posted. Namely, there is a collision if there is more than one bid at the greatest price.

We have to define first when the messages are generated and what they should contain. When to generate is obvious, the interagents will send a new message when the buyer makes a bid. For the second point is not enough just to send the bid: we need to know who has generated the message because it can be that more than one buyer makes the same bid and whether there are more buyers that have made a bid at the same value.

Thus the messages will have two fields:

1. a list of the identifiers of the buyers that have bid at price *bid*,
2. the bid itself.

From the list we can learn who has contributed to the message and if there is more than one buyer bidding at that price.

Now we have to analyze what happens when an interagent receives a message from its neighbour. When the bid in the message is different from its own, it acts as in the Leader Election algorithm: it passes the message on if the bid is greater and discards it if it is lower than its own.

The important point is what happens when it receives a message with a bid equal to its own. There are two possibilities:

1. *This is the message generated by itself* which implies that this interagent's buyer has made the greatest bid. However, this is not enough to elect itself as a winner because another buyer could have made a bid at the same value. To distinguish this case, it has to look at the list of identifiers in the first field of the message, and if there is only its identifier, it can declare itself the winner, otherwise there has been a collision, in which case it will generate a collision message in order to inform the other interagents. We will explain later how to use collision messages.
2. *Or, it is a message generated by another interagent* which indicates that other buyer has made a bid at the same price and it *could* be a collision. This is not enough for declare a collision yet because another interagent, further round the ring, could have made a greater bid. It will only be a collision if this is the greatest bid. The problem

is that the interagent has only local information and it only knows that it *could* be a collision. The interagent can only declare the collision when the message has made one complete round and it so it is sure that this is the greatest bid. All it can do is add its identifier to the list and pass on the message.

As we can see, no interagent eliminates a message with a bid equal to its own. Thus when there is a collision, this will be detected for all the interagents involved in it and each one of them will generate a collision message. Thus, after a collision, there will be one collision message for each buyer involved in the collision. In the version that we propose here, the interagents restart the round after a collision. Important remaining issues are how the collision messages are eliminated and how to ensure that each interagent receives only one collision message. The solution is that each collision message travels over the part of the ring from the interagent generating the message to the next interagent involved in the collision. Thus each interagent will receive one and only one collision message.

Another point is what should an interagent do when it knows that it has won a round. The answer is that it has to send a message around the ring in order to inform all the other interagents that the round is finished. An issue to note is *what* information should be passed on to the buyers. They could just be notified of the end of the round, but more likely they could be sent some information about the result, such as the price and/or the identity of the winner. Precise choices here depend on the conventions of the institution being modelled, but are not important otherwise to the discussion here. This message synchronizes all the interagents and subsequently the winner's interagent sends a message to the auctioneer to inform it of the result of the round and also that the round is finished.

Now we have described all the possible cases when an interagent receives a message. Hence, we can give a generic variant of the Leader Election for the resolution of bidding protocols (see Figure 2).

The last difficulty to address is what to do when no buyers make a bid. In this situation, no messages would be generated, so leading to deadlock, because each of the interagents will be waiting for messages. To avoid this, each interagent is required to generate a message for each round *unless* its buyer has not submitted a bid. These messages have a bid value of the negation of the identifier of the interagent. Thus if no one has submitted a bid, only the interagent with the lowest identifier will receive its message back. It will then detect that there have been no bids and it will notify the auctioneer that the lot is withdrawn.

Before explaining the duties of the interagent, we present an example in Figure 3. In this example there are three interagents, two of them which bid 10 and another which bids 8. This provokes a collision which is detected by both when the interagents received back their messages with more than one identifier. Then they generate a collision message, which has identifier -1. We can see that each interagent receives only one of them. The interagents which have participated in the collision wait until they receive another collision message. At that point, they eliminate the collision message and restart the round. The example finishes at that point but after that the interagents will restart the round.

1. If the interagent receives an end of round message which it *did not* generate, it passes the message to the next interagent.
2. If it receives an end of round message which it *did* generate, eliminate the message and send the result of the round to the auctioneer.
3. If it receives a collision message in which it *was not* involved, it passes the message to the next interagent and restarts the round.
4. If it receives a collision message in which it *was* involved, it eliminates the message and restarts the round.
5. If it receives a message with a bid greater than its own, it passes the message to the next interagent.
6. If it receives a message with a bid equal to its own and it *is not* its message it adds its identifier to the message and passes it to the next interagent.
7. If it receives its own message back and it only contains its identifier in the first field, it is the winner of the round and it sends an end of round message.
8. If it receives its own message back but there is more than one identifier in the first field, there is a collision and it generates a collision message.
9. If it receives a message with a bid lower than its own, it eliminates the message.

Fig. 2. Specification of the generic bidding resolution protocol

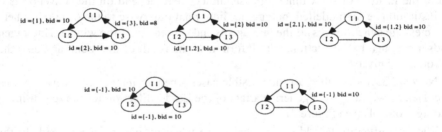

Fig. 3. Example of collision resolution

In the next section we will give the specification of the interagent in each protocol. We will explain how to apply the algorithm outlined above to each one and the modifications to take account of their individual characteristics.

5   The Interagent

As we have said earlier, the interagent has two important functions, handling communication between buyers and the institution (external) and resolving the bidding protocols (internal).

The first function gives the buyer the communication infrastructure to enable participation in the auctions by passing to the buyer the information that it needs about the state of the auctions. For example, when a round starts, the characteristics of the lot offered, if he has won a round, etc.. Furthermore, it passes the buyer messages to the other institution agents. These are the bids of the buyer and when it wants to leave the system. It also checks that the messages of the buyer follow the protocol. For example it does not allow to the buyer to make a bid at the wrong time. The idea is to abstract buyer developers from communication problems, allowing them to concentrate on bidding strategies.

The second function which is independent of the buyers, consists of deciding who won a round or whether a lot is withdrawn, using the modified Leader Election protocol with some variations depending on the auction protocol. As we have said before the buyers are not allowed to see the information passed between interagents in order to resolve a round. The interagents have to be robust and have to incorporate security measures in order to protect them from malicious buyers. Otherwise, buyers could read the messages with the bids of the others buyers and then generate new bids out of sequence with help of additional information. This is a point to be borne in mind but here we focus just on the algorithm.

From the point of view of an interagent, a round is divided in four steps as we can see in Figure 4.

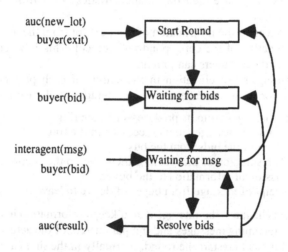

Fig. 4. The four steps of a bidding round

1. **Start Round:** This step corresponds to the period between two rounds. In that period, new buyers are added to the auction and existing participants can leave. The step finishes when the interagent receives from the auctioneer the information of the next lot to be auctioned. This step is the same for each protocol.
2. **Waiting for Bids:** This step can be seen as an initialization step. For each round it has a pre-determined time expressed in the lot information. The buyers have that time to make their first bid. Except in the English auction, that is the only moment that buyers are allowed to submit bids. When this step is finished we can be sure

that each interagent has sent its neighbour a message. It is for that reason that we say that it is an initialization period.

3. **Waiting for Next Message:** In this step an interagent waits for a message from its source interagent (the previous one in the ring) or for a message from the buyer with a new bid. In the first case it passes to the next step in order to handle that message. If it receives a message from the buyer for a new bid it generates a new message and sends it to its destination interagent (the next one in the ring). In the protocols that we specify here, only in the English auction are the buyers allowed to submit bids at that moment. In the other three they can only submit bids at the second step and this step only consists in waiting for a message from the source interagent.

4. **Resolve Bids:** This is the important point of the algorithm when an interagent uses the cases explained before with the last message received and its information to decide what it has to do. Subsequently, it returns to the previous step to handle the message.

As we can see, the first step is common for all the protocols and the others present some differences between each one. The interesting thing is that all of them follow the same pattern unless they have their own characteristics. We will focus on these three steps for each protocol.

The first step receives the information of the next lot from the auctioneer and calls the WaitingBid function of the corresponding protocol. This is when the buyers can leave the auction and new buyers can join in.

Before presenting the specification in π-calculus of each protocol we define the channels used for communication between one interagent and the others. These are:

- *in*: Receipt of messages from its predecessor in the ring.
- *out*: Transmission of messages to its successor in the ring.
- *b/int_bid*: Receipt of the bids from the buyer.
- *int/auc_res*: Transmission of the result of the round to the auctioneer.
- *int/b*: Transmission of information to the buyer.
- *b/int_exit*: Receipt of message from buyer of desire to leave the auction room.

Apart from the channels, the interagent also keeps information in order to compare it with that in the incoming messages and the parameters of the actual lot in case there is a collision and it has to restart the round. Normally in the first case it keeps the last bid submitted by the buyer — but in the English auction more information is needed: we will explain this later.

First we give the specification of the protocols. We will begin with the complete specification of First-Price/Sealed-Bid, being the simplest. Then we will explain the changes, by reference to that for the Vickrey and Dutch protocols, because they are so similar to the first one. Finally we will explain in more detail the last and more complex English auction.

6   First-Price/Sealed-Bid

The main characteristic of this kind of auctions is that you can divide it in two phases. There is a time for submission of bids and afterwards, analyzing the bids to choose a

FP-WaitingBid(id, in, out, b/int_bid, int/auc_res, int/b, $time$) =

ν ($done$, $then$, $else$)
   $\overline{int/b}\,\langle time \rangle$
   . FP-bid(b/int_bid, $time$, $done$)
   | $done(bid)$
      . $\overline{out}\,\langle bid \rangle$
      . FP-WaitingMessage(id, bid, in, out, b/int_bid, int/auc_res, int/b, $time$)

FP-bid(id, b/int_bid, $time$, $done$) =

ν ($then$, $else$, $done2$)
   delay($time$, $done2$)
   | $done2()$
      . test/1(b/int_bid, $then$, $else$)
      | $then(bid)$. $\overline{done}\,\langle bid \rangle$ + $else(junk)$. $\overline{done}\,\langle -id \rangle$

FP-WaitingMessage(id, bid, in, out, b/int_bid, int/auc_res, int/b, $time$) =

$in(id_i, n\_bid)$
   . FP-ResolveBids(id, bid, id_i, n_bid, in, out, b/int_bid, int/auc_res, int/b,
            $time$)

---

winner. For each lot there is given a time for the buyers to submit their bids and after that the interagents decide who is the winner. The winner will be the buyer who has submitted the greatest bid and this is the price that he will pay for the lot. The lots auctioned in this protocol are defined with one parameter which indicates the time that the buyers have to submit bids. The lots auctioned in this protocol are defined with one parameter which indicates the time that the buyers have to submit bids.

1. **Waiting for Bids:** This step corresponds to the time that the buyers have for submitting bids. This process uses an auxiliary process called FP-bid to check if the buyer has submitted a bid in the time given. It will generate a message with the value returned from this process and then passes to the next step of waiting for a message from its predecessor.
   The FP-bid process first waits for the time specified using the delay process (definition not given here) which waits for the units of time that it receives as a parameter. After that it uses the function test/1 in order to see if the buyer has made a bid. If it has, it returns the value of the bid, otherwise it returns the value $-id$ which indicates that the buyer has not submitted a bid.
2. **Waiting for Next Message:** In this protocol this step only waits for one message from its predecessor in the ring because the buyers are not allowed to submit multiple bids. After reading from channel in it sends a message to the process FP-ResolveBids for further processing.

3. **Resolve Bids:** This is the most complex and interesting function. It applies the algorithm explained before with its own bid and the last message received for the interagent. The algorithm here is exactly the same as explained above without changes.

$\text{FP-ResolveBids}(id, bid, id_i, n\_bid, in, out, b/int\_bid, int/auc\_res, int/b, time) =$

$\quad$ **if** $car(id_i) = -2$

$\quad\quad$ **if** $n\_bid = bid$

$\quad\quad\quad$ **if** $bid < 0$

$\quad\quad\quad\quad \overline{int/auc\_res} \langle 0, 0 \rangle$

$\quad\quad\quad$ **otherwise**

$\quad\quad\quad\quad \overline{int/auc\_res} \langle id, bid \rangle \mid \overline{int/b} \langle \text{"Winner"} \rangle$

$\quad\quad$ **otherwise**

$\quad\quad\quad \overline{int/b} \langle \text{"End of round"} \rangle$

$\quad\quad\quad \mid \overline{out} \langle -2, n\_bid \rangle$

$\quad$ **elseif** $car(id_i) = -1$

$\quad\quad$ **if** $n\_bid = bid$

$\quad\quad\quad \overline{int/b} \langle \text{"Collision"} \rangle$

$\quad\quad\quad \mid \text{FP-WaitingBid}(id, in, out, b/int\_bid, int/auc\_res, int/b, time)$

$\quad\quad$ **otherwise**

$\quad\quad\quad \overline{int/b} \langle \text{"Collision"} \rangle$

$\quad\quad\quad \mid \overline{out} \langle -1, n\_bid \rangle$

$\quad\quad\quad \mid \text{FP-WaitingBid}(id, in, out, b/int\_bid, int/auc\_res, int/b, time)$

$\quad$ **otherwise**

$\quad\quad$ **if** $n\_bid = bid$

$\quad\quad\quad$ **if** $car(id_i) = id$

$\quad\quad\quad\quad$ **if** $|id_i| = 1$

$\quad\quad\quad\quad\quad \overline{out} \langle -2, bid \rangle$

$\quad\quad\quad\quad$ **otherwise**

$\quad\quad\quad\quad\quad \overline{out} \langle -1, bid \rangle$

$\quad\quad\quad\quad\quad \mid \text{FP-WaitingMessage}(id, bid, in, out, b/int\_bid, int/auc\_res, int/b, time)$

$\quad\quad\quad$ **otherwise**

$\quad\quad\quad\quad \overline{out} \langle id_i \cup \{id\}, bid \rangle$

$\quad\quad\quad\quad \mid \text{FP-WaitingMessage}(id, bid, in, out, b/int\_bid, int/auc\_res, int/b, time)$

$\quad\quad$ **otherwise**

$\quad\quad\quad$ **if** $n\_bid > bid$

$\quad\quad\quad\quad \overline{out} \langle id_i, n\_bid \rangle$

$\quad\quad\quad\quad \mid \text{FP-WaitingMessage}(id, bid, in, out, b/int\_bid, int/auc\_res, int/b, time)$

$\quad\quad\quad$ **otherwise**

$\quad\quad\quad\quad \text{FP-WaitingMessage}(id, bid, in, out, b/int\_bid, int/auc\_res, int/b, time)$

7   Vickrey's Auction

This protocol is very similar to the one before in the sense that it is also divided in two phases and with the same processes as the previous one. The sole difference is that the winner is the buyer who has submitted the highest bid *but* the price that he has to pay corresponds to the second highest bid. That implies adding a field to the messages to contain information about the second highest bid.

We do not give the specification because the only change from first-price is that the messages have one additional field. This field, corresponding to the second highest bid, is initialized to zero when an interagent generates a message. When an interagent passes a message on it has to compare this field with its bid and it updates it, if its own is higher. The only other change is when an interagent is the winner of the round. In that case it has to send the second bid to the auctioneer.

8   Dutch Auction

The main characteristic of this protocol is that it is a descending price auction. The round starts with a high price descending until one buyer submits a bid. In real Dutch auctions it is the auctioneer who calls out the offers until one buyer bids. Here, each interagent sends independently the offers to its buyer[2]. While this confers several advantages in a distributed setting that cannot arise in the physical scenario, it does have the drawback that in contrast to a real auction, where when a buyer sees a offer he knows that no one has submitted a bid at a higher price, whereas here the buyer cannot be sure of this because each interagent is running independently from the others. This could change the bidding strategy of the buyers.

$$
\begin{aligned}
&\text{DA-bid}(id,\ b/int\_bid,\ actual\_price,\ decrement,\ reserve\_price,\ done) = \\
&\quad \nu\ (then, else, done2) \\
&\qquad \overline{int/bid}\ \langle actual\_price \rangle\ .\ \text{delay}(1, done2) \\
&\qquad |\ done2() \\
&\qquad\quad .\ \text{test/0}(b/int\_bid, then, else) \\
&\qquad\quad |\ then()\ .\ \overline{done}\ \langle bid \rangle \\
&\qquad\quad + else() \\
&\qquad\qquad .\left\{
\begin{array}{l}
\textbf{if } actual\_price - decrement > reserve\_price \\
\text{DA-bid}(id,\ b/int\_bid,\ actual\_price - decrement,\ decrement, \\
\qquad\qquad reserve\_price,\ done) \\
\textbf{otherwise} \\
\overline{done}\ \langle -id \rangle
\end{array}
\right.
\end{aligned}
$$

---

[2] This technique and its justification are presented in [13]

The parameters of this kind of auction are slightly different, being:

- *start_price*: The starting price at which the interagents start sending offers to the buyers.
- *reserve_price*: The minimum price at which the lot may be sold. If that price is reached the buyer loses the opportunity to for bid for it. If all the interagents reach this price without a bid being made, then the lot is withdrawn.
- *decrement*: The difference between successive offers.

The process that is different from First-Price/Sealed-Bid auction is FP-bid. All the other processes are identical except that the *time* parameter is replaced by the three parameters that capture the state of this protocol (given above).

The DA-bid process sends an offer to the buyer, then waits one unit of time and checks whether the buyer has submitted a bid. In that case it returns the actual price as the buyer bid, otherwise it repeats the process again. This function stops when the buyer submits a bid or the *reserve_price* is reached.

9   English Auction

This protocol is the most complex that we have specified and the one that presents the most differences with the others. Here bidding starts at a minimum price and the buyers submit increasing bids until all of them stop. Each buyer can submit as many bids as it wants before a winner is declared. In the real auctions the auctioneer says *going, going, gone* after a bid before declaring a winner. In order to model that here, before an interagent either declares itself the winner or detects a collision, its message has to make three rounds of the interagent ring.

$$
\begin{aligned}
&\textsf{EA-WaitingMessage}(id, bid, in, out, b/int\_bid, int/auc\_res, int/b, l\_id, l\_bid, count, \\
&\qquad\qquad\qquad start\_price, decrement, reserve\_price) = \\
&\left\{
\begin{array}{l}
\textbf{if } l\_bid < 0 \lor counter = 2 \\
in(id_i, n\_bid) \\
.\ \textsf{EA-ResolveBid}(id, bid, id_i, n\_bid, in, out, b/int\_bid, int/auc\_res, int/b, \\
\qquad\qquad\qquad l\_id, l\_bid, count, start\_price, decrement, reserve\_price) \\
\textbf{otherwise} \\
in(id_i, n\_bid) \\
.\ \textsf{EA-ResolveBid}(id, bid, id_i, n\_bid, in, out, b/int\_bid, int/auc\_res, int/b, \\
\qquad\qquad\qquad l\_id, l\_bid, count, start\_price, decrement, reserve\_price) \\
+\ b/int\_bid(n\_bid) \\
\quad .\ \overline{out}\ \langle\{id\}, n\_bid\rangle \\
\quad .\ \textsf{EA-WaitingMessage}(id, n\_bid, in, out, b/int\_bid, int/auc\_res, int/b, id, \\
\qquad\qquad\qquad n\_bid, 0, start\_price, decrement, reserve\_price)
\end{array}
\right.
\end{aligned}
$$

This protocol starts with a descending bidding protocol as in the Dutch auction until one buyer submits a bid. After that the auction follows the pattern just described, with the bids going up.

In order to count the laps of the message with the greatest bid received, each inter-agent has to keep more information. It has to keep the last message that it has passed on because it is the one with the greatest bid so far, and the number of times that it has received it in order to count the laps.

$\text{EA-ResolveBid}(id, bid, id_i, n\_bid, in, out, b/int\_bid, int/auc\_res, int/b, l\_id, l\_bid, count, start\_price,$
$\quad\quad\quad decrement, reserve\_price) =$

if $car(id_i) = -2$
 if $n\_bid = bid$
  if $bid < 0$
  $\overline{int/auc\_res}\,\langle 0, 0\rangle$
  otherwise
  $\overline{int/auc\_res}\,\langle id, bid\rangle \mid \overline{int/b}\,(\text{"Winner"})$
 otherwise
 $\overline{int/b}\,(\text{"End of round"})$
 $\mid \overline{out}\,(-2, n\_bid)$
elseif $car(id_i) = -1$
 if $n\_bid = bid$
 $\text{EA-WaitBid}(id, in, out, b/int\_bid, int/auc\text{-}res, int/b, start\_price, decrement, reserve\_price)$
 otherwise
 $\overline{out}\,(-1, n\_bid)$
 $\mid \text{EA-WaitBid}(id, in, out, b/int\_bid, int/auc\text{-}res, int/b, start\_price, decrement, reserve\_price)$
elseif $car(id_i) = l\_id \wedge n\_bid = l\_bid$
 if $n\_bid > bid$
 $\overline{out}\,(id_i, n\_bid)$
 $\mid \text{EA-WaitingMessage}(id, bid, in, out, b/int\_bid, int/auc\text{-}res, int/b, l\_id, l\_bid, count + 1,$
      $start\_price, decrement, reserve\_price)$
 elseif $count = 2$
  if $|id_i| = 1$
  $\overline{out}\,(-2, bid)$
  $\mid \text{EA-WaitingMessage}(id, bid, in, out, b/int\_bid, int/auc\text{-}res, int/b, l\_id, l\_bid, count,$
      $start\_price, decrement, reserve\_price)$
  otherwise
  $\overline{out}\,(-1, bid)$
  $\mid \text{EA-WaitingMessage}(id, in, out, bid, bm\_nbi2, b/int\_bid, int/auc\text{-}res, int/b, l\_id, l\_bid, count,$
      $start\_price, decrement, reserve\_price)$
 otherwise
 $\overline{out}\,(id_i, n\_bid)$
 $\mid \text{EA-WaitingMessage}(id, bid, in, out, b/int\_bid, int/auc\text{-}res, int/b, l\_id, l\_bid, count + 1,$
      $start\_price, decrement, reserve\_price)$
elseif $n\_bid = l\_bid \wedge count > 0$
$\overline{out}\,(id_i, n\_bid)$
$.\ \text{EA-WaitingMessage}(id, bid, in, out, b/int\_bid, int/auc\text{-}res, int/b, l\_id, l\_bid, count,$
     $start\_price, decrement, reserve\_price)$
elseif $n\_bid > bid$
$\overline{out}\,(id_i, n\_bid)$
$.\ \text{EA-WaitingMessage}(id, bid, in, out, b/int\_bid, int/auc\text{-}res, int/b, car(id_i), n\_bid, 0,$
     $start\_price, decrement, reserve\_price)$
elseif $n\_bid = bid$
$\overline{out}\,(id_i \cup \{id\}, bid)$
$.\ \text{EA-WaitingMessage}(id, bid, in, out, b/int\_bid, int/auc\text{-}res, int/b, l\_id, l\_bid, count,$
     $start\_price, decrement, reserve\_price)$
otherwise
$\text{EA-WaitingMessage}(id, bid, in, out, b/int\_bid, int/auc\text{-}res, int/b, l\_id, l\_bid, count,$
     $start\_price, decrement, reserve\_price)$

There is another important point in which it differs from real auctions. There are two situations where the buyer is not allowed to submit bids but where they can be allowed later. The first one is when the buyer has not made a bid at the waiting for bids step. After that the buyer will be allowed to make bids if the interagent receives a bid from another one. The second situation is when the interagent receives a message for the third time. From the point of view of the interagent the round is over. Although there is one possibility it may not be: if another buyer submits a greater bid before it has received the message three times. In the real auctions this does not happen because the auctioneer declares the end of the rounds in a centralized way. When the auctioneer declares that a lot is withdrawn or there is a winner there is no possibility of continuing the round.

So, when an interagent receives a new message it has to compare it with the one that it has kept. If the bid is lower it discards the new message. If the bid in the new message is greater then it keeps it, it sets the counter to zero and it passes the message on.

We have to bear in mind that there can be more than one message in the ring with the same bid value because no interagent discards any message with a bid equal to its own. So, when an interagent receives a message with a bid equal to that in the message that it has kept it compares the identifiers to see if they are the same message. If not it passes the message on and waits for another one. If they are the same and the counter is less than two it passes the message on and increments the counter by one. If the counter is equal to two it checks if it is its own message. In that case it declares itself as a winner if there is only its identifier and the bid is greater than zero. It declares the lot withdrawn if the bid is lower than zero and a collision if there is more than one identifier in the message. If it is not its message then it passes the message on but its buyer will not be allowed to make more bids unless it receives a new message with a greater bid as we have explained above.

One point here is that the identifiers in the list are always added at the end. So, in order to determine if two messages with the same bid are from the same buyer, it is enough to compare the first identifier of each one.

The last point to consider is that a buyer has always to submit a greater bid than the last that it received. Given this constraint, an interagent can only possibly receive a message that it has not generated with an equal bid to its own when its message is in the first lap around the ring. In this situation it has to add its identifier to the list in the first field of the message.

The first step is the same as in the Dutch auction, starting at one price and going down. Therefore, we will just specify the other two.

10   Related and Future Work

As we proposed at the beginning, we have presented a distributed method for the resolution of the classic bidding protocols. For that purpose we have distributed the task from the auctioneer to the interagents. Thus the load of messages is also distributed because in the centralized versions all the messages go from the auctioneer to each interagent or from each of them to the auctioneer.

With the use of interagents this very significant change can be done without affecting the buyers which can run without any knowledge of the way in which the bids are resolved. The interagents also define the communication infrastructure and thus the buyers can focus on bidding strategies.

The specification given has been satisfactorily implemented using Pict [15], a π-calculus interpreter, giving some confidence in the validity of the method, although without a directly executable specification, it does nothing to verify the specification.

We have given the specification of four protocols but we have defined the general steps in order to resolve bidding protocols in a distributed way. Thus it may simplify the specification of new auction protocols in a distributed manner. All that is necessary is the definition of the three steps for the new protocol.

Another important point is that the fact that in basing our algorithm on the Leader Election, we can use the theoretical results established for Leader Election. This includes the algorithmic improvements mentioned in the introduction and, more importantly, its combination with techniques for termination detection and handling of stopping and Byzantine failure, which is an important aspect of our future (implementation) work.

Our plans for the immediate future are an implementation in the framework of the FishMarket, so that we will have two ways of resolve the bidding protocols in our electronic auction house. The FM already uses interagents for communication with the buyers and with the other agents and so all have to do is modify them to handle bid resolution as outlined here. In consequence we can take benefit from all the other infrastructure of the FM in order to get our specification running easily.

References

1. James Bushnell and Shmuel Oren. Two dimensional auctions for efficient franchising of public monopolies. Technical Report ERL-93-41, University of California, Berkeley, 1993.
2. S. Clearwater (ed.). *Market-Based Control: A Paradigm for Distributed Resource Allocation*. World Scientific Press, 1995.
3. M. Franklin and M. Reiter. The Design and Implementation of a Secure Auction Service. *IEEE Transactions on Software Engineering*, 22(5):302–312, 1996.
4. Ross A. Gagliano, Martin D. Fraser, and Mark E. Schaefer. Auction allocation of computing resources. *Communications of the ACM*, 38(6):88–102, June 1995.
5. Pere Garcia, Eduard Giménez, Lluís Godo, and Juan A. Rodríguez-Aguilar. Possibilistic-based design of bidding strategies in electronic auctions. In *The 13th biennial European Conference on Artificial Intelligence (ECAI-98)*, 1998.
6. B. A. Huberman and S. Clearwater. A multi-agent system for controlling builging environments. In *Proceedings of the First International Conference on Multi-Agent Systems (ICMAS-95)*, pages 171–176. AAAI Press, June 1995.
7. Leslie Lamport, Robert Shostak, and Marshall Pease. The Byzantine generals problem. *ACM Transactions on Programming Languages and Systems*, 4(3):382–401, July 1982.
8. Nancy Lynch. *Distributed Algorithms*. Morgan Kaufmann, 1996. ISBN 1-55860-348-4.
9. Francisco J. Martín, Enric Plaza, and Juan Antonio Rodríguez-Aguilar. An infrastructure for agent-based systems: An interagent approach. *International Journal of Intelligent Systems*, 1998.
10. Robin Milner. The Polyadic π-Calculus: a Tutorial. Preprint of Proceedings International Summer School on Logic and Algebra of Specification, 1991.
11. Uwe Nestmann. Calculi for mobile processes. available through
    http://www.cs.auc.dk/mobility/.

12. D. North. *Institutions, Institutional Change and Economics Perfomance*. Cambridge U. P., 1990.
13. J.A. Padget and R.J. Bradford. A π-calculus model of the spanish fishmarket. In *Proceedings of AMET'98*, volume 1571 of *Lecture Notes in Artificial Intelligence*, pages 166–188. Springer Verlag, 1999.
14. Benjamin C. Pierce. Foundational calculi for programming languages. In Allen B. Tucker, editor, *Handbook of Computer Science and Engineering*, chapter 139. CRC Press, 1996.
15. Benjamin C Pierce and David N Turner. Pict: A Programming Language Based on the Pi-Calculus. Technical Report 476, Indiana University, March 1997.
16. J.A. Rodríguez, F.J. Martin, P. Garcia, P. Noriega, and C. Sierra. Towards a formal specification of complex social structures in multi-agent systems. In Julian Padget, editor, *Proceedings of the workshop on Collaboration Between Human And Artificial Societies*, volume 1624 of *LNAI*, pages 289–305. Springer Verlag, 1999.
17. J.A. Rodríguez, P. Noriega, C. Sierra, and J.A. Padget. FM96.5 A Java-based Electronic Auction House. In *Second International Conference on The Practical Application of Intelligent Agents and Multi-Agent Technology: PAAM'97*, 1997.
18. Hal R. Varian. Economic mechanism design for computerized agents. In *First USENIX Workshop on Electronic Commerce*, pages 13–21, New York, July 1995. USENIX.
19. Fredrik Ygge and Hans Akkermans. Power load management as a computational market. In *Proceedings of the Second International Conference on Multi-Agent Systems (ICMAS-96)*, 1996.
20. Fredrik Ygge and Hans Akkermans. Making a case for multi-agent systems. In Magnus Boman and Walter Van de Velde, editors, *Advances in Case-Based Reasoning*, number 1237 in Lecture Notes in Artificial Intelligence, pages 156–176. Springer-Verlag, 1997.
21. The FishMarket Project. http://www.iiia.csic.es/Projects/fishmarket.

Author Index

Bouttilier, Craig, 131

Collins, John, 113
Conan, Vania, 40

Dailianas, Apostolos, 153
Das, Rajarshi, 180
Dellarocas, Chrysanthos, 24

Esteva, Mark, 220

Foss, Marten, 40

Gini, Maria, 113
Goldszmidt, Moisés, 131
Gottemukkala, Vibby, 153
Greenwald, Amy R., 1

Jhingran, Anant, 153

Kephart, Jeffrey O., 1, 180
Kim, Juneha, 102
Kim, SooWoong, 102
Klein, Mark, 24

Lenda, Peter, 40
Louveaux, Sophie, 40

MacKie-Mason, Jeffrey K., 180
Mobasher, Bamshad, 113
Monteleoni, Claire, 131

Padget, Julian, 220
Parkes, David C., 206

Sabata, Bikash, 131
Sairamesh, Jakka, 153
Salaun, Anne, 40
Sundareswara, Fashmi, 113

Walsh, William E., 94
Wellman, Michael P., 94

Ygge, Fredrik, 68
Yoon, Shim, 102
Yun, Ju Young, 102

Lecture Notes in Artificial Intelligence (LNAI)

Vol. 1720: O. Watanabe, T. Yokomori (Eds.), Algorithmic Learning Theory. Proceedings, 1999. XI, 365 pages. 1999.

Vol. 1721: S. Arikawa, K. Furukawa (Eds.), Discovery Science. Proceedings, 1999. XI, 374 pages. 1999.

Vol. 1724: H.I. Christensen, H. Bunke, H. Noltemeier (Eds.), Sensor Based Intelligent Robots. Proceedings, 1998. VIII, 327 pages. 1999.

Vol. 1730: M. Gelfond, N. Leone, G. Pfeifer (Eds.), Logic Programming and Nonmonotonic Reasoning. Proceedings, 1999. XI, 391 pages. 1999.

Vol. 1733: H. Nakashima, C. Zhang (Eds.), Approaches to Intelligent Agents. Proceedings, 1999. XII, 241 pages. 1999.

Vol. 1735: J.W. Amtrup, Incremental Speech Translation. XV, 200 pages. 1999.

Vol. 1739: A. Braffort, R. Gherbi, S. Gibet, J. Richardson, D. Teil (Eds.), Gesture-Based Communication in Human-Computer Interaction. Proceedings, 1999. XI, 333 pages. 1999.

Vol. 1744: S. Staab, Grading Knowledge: Extracting Degree Information from Texts. X, 187 pages. 1999.

Vol. 1747: N. Foo (Ed.), Adavanced Topics in Artificial Intelligence. Proceedings, 1999. XV, 500 pages. 1999.

Vol. 1757: N.R. Jennings, Y. Lespérance (Eds.), Intelligent Agents VI. Proceedings, 1999. XII, 380 pages. 2000.

Vol. 1759: M.J. Zaki, C.-T. Ho (Eds.), Large-Scale Parallel Data Mining. VIII, 261 pages. 2000.

Vol. 1760: J.-J. Ch. Meyer, P.-Y. Schobbens (Eds.), Formal Models of Agents. Poceedings. VIII, 253 pages. 1999.

Vol. 1761: R. Caferra, G. Salzer (Eds.), Automated Deduction in Classical and Non-Classical Logics. Proceedings. VIII, 299 pages. 2000.

Vol. 1771: P. Lambrix, Part-Whole Reasoning in an Object-Centered Framework. XII, 195 pages. 2000.

Vol. 1772: M. Beetz, Concurrent Reactive Plans. XVI, 213 pages. 2000.

Vol. 1775: M. Thielscher, Challenges for Action Theories. XIII, 138 pages. 2000.

Vol. 1778: S. Wermter, R. Sun (Eds.), Hybrid Neural Systems. IX, 403 pages. 2000.

Vol. 1788: A. Moukas, C. Sierra, F. Ygge (Eds.), Agent Mediated Electronic Commerce II. IX, 239 pages. 2000.

Vol. 1792: E. Lamma, P. Mello (Eds.), AI*IA 99: Advances in Artificial Intelligence. Proceedings, 1999. XI, 392 pages. 2000.

Vol. 1793: O. Cairo, L.E. Sucar, F.J. Cantu (Eds.), MICAI 2000: Advances in Artificial Intelligence. Proceedings, 2000. XIV, 750 pages. 2000.

Vol. 1794: H. Kirchner, C. Ringeissen (Eds.), Frontiers of Combining Systems. Proceedings, 2000. X, 291 pages. 2000.

Vol. 1804: B. Azvine, N. Azarmi, D.D. Nauck (Eds.), Intelligent Systems and Soft Computing. XVII, 359 pages. 2000.

Vol. 1805: T. Terano, H. Liu, A.L.P. Chen (Eds.), Knowledge Discovery and Data Mining. Proceedings, 2000. XIV, 460 pages. 2000.

Vol. 1809: S. Biundo, M. Fox (Eds.), Recent Advances in AI Planning. Proceedings, 1999. VIII, 373 pages. 2000.

Vol. 1810: R. López de Mántaras, E. Plaza (Eds.), Machine Learning: ECML 2000. Proceedings, 2000. XII, 460 pages. 2000.

Vol. 1813: P.L. Lanzi, W. Stolzmann, S.W. Wilson (Eds.), Learning Classifier Systems. X, 349 pages. 2000.

Vol. 1821: R. Loganantharaj, G. Palm, M. Ali (Eds.), Intelligent Problem Solving. Proceedings, 2000. XVII, 751 pages. 2000.

Vol. 1822: H.H. Hamilton, Advances in Artificial Intelligence. Proceedings, 2000. XII, 450 pages. 2000.

Vol. 1831: D. McAllester (Ed.), Automated Deduction – CADE-17. Proceedings, 2000. XIII, 519 pages. 2000.

Vol. 1834: J.-C. Heudin (Ed.), Virtual Worlds. Proceedings, 2000. XI, 314 pages. 2000.

Vol. 1835: D. N. Christodoulakis (Ed.), Natural Language Processing – NLP 2000. Proceedings, 2000. XII, 438 pages. 2000.

Vol. 1836: B. Masand, M. Spiliopoulou (Eds.), Web Usage Analysis and User Profiling. Proceedings, 2000. V, 183 pages. 2000.

Vol. 1847: R. Dyckhoff (Ed.), Automated Reasoning with Analytic Tableaux and Related Methods. Proceedings, 2000. X, 441 pages. 2000.

Vol. 1849: C. Freksa, W. Brauer, C. Habel, K.F. Wender (Eds.), Spatial Cognition II. XI, 420 pages. 2000.

Vol. 1860: M. Klusch, L. Kerschberg (Eds.), Cooperative Information Agents IV. Proceedings, 2000. XI, 285 pages. 2000.

Vol. 1861: J. Lloyd, V. Dahl, U. Furbach, M. Kerber, K.-K. Lau, C. Palamidessi, L. Moniz Pereira, Y. Sagiv, P.J. Stuckey (Eds.), Computational Logic – CL 2000. Proceedings, 2000. XIX, 1379 pages.

Vol. 1864: B. Y. Choueiry, T. Walsh (Eds.), Abstraction, Reformulation, and Approximation. Proceedings, 2000. XI, 333 pages. 2000.

Vol. 1866: J. Cussens, A. Frisch (Eds.), Inductive Logic Programming. Proceedings, 2000. X, 265 pages. 2000.

Lecture Notes in Computer Science

Vol. 1832: B. Lings, K. Jeffery (Eds.), Advances in Databases. Proceedings, 2000. X, 227 pages. 2000. Vol. 1833: L. Bachmair (Ed.), Rewriting Techniques and Applications. Proceedings, 2000. X. 275 pages. 2000.

Vol. 1834: J.-C. Heudin (Ed.), Virtual Worlds. Proceedings, 2000. XI, 314 pages. 2000. (Subseries LNAI).

Vol. 1835: D. N. Christodoulakis (Ed.), Natural Language Processing – NLP 2000. Proceedings, 2000. XII, 438 pages. 2000. (Subseries LNAI).

Vol. 1836: B. Masand, M. Spiliopoulou (Eds.), Web Usage Analysis and User Profiling. Proceedings, 2000. V, 183 pages. 2000. (Subseries LNAI).

Vol. 1837: R. Backhouse, J. Nuno Oliveira (Eds.), Mathematics of Program Construction. Proceedings, 2000. IX, 257 pages. 2000.

Vol. 1838: W. Bosma (Ed.), Algorithmic Number Theory. Proceedings, 2000. IX, 615 pages. 2000.

Vol. 1839: G. Gauthier, C. Frasson, K. VanLehn (Eds.), Intelligent Tutoring Systems. Proceedings, 2000. XIX, 675 pages. 2000.

Vol. 1840: F. Bomarius, M. Oivo (Eds.), Product Focused Software Process Improvement. Proceedings, 2000. XI, 426 pages. 2000.

Vol. 1841: E. Dawson, A. Clark, C. Boyd (Eds.), Information Security and Privacy. XII, 488 pages. 2000.

Vol. 1842: D. Vernon (Ed.), Computer Vision – ECCV 2000. Part I. Proceedings, 2000. XVIII, 953 pages. 2000.

Vol. 1843: D. Vernon (Ed.), Computer Vision – ECCV 2000. Part II. Proceedings, 2000. XVIII, 881 pages. 2000.

Vol. 1844: W.B. Frakes (Ed.), Software Reuse: Advances in Software Reusability. Proceedings, 2000. XI, 450 pages. 2000.

Vol. 1845: H.B. Keller, E. Plöderer (Eds.), Reliable Software Technologies Ada-Europe 2000. Proceedings, 2000. XIII, 304 pages. 2000.

Vol. 1846: H. Lu, A. Zhou (Eds.), Web-Age Information Management. Proceedings, 2000. XIII, 462 pages. 2000.

Vol. 1847: R. Dyckhoff (Ed.), Automated Reasoning with Analytic Tableaux and Related Methods. Proceedings, 2000. X, 441 pages. 2000. (Subseries LNAI).

Vol. 1848: R. Giancarlo, D. Sankoff (Eds.), Combinatorial Pattern Matching. Proceedings, 2000. XI, 423 pages. 2000.

Vol. 1849: C. Freksa, W. Brauer, C. Habel, K.F. Wender (Eds.), Spatial Cognition II. XI, 420 pages. 2000. (Subseries LNAI).

Vol. 1850: E. Bertino (Ed.), ECOOP 2000 – Object-Oriented Programming. Proceedings, 2000. XIII, 493 pages. 2000.

Vol. 1851: M.M. Halldórsson (Ed.), Algorithm Theory – SWAT 2000. Proceedings, 2000. XI, 564 pages. 2000.

Vol. 1853: U. Montanari, J.D.P. Rolim, E. Welzl (Eds.), Automata, Languages and Programming. Proceedings, 2000. XVI, 941 pages. 2000.

Vol. 1854: G. Lacoste, B. Pfitzmann, M. Steiner, M. Waidner (Eds.), SEMPER — Secure Electronic Marketplace for Europe. XVIII, 350 pages. 2000.

Vol. 1855: E.A. Emerson, A.P. Sistla (Eds.), Computer Aided Verification. Proceedings, 2000. X, 582 pages. 2000.

Vol. 1857: J. Kittler, F. Roli (Eds.), Multiple Classifier Systems. Proceedings, 2000. XII, 404 pages. 2000.

Vol. 1858: D.-Z. Du, P. Eades, V. Estivill-Castro, X. Lin, A. Sharma (Eds.), Computing and Combinatorics. Proceedings, 2000. XII, 478 pages. 2000.

Vol. 1860: M. Klusch, L. Kerschberg (Eds.), Cooperative Information Agents IV. Proceedings, 2000. XI, 285 pages. 2000. (Subseries LNAI).

Vol. 1861: J. Lloyd, V. Dahl, U. Furbach, M. Kerber, K.-K. Lau, C. Palamidessi, L. Moniz Pereira, Y. Sagiv, P.J. Stuckey (Eds.), Computational Logic – CL 2000. Proceedings, 2000. XIX, 1379 pages. (Subseries LNAI).

Vol. 1862: P. Clote, H. Schwichtenberg (Eds.), Computer Science Logic. Proceedings, 2000. XIII, 543 pages. 2000.

Vol. 1863: L. Carter, J. Ferrante (Eds.), Languages and Compilers for Parallel Computing. Proceedings, 1999. XII, 500 pages. 2000.

Vol. 1864: B. Y. Choueiry, T. Walsh (Eds.), Abstraction, Reformulation, and Approximation. Proceedings, 2000. XI, 333 pages. 2000. (Subseries LNAI).

Vol. 1866: J. Cussens, A. Frisch (Eds.), Inductive Logic Programming. Proceedings, 2000. X, 265 pages. 2000. (Subseries LNAI).

Vol. 1868: P. Koopman, C. Clack (Eds.), Implementations of Functional Languages. Proceedings, 1999. IX, 199 pages. 2000.

Vol. 1869: M. Aagaard, J. Harrison (Eds.), Theorem Proving in Higher Order Logics. Proceedings, 2000. IX, 535 pages. 2000.

Vol. 1872: J. van Leeuwen, O. Watanabe, M. Hagiya, P.D. Mosses, T. Ito (Eds.), Theoretical Computer Science. Proceedings, 2000. XV, 630 pages. 2000.

Vol. 1880: M. Bellare (Ed.), Advances in Cryptology – CRYPTO 2000. Proceedings, 2000. XI, 545 pages. 2000.

Vol. 1893: M. Nielsen, B. Rovan (Eds.), Mathematical Foundations of Computer Science 2000. Proceedings, 2000. XIII, 710 pages. 2000.